$13⁵⁵

Shakespeare & the French Poet

Shakespeare &

the French Poet

YVES BONNEFOY

Edited & with an Introduction by JOHN NAUGHTON

Including an Interview with YVES BONNEFOY

THE UNIVERSITY OF CHICAGO PRESS   Chicago & London

Poet, critic, and professor emeritus of comparative poetics at the Collège
de France, YVES BONNEFOY was awarded the Prix Goncourt for Poetry
in 1987. JOHN NAUGHTON is professor of Romance languages and
literatures at Colgate University. He is the principal translator of
Bonnefoy's work into English.

The University of Chicago Press, Chicago 60637
The University of Chicago Press, Ltd., London
© 2004 by The University of Chicago
All rights reserved. Published 2004
Printed in the United States of America
13 12 11 10 09 08 07 06 05 04   5 4 3 2 1

ISBN (cloth): 0-226-06442-5
ISBN (paper): 0-226-06443-3

Grateful acknowledgment is made to Mercure de France for permission to
publish English translations of these essays, which appeared in French in
Théâtre et poésie: Shakespeare et Yeats, © Mercure de France 1998, and *Sous
l'horizon du langage,* © Mercure de France 2002.

Library of Congress Cataloging-in-Publication Data

Bonnefoy, Yves.
    [Essays. English. Selections]
    Shakespeare and the French poet : with an interview with Yves
Bonnefoy / Yves Bonnefoy ; edited and with an introduction by John
Naughton.
        p.   cm.
    Essays originally published in French in Théâtre et poésie:
Shakespeare et Yeats and in Sous l'horizon du langage.
    Includes bibliographical references and index.
        ISBN 0-226-06442-5 (alk. paper)—ISBN 0-226-06443-3
(pbk. : alk. paper)
        1. Shakespeare, William, 1564–1616—Translations into French—
History and criticism. 2. Shakespeare, William, 1564–1616—
Criticism and interpretation. 3. Shakespeare, William, 1564–
1616—Appreciation—France. 4. Shakespeare, William, 1564–
1616—Influence. 5. English language—Translating into French.
6. Translating and interpreting—France. I. Naughton, John T.
II. Title.
    PR2881.5.F74B66   2004
    822.3'3—dc22

                                                    2003023393

♾ The paper used in this publication meets the minimum requirements of
the American National Standard for Information Sciences—Permanence
of paper for Printed Library Materials, ANSI Z39.48-1991.

Contents

Introduction

I HAVE, ON other occasions, been asked to introduce Yves Bonnefoy to English-speaking readers,[1] and it is a pleasure to do so again under these circumstances. Bonnefoy has translated and written about Shakespeare—especially in relation to French poetic tradition and practice—over a nearly fifty-year period. The essays collected here, though they are not the totality of Bonnefoy's reflections, do offer a representative and comprehensive view of the French poet's ideas about what is most fundamental to the study of Shakespeare, while isolating the most essential differences between English and French as poetic languages.

Bonnefoy has entitled his great study of Alberto Giacometti the *biographie d'une oeuvre*, underscoring his conviction that, as he once wrote in an essay on Degas, "it hardly matters what a man's life was; it is not necessary to know about it to get a sense of what he has accomplished, all the more so in that his life grows simpler the moment his work touches greatness." And it is true that Bonnefoy's own life may be succinctly summarized. In some ways, it is as simple and straightforward as his work is complex and multifaceted.

Born in Tours in 1923 and educated there, Bonnefoy is the son of a railroad foreman and a schoolteacher mother. He lost his father when he was only thirteen. After doing university work in mathematics and philosophy, he came in 1943 to occupied Paris, where he frequented some surrealist circles and later became acquainted with André Breton. He would eventually break

---

1. See *The Poetics of Yves Bonnefoy* (University of Chicago Press, 1984); *The Act and the Place of Poetry* (University of Chicago Press, 1989); *In the Shadow's Light*, (University of Chicago Press, 1991); *Yves Bonnefoy: New and Selected Poems* (University of Chicago Press, 1995).

with Breton to pursue his own path. The publication in 1953 of his first book of poems, *Du Mouvement et de l'immobilité de Douve* (*On the Motion and Immobility of Douve*), made him one of the most highly regarded poets of his generation. Six other books of poetry have since appeared: *Hier régnant désert* (*Yesterday's Wilderness Kingdom*), 1958; *Pierre écrite* (*Words in Stone*), 1965; *Dans le leurre du seuil* (*In the Lure of the Threshold*), 1975; *Ce qui fut sans lumière* (*In the Shadow's Light*), 1987; *Début et fin de la neige* (*The Beginning and the End of the Snow*), 1991; *Les Planches courbes* (*The Curved Planks*), 2001. To this steady production of poetry may be added a number of poetic prose collections, art and literary criticism, autobiography (*L'Arrière-pays*), editing of the review *L'Éphémère* and of the acclaimed *Dictionary of Mythologies*, interviews, and his many translations—of Shakespeare, Donne, Keats, Yeats, Leopardi. (For Bonnefoy's principal works, see the bibliography at the end of this volume.)

Bonnefoy's work, it may be said, is his life. Still, this life has been enriched by the many trips he has made around an earth he has always seen "as a variety of propositions about existence" and in particular by moments spent in a house in Provence, a place that at one time had been a monastery, which after the Revolution was converted into some kind of farmhouse. The dwelling, in its state of dilapidation, with its gaping holes and missing stones, with its need for constant care and restoration, became for Bonnefoy the locus of a simple and persistent, if menaced and precarious, sacred order. Much of his poetry since the 1960s is marked by his attachment to this place.

The man who once equated poetry with wandering, with searching, has himself been an indefatigable traveler. He has been a regular visitor to the United States, where he has been a guest professor at such places as the City University of New York, Harvard, Princeton, Yale, Wesleyan, Brandeis, Williams College, and the University of California. He has lectured in many places in Europe, as well as in Japan, Great Britain, and Ireland. He has won the Prix Montaigne, the Prix Balzan, and the *Hudson Review*'s Bennett Award among other prizes, and has been the recipient of many distinctions, including doctorates from Trinity College, Dublin, the University of Chicago, the University of Edinburgh, and the University of Rome. In 2001, he was made a member of the American Academy of Arts and Letters. Anyone flipping through the *Résumés des cours et travaux* published during his years at the *Collège de France* (1981–94) will be astonished at the breadth and variety of Bonnefoy's scholarly interest and activity, which nothing has diminished in the almost ten years since he left the *Collège*.

As young French students to this day still do, Bonnefoy read passages from Shakespeare in his high school English classes. As he says in the interview included at the end of this book, he was struck, even as a young reader, by Mark Antony's famous "Friends, Romans, countrymen" speech because in it he could sense what he would later identify as the dialectic between rhetoric and poetry, the former used to manipulate the crowd, the latter remembering the living presence of the now dead Caesar—"on a summer's evening in his tent." Bonnefoy would develop these early intuitions nearly fifty years later in the essay on *Julius Caesar* published here.

It was, of course, many years after these first encounters with Shakespeare that Bonnefoy would undertake to translate whole plays. The translations began thanks to the encouragement of Pierre Jean Jouve, who, though never much studied in Great Britain or the United States, was nonetheless one of the most important poets of the first half of the twentieth century in France and a man Bonnefoy greatly admired. Jouve suggested to Pierre Leyris, who was putting together a complete Shakespeare in translation, that he give the young Yves Bonnefoy a work to translate. Leyris proposed *Julius Caesar*, though he asked to see a sample scene before signing him on. Bonnefoy did the first scene of the play—"Hence! home, you idle creatures, get you home!"—with such fervor and mastery that Leyris asked him to translate *Hamlet* as well.

This was the beginning of one of the most important dimensions of Bonnefoy's poetic activity. Over a period of almost half a century, various plays and poems have appeared: in addition to *Hamlet* and *Julius Caesar*, he has published translations of *Henry IV, part one; The Winter's Tale; Venus and Adonis; The Rape of Lucrece; King Lear; Romeo and Juliet; Macbeth; The Tempest; Antony and Cleopatra; Othello; As You Like It;* a number of the sonnets; *The Phoenix and Turtle*. It is the translator's uniquely intimate experience of the text that has led to the special kinds of insight that animate Bonnefoy's readings of these plays and poems.

For Bonnefoy, the exercise of translating Shakespeare has never meant reviewing and correcting preexisting translations. As he puts it, it has rather involved seeking to "make someone else's words live again in my own." Translation thus becomes an activity that requires the translator to study himself even while reading another, for, as Bonnefoy observes (in "Translating Shakespeare's Sonnets"), "the material of the translator is less the 'meaning' possessed by the text . . . than the translator's own experience of this meaning." Readers familiar with his work know that for Bonnefoy translating from English to French has meant the "'testing' of one way of thinking by another," since for Bonnefoy an "opposing metaphysics" governs the French and English languages. If English, in Bonnefoy's view, "concerns itself naturally with tangible aspects," the French language seems to encourage poets not so much to describe external reality, as to shut themselves in "with certain selected precepts in a simplified, more circumscribed world." And this more coherent world of intelligible essences replaces the "bewildering diversity" of the real world by closing its eyes to "the very existence of time, everyday life and death." And so French *excludes* rather than describes, is fascinated by the idea or the essence of things rather than with things themselves. French poetry is thus inherently Platonic, while Shakespeare's reflects "a sort of passionate Aristotelianism." English poetry, then, "is like a mirror, French poetry like a crystal sphere." This being so, how can a language as different as French translate an English poet as rich as Shakespeare? How can it avoid its fatal tendency to "tone down and dim" particular realities? How can the French poet preserve the alternation of prose and verse in Shakespeare, the word play, the punning? Should he not resign himself to the impossibility of his task?

In Bonnefoy's view, the practice of French poetry since Baudelaire and Rimbaud has prepared it as never before to undergo an examination of its own resources, and "it is at the level of their deepest intuitions that the realism of Shakespeare and recent French poetry's denial of idealism" may enter into a significant new relation. The study of Shakespeare, the effort to translate him, requires French poets to reflect upon one way of thinking by looking closely at another; it thus becomes the struggle of a language with its own nature. And modern French poetry's attention to "the being of things, their metaphysical *thereness*, their presence . . . remote from verbalization" places it in an unprecedented position for approaching Shakespeare's universe. Its sense of spiritual disinheritance is Hamlet's; its need to love a world no transcendant order has founded is encouraged by the lessons of *Lear* and *The Winter's Tale*.

In part two of this volume, the reader will find a sampling of Bonnefoy's reflections on the problems the French poet faces when attempting to translate Shakespeare. Since for Bonnefoy form and meaning emerge simultaneously, the translator's first obligation would seem to be the need to find the proper *form*, and in any case a *poetic* form, for the translation of a poetic text.

Thus Bonnefoy will argue, as in his essay "Shakespeare and the French Poet," that the translator of Shakespeare must seek to preserve "the poetic line and its lofty tragic quality without giving the impression that the English poet believed in a hieratic and unreal world." In order to translate Shakespeare's pentameter, this will mean using free verse: a verse in the space of which a line of eleven syllables is often recurrent—a line that begins with six syllables, as the dream of a participation in the Ideal, but ends with five, which "gather and secularize, like facts open to the future of other facts," thus assuring that "real and sacred are, by this verse's offices, in dialectical relation, as they are in the great decisions of life that the theater wants to evoke, especially the theater of Shakespeare."

On the other hand, in "Translating into Verse or Prose," Bonnefoy attempts to justify what was for him the very painful decision to violate his own most basic "principle" and to translate Shakespeare's verse narratives *Venus and Adonis* and *The Rape of Lucrece* in prose so as better to preserve their pictorial quality. But whether urging the use of verse or defending the recourse to prose, a similar concern guides his choices and animates his project—and that is to recover, to relive, what is genuinely poetic.

III

What may constitute the principal interest of this volume for many readers, of course, is the meditation, independent of the problems of translating them, on the plays themselves. But readers unfamiliar with Bonnefoy's mode of thought and with the philosophical categories subtending it may feel that a word or two of introduction, if not of explanation, are in order, especially as it is a unified and consistent, if somewhat elusive, body of thought that is brought to bear on each of the plays Bonnefoy discusses, and always with the same gravity, passion, and conviction.

There is a fundamental dialectic that grounds Bonnefoy's poetics: the opposition between *image* and *presence*. Appearances are the material for the creation of images, which Bonnefoy sees as the source of our alienation from one another and the world. It is our tragedy to live much of life on the level of images: in the form of the reductivist way in which we read other people or things, or in our adherence to governing ideologies, or in our capacity for what in his essay on *Romeo and Juliet* Bonnefoy calls "daydreaming." It is a similar attachment to the "image-world," a comparable failure to connect with reality and the beings in it, that creates the affinity between two such seemingly different types as Macbeth and Romeo, since both have to a dangerous degree "bet on dream"—a proclivity which is at the root of what devastates society, especially in the modern period when faith in the unified medieval world picture has waned. Likewise, Bonnefoy perceives in Brutus a struggle similar to the one that cripples Hamlet. In Bonnefoy's reading of the plays, *Julius Caesar* ceases to be the "Roman" work built solely on logic, clarity, and rational discourse, as opposed to the "modern" subjectivity and obscurity of *Hamlet*. The central preoccupation of *Julius Caesar* is not political, according to this view. The main focus of the play is rather the "study of the soul eternally torn between the intelligible and existence," just as it is in *Hamlet*.

It is, in fact, characteristic of Bonnefoy's approach to Shakespeare's work to bring together two plays for purposes of comparison and contrast. Thus in "Readiness, Ripeness: *Hamlet, Lear*," Bonnefoy analyzes two opposing responses to the sense that the older sacred order governing the world has collapsed. On the one hand, Hamlet's "readiness" expresses his sense that "a single act still has some logic and is worthy of being carried out: and that is to take great pains to detach oneself from every illusion and to be ready to accept everything—everything, but first of all, and especially, death, the essence of all life—with irony and indifference." The "ripeness" that emerges in *King Lear*, on the other hand, is the loving and compassionate acceptance of mortality, the understanding that finitude binds human beings together and that, while it strips them of their vain illusions, it can open them to their essential oneness. *Lear* thus evokes "the quintessence of the world's order, the unity of which one seems to breathe," whereas *Hamlet* deploys "the reverse side of that order, when one no longer sees anything in the grayness of the passing days but the incomprehensible weave."

The artist himself participates to a special degree in the alienation that afflicts society, since he can only offer a partial and incomplete version of reality when he is not attempting to fabricate a competing form of it—the nature of which is represented as superior, if artificial—by an art practiced as an end in itself. Of necessity, then, the artist is himself the creator of illusion, of images; and even if the thrust of his work is to denounce their unreality, as would seem to be the case in *The Winter's Tale*, it remains nonetheless true that a work of art can never rival "nature." This idea is made central in Bonnefoy's discussion of *The Winter's Tale*, in the course of which he calls attention to the fact that Shakespeare has placed what should have been the most important scene of the play—the mutual recognition of a father and a daughter—offstage, as if to remind us that it remains a representation in a work of art and, as such, a form of promise, a suggestion concerning an authentic goal of aspiration in real life, and nothing more.

Similarly, the magic practiced by Prospero in *The Tempest*, and his aim of "bettering" his mind, are analyzed by Bonnefoy as constituting a rarefied form of alienation since they are predicated on a lack of involvement with other human beings. Shakespeare knows that Prospero's magic has affinities with the magic of the theater itself, and so when he has Prospero denounce his magic, when he has him solicit the prayers of the "real" audience, Shakespeare may be said to establish the priority of human communion over the claims, over the "charms," of the art he thereby "overthrows."

Finally, in societies dominated by men and by male values, it is women, because of the imposition of restricting and impoverished images, who will be most deprived of being. Bonnefoy's readings of *The Tempest*, *Antony and Cleopatra*, and *Othello* all share a focus on the fate of the women characters when the prestige of images is preferred to the values of existence. To this degree, then, the analyses of these plays have a "feminist" perspective, although this perspective needs to be placed in the context of the larger ontological evaluation that is Bonnefoy's guiding principle. He distinguishes between an "I" in full relation to being, to "itself" and to others, and an "ego," a "me"— what Bonnefoy calls *le moi*—which is constituted by social and cultural codes and values, by language itself. This self will always exist more superficially, less authentically, than the "I," despite the moments of profound intensity—of *tragedy*—it may experience.

Against the world of the image, Bonnefoy posits a world of *presence*. Now a *presence* can only become manifest in the context of finitude. Mortal being invades the timeless world of the idea and disrupts conceptual orders, as well as the words and ideas that stand for things; it asserts itself against the backdrop of its eventual disappearance. The world of *presence* comes to be through love, through an acceptance of "what is," which is to say, of chance and death. And this loving acceptance of "finitude" involves an act of will—the will *to be*—which must be affirmed against the various forms of alienation that endanger it. This will in us burns, Bonnefoy would have us see, like the taper in Brutus's tent, despite the power of the night.

The centering of the will on what is essential involves, then, the acceptance of death as an existential starting point. Cleopatra understands this when in an effort to reorient her relation to Antony—whose being has been unduly determined by considerations of power and prestige, to the detriment of all other concerns—she sends him news of her death. Lear takes the same "physic" when he learns what "unaccommodated" being is, when he comes to see that suffering and death are the bonds that unite people, even while they divest them of their "pomp." Now conceptual language conceals death, and, as Bonnefoy has often insisted, "discourse is false because it removes one thing from the world—death—and thus nullifies everything." Nothing, he goes on to say, "exists except through death, and nothing is true that is not proved by death." Bonnefoy wrote these words in a 1955 essay on Baudelaire, and what he said of Baudelaire is certainly true of himself: "Baudelaire chose death that death might grow in him like a conscience, that he might know through death."

There is another reference worth mentioning here—one that Bonnefoy makes constantly in his essays on Shakespeare—and that is the reference to the French poet Arthur Rimbaud. Rimbaud felt that "true life was missing," was absent in a world dominated by conventional forms of discourse and by false representations of the human person's relation to the world. Love in particular, he felt, needed to be "reinvented." Bonnefoy uses these categories of thought and feeling as he analyzes Shakespeare's plays, investing them with something of the child-poet's vision but doing so reciprocally, shedding new light on Rimbaud through the association with Shakespeare. When Rimbaud, at the end of *A Season in Hell*, exclaims that he has been thrown back to earth with a duty to find and "rough reality" to embrace, he reiterates a movement Bonnefoy often finds in Shakespeare, since this reality is predicated on the acceptance of limitation and death, which it takes as its starting point.

Bonnefoy's essays on Shakespeare focus on the fascination in Shakespeare's work with the "weakening of that faith in the meaning of the world that ensured the survival of society" and stress the fact that this is the obsessional center around which his entire opus turns. And surely this spiritual insecurity was something that French poets of the postwar era could share with Shakespeare. Nonetheless, Bonnefoy will insist that "in spite of the collapse of the 'goodly frame' which the Christian Middle Ages had built with heaven and earth around man created by God, this poet of a harsher time felt that an order still remained in place, in nature and in us—a deep, universal order, the order of life, which, when understood, when recognized in its simple forms, when loved and accepted, can give new meaning through its unity and its sufficiency to our condition of exiles from the world of the Promise—just as grass springs up among ruins."

One last matter. Readers may certainly want to question what may seem to be a sweeping indictment of language as a source of alienation from immediacy and from the simpler forms of one's relation to oneself and to life that runs from one end of these essays to the other. Isn't it language that allows us to organize the world, to differentiate among phenomena, to control the natural forces surrounding us? What would we do without language? Does the relation to unity, to the "self-evident," to the presence of things imply a kind of anti-intellectualism? Must one come to know "the bliss of animals," or "the innocence of limbo," as Rimbaud said, in order to recover this unity beyond or beneath words? No contemporary writer is more an advocate of intellectual pursuits than Yves Bonnefoy, and it is one of the most arresting aspects of his work that it manages to affirm a life of presence ("which has no name in the world of the Idea") through a series of intellectual and artistic projects that make full use of abstract categories. And if he is inclined to celebrate the real in the most "essential" and intellectual of discourses, it is because there is a contradiction at the heart of his undertaking that he has always fully acknowledged. In order for the return to immediacy to be "more than mere simulation," he once wrote, "it is essential that the two terms of the contradiction be kept face to face, and that this separated and unhappy life of the mind be itself affirmed to the very end in its profound difference. . . . We are from the Western world, and this cannot be denied. We have eaten of the tree of knowledge, and this cannot be denied. And far from dreaming of a cure for what we are, it is through our irrevocable intellectuality that we must try to reinvent presence, which is salvation."

What Bonnefoy is above all contesting are the systems of discourse that, when absolutized, deprive us of our relation to ourselves, since these systems, especially when they are ends in themselves, tend to separate us from what is most fundamental. Imagine, Bonnefoy said during his inaugural address at the Collège de France, the survivors of some disaster struggling to reestablish their lives. These people will decide, even without thinking about it, "that *there is being*, that one's relation to oneself, even if nothing founds it, is origin and suffices to itself." And so they learn "that *what is* is what responds to [their] project, what allows for exchange, and must first of all have done this to find a place in language." The poet's task is to recover something of this simpler, deeper, and more focused relation to the world, to dispel the power and pretension of an inauthentic self and to "reorient words, beyond the confines of dream, on our relation to others, which is the origin of being." His obligation, then, is not "to reabsorb what is in a formula, but, on the contrary, to reabsorb the formula in a participation in the real."

For Yves Bonnefoy, as for Martin Buber, there are two fundamental attitudes toward the world. One is concerned with knowing and using it, the other with meeting it. The first is concerned with objects, the second with relation and mutuality. The first kind of attitude to the world creates "individuality," reveling in its special being, in its difference and distinction. The second always involves relation in the present—in the *hic et nunc,* as Bonnefoy loves to insist. This second kind of relation invests the world with irrefutable significance and coherence. It does not begin as words. "We would have very little if we only had words," Bonnefoy has written. "What we need are the presences that words in themselves will never know how to restore to life." But all forms of language, even conceptual language, are enriched by the remembrance of this relation to presence. And each in its own way may seek to contribute to a "common speech"—one that is "no longer concerned with what is separated, closed off," one that sets about to "dissipate the last enchantments of the mythical self" and to speak of "the simplest of human desires in the presence of the simplest of objects, which is being." This use of language strives to "bring together the universal self."

IV

The reader should note that all the essays in this volume were originally published as prefaces to Bonnefoy's various translations of Shakespeare. Bonnefoy's readings are therefore based, as I have already suggested, on the translator's uniquely intimate contact with the very substance of the work he is translating. On the other hand, the reader will notice a certain degree of repetitiveness, since each essay originally stood alone, and the project of putting them together developed only after each was published. As penetrating as it is with respect to particulars, to details in the plays, the attention paid to them is always placed in the context of the larger preoccupations. These preoccupations, by Bonnefoy's own admission, are fundamentally "ontological." They lead him to read Shakespeare from the perspective of an overriding concern for the relation to being that Shakespeare's work may be said to show forth. I have mentioned the taper that burns in Brutus's tent. Bonnefoy's eye is constantly drawn to such details: the chess game that Miranda and Ferdinand play, which Bonnefoy sees as a bad omen for their future relation; the "willow song" sung by Desdemona, which Bonnefoy reads as an affirmation of life even in the face of impending death. These analyses, it has to be said, focus primarily on the plays as texts, and are the result of the kind of close and painstaking scrutiny that translation inevitably involves. They are very rarely based on considerations that recognize the plays as products of and for the theater. This is not to say that such considerations are totally absent from Bonnefoy's readings, but his focus is clearly on the mind that produced the dramas.

v

In the essays that deal with questions having to do with the translation of Shakespeare into French, Bonnefoy underscores the seemingly insurmountable difficulties the French poet must face. On a different scale, the English translator of Bonnefoy's French encounters his own problems, since the sentences he must translate are extraordinarily long, dense, and subtly nuanced. Our challenge was to preserve something of the complexity of the French sentences without at the same time creating phrases so heavy and unwieldy as to alienate the English-speaking reader. In this effort we have probably failed, since our task was made more difficult still by Bonnefoy's constant recourse to a vocabulary that is grounded in philosophy and linguistics. Bonnefoy's thought is pitched at a very high level. There is an intensity of commitment to a fundamental set of values that drives what otherwise might seem overly rhetorical, even sentimental. Doubtless he reads himself into Shakespeare, but Shakespeare is surely none the worse for it. If anything at all of that *gravité enflammée* of which Philippe Jaccottet once spoke, and which so characterizes both Bonnefoy's poetry and his prose, has been preserved, we will consider that we will have done the most important part of our job.

Special thanks are due my friend and colleague Robert Garland, chair of the Classics Department at Colgate University. His formidable knowledge of the ancient world, together with his abiding enthusiasm for Shakespeare, made him an ideal reader of many of these essays, and the comments he made concerning their articulation in English proved invaluable. Stephen Romer, who helped to translate one of the essays in this volume, also gave me the benefit of his careful readings of several of the other essays here presented, and Mark Hutchinson brought his exceptionally discerning eye to yet others. It seems especially appropriate that the force of friendship and collaboration should be a guiding feature of this book. The impressive number of French scholars who offered to help in the translation of this work did so not only because of a profound awareness of its importance, but also because of the feelings of gratitude and friendship they have for Bonnefoy himself. He is, in every way, a writer who rewards those who study him—and in his case, Glendower's boast applies, for he is indeed "not in the roll of common men."

JOHN NAUGHTON

Author's Note

I HAVE ASKED John Naughton's permission to add a few words of my own to his acknowledgments, for how could I let this book appear without expressing my sense of profound gratitude toward its editor and toward all those who gave such energy and attention to these translations. The reader of this book may not know how very difficult it was to translate. Its author has made use of a great many of the idiomatic resources of his language. He cannot resist listening to the rhythm of his sentences at the very moment he is writing them, which sometimes means that what he says is extremely elliptical. On the other hand, he also favors sentences that follow the movement of thought as it develops, and so some of these may extend to thirty or forty lines. All of which results in a text that could discourage translators or make them give up entirely, had they not the courage, the determination, the self-sacrifice, and the intelligence of John and his friends.

All my thanks go to them for so many months of hard work. At a moment like this, I realize more than ever what friendship is—friendship I feel motivating not only my translators but also the University of Chicago Press, which for many years now has supported and encouraged the publication of my work in English.

PART ONE

CHAPTER ONE

Shakespeare's Uneasiness

W HY CONNECT *Macbeth* with *Romeo and Juliet?* The one a drama shrouded in mist, stained with blood, pierced by cries of terror, the most Nordic and nocturnal of Shakespeare's works; the other, on the contrary, a romantic tragedy, essentially Mediterranean, a poem such as Pisanello might have chosen to illustrate in a fresco, in one of those beautiful palaces where music and dance seem to release desire from its matrix of primitive violence?

Whereas Macbeth seems to us to represent guilt in the absolute, without anything about him to arouse that compassion which to Western thought is the principle explaining our interest in tragedy, Romeo and Juliet are, or at least appear to be, the wholly innocent victims of a conspiracy between human folly and their unlucky stars. They die, but as though to prove that nobility and purity are not merely ideas. Day dawns when the play ends.

Let us begin, however, by observing that Italy was not for the Elizabethans what nowadays we fancy it must have been for them. No doubt they saw it as the realm of culture, beauty, and sensuous delight, but the revolutionary thought of Machiavelli had spread through Europe like a threat to be vanquished, and in Protestant countries this opposition took a complex form, entailing a suspicion of culture even while its benefits were acknowledged. Machiavelli was likened to Satan, as were the Jesuits, agents of the Counter-Reformation and instruments of the devil, and Italy was identified as the land of treachery, poison, and murder. Iago is Italian, and in *Hamlet* the "play within the play" that tells the sinister story of a nephew's murder of his uncle by pouring poison into his ear while he sleeps is "writ in choice Italian." The Gothic novel is here prefigured. The South provides as apt an occasion as the North for meditation on the darker sides of the soul, in jeopardy since the Fall.

Such meditation occurs in *Romeo and Juliet*, an early play, and in *Macbeth*, the work of Shakespeare's maturity, in not too dissimilar a fashion, so that a comparison of the two plays sheds fresh light on each of them. Is Macbeth evil incarnate, while Romeo represents love unjustly, mysteriously victimized? Yet Shakespeare has shown from the opening words of *Macbeth* that his hero is the victim of an attack as hard to combat as it is pregnant with consequences. He was, we are told, the essence of loyalty and valor, but the forces of evil decide, then and there, on the stage before our eyes, to involve him in a plan that reaches far beyond his personal lot, since it concerns the fate of a dynasty that was still in power in Scotland and in England when the play was written. And for Shakespeare's contemporaries, these forces existed; one and all felt threatened by them. That they should attack Macbeth, that his was the soul they had to capture, and that they were able to persuade him to his criminal projects by proving that they had the gift of reading the future were surely singular misfortunes for this obscure clan chieftain.

It is true that the three female demons who catch him in their net could prevail over his will only because it was potentially or already flawed: in spite of the vestiges of paganism that Shakespeare can discern in Scotland, we are still in the Christian world of free will, where the devil has great power but within precise limits. Macbeth, who yields so readily and is soon to become so black a figure, cannot originally have been a truly righteous man, and a pure soul. But the choice that has been made of him, and which has jeopardized him further, shifts our attention from one level of evil to another, more inward and less easily discernible—even by the man within whom it dwells—than mere ambition or a taste for plundering or murder. Macbeth is not innocent, but his soul was so insidiously affected to begin with that it did not know its own guilt.

This is confirmed, moreover, by a whole series of indications that Shakespeare gives us from the start or, rather, that he sees developing, albeit sometimes indistinctly, in a figure who rapidly becomes strikingly real to us, thanks to the sympathy that Shakespeare feels (and this is the essence of his genius) for everything that lives and dies. What he first shows us about Macbeth—and only a genius could have had such an intuition about a warrior famous for his courage in battle—is fear, omnipresent fear. Macbeth does not dread his adversary's sword, but an old wives' tale sets him trembling. Hardly has he envisaged his crime when he is beset with terrifying visions. Banquo's ghost signifies his remorse, no doubt, his quite natural dread of the wrath of heaven, but it frightens him far more than any flesh-and-blood judge could because it comes from that world of the unseen whose awesome presence he has always sensed around him. This fear is metaphysical in essence, and shows Macbeth as subject to that insidious, almost covert alienation that we have begun to sense at work in him. In the presence of nature, where others would see only cause for praising God, this uneasy spirit is on the alert. He is not so much a being who consciously wills evil as one who lives in constant dread of it, like a dizziness that paralyzes his capacity to love and over which his will has little power.

We realize, furthermore, from the very first dialogue with the witches, that Macbeth has an obsession of which he is similarly unconscious, though it is the source of many of his thoughts and actions. This is the obsession with fatherhood, a joy denied him (since for all his apparent virility he has no children), and jealousy of others' progeny. "Your children shall be kings," he says to Banquo, as the witches, those Fates, vanish into the mist. This thought already spoils the future promised him, and later drives him back to the priestesses of Hecate, to the very door of hell, because he wants at all costs to hear them repeat what he already knows but refuses to admit. And his wife, on two occasions, refers with singular violence to the children she has apparently had but in any case has lost. In terrible words, she sets her murderous plans above the child she has suckled. We are given to understand that the assassination of the king, the usurpation of power, is to be the new offspring of this man and this woman—an offspring born in the anguished hours before the dawn and soon to be the only bond between the couple.

Now one of the more important features of the medieval mind, one that still prevailed in Shakespeare's day, was the sense that God's world was a vast and perfect form, and that within it every creature had its place in the overall structure, which was an emanation of the Divine, and was therefore expected to compensate for the damage done by its death to the plenitude of the cosmos by procreating other lives to take its place. The destiny of being is thus entrusted to the ardor specific to every creature, and this is particularly true of man, who has been endowed with freedom of choice. If he has children, that is a positive sign in his favor. If he has none, he must feel himself indebted and so must rise through an effort of the mind to that participation in the form of the universe from which he is debarred physically.

Macbeth shows no signs of such a capacity for contemplation; on the contrary, his fear reveals that earth and heaven are alien to him, and his jealousy shows that other beings are rivals and enemies rather than kindred spirits. Whether his sterility is the cause or the consequence of his terror in the face of existence, this lack of children intensifies the terror, making the created world into a hostile and enigmatic place. And thus in two furtive but convergent ways, Macbeth is shown to be in a state of severance from the whole, of retreat into the self, which can be recognized as that vague but very deep and very dangerous malignity of which the Evil One has taken advantage. Does Shakespeare portray a creature of unbridled violence and ambition, whose crimes stem naturally and directly from obvious and dominating impulses, such as motivate Richard III, or Edmund in *King Lear*? No, he has probed more deeply, at the unconscious level where desire is contaminated almost at the moment of its birth, a moment when the wrong choice is made without a clear awareness of its consequences, which soon prove criminal. Whence the astonishment of Macbeth, overtaken in his own fate by some unknown power. Lacking desire at the outset, fearful of a world to whose beauty he is indifferent, then carried away by a dark desire, which perhaps is only a mask to hide that emptiness, he remains to the end a man who fails to understand. Remember his reflections on learning of his wife's death. They clearly display that incomprehension of the created world which, for a Christian of the Renaissance, was the most radical sin of all:

> Out, out, brief candle!
> Life's but a walking shadow, a poor player
> That struts and frets his hour upon the stage
> And then is heard no more: it is a tale
> Told by an idiot, full of sound and fury,
> Signifying nothing.

When alienation has reached this point, we are no longer dealing with the common sort of violence and treachery. An aching can be sensed, a yearning for love: however many misdeeds this sinner has accumulated, however far gone he is in crime, Shakespeare yet perceives him at a level so profound, so close to the painful recesses of our original being-in-the-world, that in spite of everything this man Macbeth embodies our universal condition, grasped at that mysterious point where one can still choose what to be, but where it is late, terribly late, in one's relation to oneself.

In *Macbeth*, Shakespeare is undoubtedly the playwright forcefully depicting visible violence and its explicit intentions; but he is also, without using specific words but by means of brief notations based on intuition, the theologian probing the most secret region of the soul—the latter being defined of course according to the Christian doctrine that is its frame of reference.

And if we now return to *Romeo and Juliet*, which predates the period when Shakespeare was to deal openly with the question of evil, we find that what we have learned from *Macbeth* sheds light upon the earlier play and that a greater complexity of meaning is revealed. The problem of *Romeo and Juliet*, at first glance, is that of the sufferings of the righteous, or the silence of God. The Elizabethan thinker recognizes that the fall of man has disturbed the workings of the world and that the very course of the stars has lost that harmonious coordination which should have ensured for mankind, through a play of influences involving the elements and the humors, an untroubled destiny. Nevertheless, there are too many setbacks in the fate of these two lovers, who seemingly had sought only to conform to the great law of life that is also God's law and the law of the heavenly bodies. Should we assume that the hard but noble task of the just man afflicted by misfortune is to rise above adversity? And yet this unfortunate pair has scarcely had time to prepare for such a life, let alone live it; it is as though heaven had decided that the finest people, because of their love, would be subjected to despair and therefore have recourse to suicide, which leads to hell.

But just as in *Macbeth*, where the protagonist's guilt is fully revealed only by a profoundly searching insight that discloses the metaphysical vice underlying crude impulses, it may be that in *Romeo and Juliet* what determines the action of the play is no more than its surface reality and that the misfortunes that ravage two lives are caused not by mere chance but by the difficulty one of the two protagonists finds in adapting to the world in which he must live. Is Romeo really that lover whose emotion, in harmony with the will of all creation, is so pure and so intense that Shakespeare will use it as a point of reference, standing out like a bright color against blacks and grays? In fact, as is made clear in the first act, he is the figure of melancholy as studied by the Elizabethans, the sad youth who, before becoming enamored of Juliet, fancied himself in love with a certain Rosaline, who was nothing but a mirage and an excuse for him to shun the world. At this point Romeo lived only by night, avoiding his friends, and all his words expressed only a vast dream that substituted a simplified image for the practical experience of everyday reality. This may seem like intensity and purity, but it means being oblivious to people as they exist in ordinary life, hence a lack of compassion, which is potentially evil.

It may be objected that this is only the beginning of the play and that the evil vanishes later with the meeting of Romeo and Juliet and the discovery of mutual love. But a careful reading of the tragedy reveals that, on the contrary, when Shakespeare dramatized the story told by Bandello and Arthur Brooke, he introduced an element of suspicion that brings out and enhances a number of facts of particular concern to him. When Romeo goes to the house of his enemies the Capulets, he does so with a sense of foreboding, as though driven by a malevolent force already at work within his very being. He has "dreamed a dream last night," which Mercutio's interruption prevents him from relating, so that one is tempted to believe that what he was about to tell us is what takes place that evening or the next day, already partly delineated in his own unconscious desire. Surely he is the kind of man who can only love if some obstacle intervenes, distancing the beloved object, haloing it with transcendence. Note that Juliet is still far off in the great hall when he is stirred by her beauty, which he claims is "too rich for use, for earth too dear," and that it is again as an image that he sees her at her window at the beginning of the balcony scene. The ecstatic words with which he greets this lovely nocturnal vision suggest not a real person but a cosmic form, whose two bright eyes are about to take their place among the stars, and this silent apparition seems to emit a disturbing light, anticipating the dream-visions of Edgar Poe. Ill-omened, too, is the secret marriage, which will render impossible any meeting in ordinary reality. Sexual possession is not incompatible with dream when it is confined to the mere physical act by the furtive character of the lovers' meetings. For this kind of lover, Juliet may well be another Rosaline, a proof that one can reject the world for the sake of beauty, and meanwhile know nothing of the true nature of the person one thinks one loves at other moments of her existence.

Now this experience of being, even if it involves no sense of guilt, resembles that negative disposition that Shakespeare shows to be at the origin of Macbeth's wrong choices; and here again it can have fatal consequences. To stake everything on a dream, to bank on appearance instead of confronting presence, is to place oneself in a difficult position between reality and mirage, where impatience lays down the law, where actions are more hazardous, and where consequently the risks are more dangerous and disaster strikes at last. "He was asking for it," proverbial wisdom says in such cases. And we may suspect that Romeo, in the depths of his being, was asking for what he thought he was simply enduring. We can see in his decision to kill himself, taken like a flash of lightning, as sudden as his love has been, the consequence not so much of his misfortune as of the alienation that has always warped his view of the world and submerged action in dream.

We must realize, too, that he is responsible not only for his own misfortune but for others that occur in the play, first and foremost for Juliet's. Married in secret and by the same token exposed to dangers such as the marriage planned for her by her father, which involves her in the most terrifying and traumatic experiences, Juliet seems robbed of her destiny, and Romeo may thus be thought to have seduced rather than married her, to have raped a willing victim, although an alternative solution was possible, as is hinted at several times. On more than one occasion, Shakespeare gives us to understand that the quarrel between the Montagues and the Capulets was dying down, and was kept aflame only by the folly of servants and the arrogance of young Tybalt, whose high-flown fantasy echoes, on a more vulgar note, that refusal to accept reality which is characteristic of Romeo. The head of the house of Capulet, who wants to get his daughter married, speaks in praise of Romeo ("a virtuous and well-governed youth") and accepts him in his house. Romeo might have remembered the words that express the essence of Christianity: "Knock and it shall be opened unto you." Antagonisms, at that time, were often brought to an end by marriages. Romeo's better self, with greater trustfulness, might have brought about that great reconciliation that Friar Laurence imagined, and which was achieved by his death, only too late and at such cost.

III

In *Romeo and Juliet*, Shakespeare raises somewhat the same problem as in *Macbeth*, responding to a similar enigma in the same kind of way. The question in each case, the dilemma that disturbs a mind accustomed to the idea of heaven's vigilance,[1] is that of chance, which seems to contradict this vigi-

---

1. In *King Lear*, when Edgar takes up Edmond's challenge, who can doubt that he will be victorious in this decisive battle? The economy of the play makes it unthinkable that the righteous man would perish through God's judgment at this moment.

lance, less because of the manifold vicissitudes it inflicts on the righteous than through the traps it seems to lay in their path, which the devil turns to his advantage. And the answer is not only to recognize in these victims of chance the fact of a preexistent fault, which exonerates heaven from the reproach of indifference, but also to disclose that fault in a remote recess of the soul, where lesser writers, satisfied with the virtues and vices current in ordinary behavior, would not have thought to search. Shakespeare, in short, is held back neither by horror nor by compassion, although he experiences both. By the power of his sympathy—which is denied to none of his characters, whence the impression of universality he conveys despite his highly personal sensibility and the assertion of his own opinions—he is aware of frustrated longings, naive aspirations, latent alienations, and morbid tendencies however slight; and, like a theologian although his language is not philosophical, he discovers in these indications of man's relation to the world the mysterious root—the still voiceless mandrake—of that which later in life, in altered circumstances, will take the form of evil. Like a theologian, but also like the devil, who, let us remark in passing, does exactly the same thing. But in the latter case the aim is evil, whereas if Shakespeare holds a mirror up to society, it is only so that the Christian soul, more readily aware of its own failings and of the dangers it faces, might escape the grasp of the great adversary. In *Romeo and Juliet* and in *Macbeth*, Shakespeare, who knows full well both the appalling consequences and the all but imperceptible origins of evil, does not trace out the intermediary stages of its development. The language of inner experience was not yet sufficiently diversified or recognized on the Elizabethan stage to make readily available to him those monologues that are like windows opening onto the relations between action and the unconscious mind. In *Hamlet* and *Othello*, on the other hand, it is precisely these moments of groping deliberation that he seeks to focus on, moments of world-weary ennui when the time seems out of joint, or of sudden eruption into madness or crime.

Which leads to one final observation. In contrast to Marlowe, whom he had studied closely, Shakespeare seems an optimist, for in tracing back the sources of crime or injustice to states of mind that are difficult but are not impossible to localize, to study, to understand, he refuses to admit the radical senselessness of any human situation. It may seem odd to use the term "optimist" of a poet so conscious of the black depths of which mankind is capable, who puts Iago beside Othello, and can create a Richard III of whom one wonders whether he has ever been capable of choosing between good and evil. But Shakespeare is obviously unwilling to see these few monsters as other than exceptional, a sort of countermiracle to be explained by some prior fault or a design of Providence; and whenever he can, Shakespeare tends toward the idea of liberty, recognizing the original fact of man's Fall and its consequences, the weakening of the human will, but describing subsequent lapses only against the background of virtues that persevere and new beginnings that mean hope. How often in Shakespeare's plays the action ends as day breaks, when order, which has been shaken and ravaged, is finally restored, when positive values are reasserted, either suddenly as in *Romeo and Juliet* or, as in *Macbeth*, by the action of the forces of good, ever more clearly at work toward the end of the play! Evil, for Shakespeare, is always at the basis of his study of human destiny, but it is a relative evil, outlined against a background of divine light and circumvented by Grace.

Optimism? Yet not without genuine disquiet, shown throughout his work by various frequently recurring signs. Is evil only a sort of dizziness before the plenitude of being, something one can get rid of simply by arising and walking away? But how swiftly some barely perceptible twist in the soul may sometimes spread, and with what tremendous consequences for the individual and the state, even sometimes for nature itself, which in *Macbeth*, *Julius Caesar*, and *Lear* we see thrown into a disorder that reflects the turmoil in human consciences! If Shakespeare, as I have said, does not dwell on the intermediate stages, it is because his sources all tell him that the disaster happens immediately, with no trace remaining of the moments that preceded it in the deterioration of his characters. And yet so many of these have seemed, at the beginning, so rich in virtues and gifts! Leaving aside Macbeth, who was never more than a brutal warrior in a still-barbarous age that seems pre-Christian and thereby almost reassuring, consider Romeo, the fine flower of a Christian society in which art, music, and rhetoric could shore up a troubled conscience. His good intentions, his will to love, are manifest, as is that physical beauty which to the Renaissance mind is the outward sign of moral quality, of purity of soul. Surely it is cause for alarm to see that the taint is in him too and will spoil everything in two days, like the canker in the rose.

Shakespeare is certainly alarmed. This is indicated by the insistence with which, fascinated by such a contradiction, he speaks both of Romeo's melancholy and of his rich virtues, calling to witness Mercutio, another melancholic but a clear-sighted one, whom we may take to represent the author at the heart of his creation. And Shakespeare's alarm is also indicated by his increasing concentration in subsequent plays on the rift between mind and world, on the repudiation of life, on excarnation—a concern already voiced in the sonnets, where the fair young man's perfection is worthless, since his refusal to marry and beget a child suggests metaphysical avarice. And so, not long after Romeo, we find Brutus in the harsh Roman world, and soon there will be Hamlet. The prince of Denmark, melancholy, skeptical, sickened by life, is a more self-aware Romeo who knows the flaw in his love, of which Ophelia, nonetheless, will be as much a victim as Juliet. The most famous and modern of Shakespeare's tragedies openly tackles the problem that was only latent in his most romantic one; and does so with an anguish—despite the ending, which restores order—metaphorically conveyed from the start by the cold night, the deserted battlements, the warlike preparations, the threat of the unseen.

Remember, we are in the Renaissance. Artistic creation, beautiful objects, poems reviving old myths, and the fuller acknowledgment of physical beauty are liable to ensnare one with charms that may prove illusory. The dream spreads, it permeates life itself, it seems victorious. In philosophy, in moral life, even and above all in forms of mystical experience, Neoplatonic thought, which Shakespeare knew through Spenser, seemed to justify a preference for the mirage, though this resulted in the melancholia of those young men who sit silently, chin in hand, their shoulders draped in inky cloaks.

And if, as the century drew to its close, there was Shakespeare, so deep a gaze scanning so wide a realm, it was not only because a mirror had to be held up to virtue so that it could see itself without complacency—the danger being only a failure to recognize those initial moods of dejection which can so quickly lead to despair, madness, and crime—but also because the trust that medieval man had placed in the world had now been undermined and so had to be restored; and this required a probing investigation of all the enigmas the poet perceived, all the dramas unfolding beneath his gaze, every sort of dream. The great writer is one who senses the weakening of that faith in the meaning of the world that ensures the survival of society, if not its happiness; and who makes this decline his sole concern, unafraid of its very monotony, which enables him to take in the immense diversity of situations and of human beings.

TRANSLATED BY JEAN STEWART AND JOHN NAUGHTON

CHAPTER TWO

Readiness, Ripeness: *Hamlet, Lear*

JUST AFTER he agrees to fight with Laertes—but not without a sense of foreboding that he tries to suppress—Hamlet concludes that "the readiness is all." And toward the end of *King Lear*, Edgar, son of the earl of Gloucester, persisting in his efforts to dissuade his father from suicide, asserts that "ripeness is all." And shouldn't we suppose that Shakespeare consciously established the opposition in these two phrases that are so closely related and come at two moments so dense with meaning—and that they therefore speak of one of the tensions at the very heart of his poetics? I would like to understand more clearly the "readiness" in *Hamlet* and the "ripeness" in *King Lear*.

But first a preliminary remark which, though it has been made before, seems nevertheless useful to bear in mind when we raise questions about Shakespeare's work. As we study the history of Western society, we discover at one moment or another, and on every level of life, especially on the level of self-awareness, a deep fissure that marks the point of separation between a previous and now seemingly archaic era and what might be called the modern world. The time "before" was a time when a conception of oneness, of unity, experienced as life, as presence, governed every relationship one could have with specific realities. Each of these realities thus found its place in a precisely defined order, which in turn made each reality into a presence, a kind of soul alive to itself and to the world among the other realities endowed with the same life, and assured to each a meaning of which there could be no doubt. The most important and most fortunate consequence of this fact of an order and a meaning was that human beings, who knew themselves to be an element in this world and sometimes even thought themselves the center of it, had no occasion to call into doubt their own being or the fact that they stood for the absolute. Whatever may have been the high and low points of their existence, in which chance often came into play, human beings were still able and compelled to honor their essence, which preserved a divine spark: herein is the whole substance of the teaching of the Christian Middle Ages with its theology of salvation. But a day came when technology and science began to discover, in what as a result became simply objects, features that could not be integrated into the structures of traditional meaning. The established order fell into fragmentation; the earth of signs and promises became nature once again, and life matter; the relation of the person to himself or herself was all at once an enigma, and destiny a solitude. This is the fissure I was speaking of, the final settlings of which have not yet been determined.

And it should also be noticed that the first truly irrevocable manifestation of this crisis, which engendered the civilization—if the word still applies—that today we contrast to the rest of the planet, took place at various moments (depending on the country as well as the social milieu) of the end of the sixteenth and beginning of the seventeenth century, the years during which Shakespeare wrote his plays. The fracture line that broke the horizon of atemporality and gave over the history of the world to its ever more uncertain and precipitous development passes through *Hamlet;* it is obviously one of the causes of the play and could be said to run right through its heart. Without attempting a detailed analysis, for these few pages would hardly be the place for it, I can at least emphasize, as an example of what I mean, the central importance of the opposition of two beings who clearly represent the succession of the two eras, a contrast all the more striking for being established between a father and a son who bear the same name. On this scarcely realistic stage, where aspects of the high Middle Ages are boldly combined with others that reflect the life of Shakespeare's own time and even its philosophical avant-garde—the references to Wittenberg, for instance, the stoicism of Horatio—the old Hamlet, the king who furthermore is already dead although he continues to make himself heard, clearly represents, as is even made explicit, the archaic mode of being. Not only does he wear the dress and bear witness to the customs of feudal society; even his need for vengeance signifies his adherence to the dying tradition, since this demand, which bears the stamp of a sacred right, implies among other things the certainty that the entire state suffers when legitimacy is violated. And beyond this, his status as battling and triumphant sovereign of being is an excellent metaphor for the domination that a Christian, in the era before the new astronomy, thought he exercised over a world on the peripheries of which the devil might nonetheless be prowling. And, finally, the first Hamlet is a father without the slightest apprehension, with hope even—at least at the beginning of the play—which means that he has confidence in established values, in continuity. Claudius, who puts an end to the reign, has no children.

As for the other Hamlet, the son called upon to reestablish the traditional order and thus to assume his royal function, it is easy to see that if he is the hero of Shakespeare's tragedy, it is because the values evoked by the Ghost, which Hamlet immediately tries to inscribe in the "book" of his memory, have now almost no reality in his eyes. His goodwill is nevertheless quite real; he burns with the desire to vindicate his father, and he admires two other sons who do not hesitate to take their place in the society they believe still exists; and if for a moment he thinks of marriage, he who has been filled with disgust for things sexual by his mother's new relationship, it is, I think, in the hope that the very real love he feels for Ophelia might reconcile him to life as it is, and to the idea of generation, which in turn could help him to vanquish the skepticism that saps his energy and turns him from action. But this desire to do what is right sets off even more strikingly the extent to which his vision of the world, like a paralyzing if not completely destructive fatality, no longer recognizes its once perfect organization—that organization which is, in fact, already in disarray in the comportment of the "Danish" court, prey to a symptomatic corruption. One remembers his moving words on the earth, that sterile promontory, on the heavens, that foul and pestilent congregation of vapors. Similarly, he fails with Ophelia, although there is nothing really wrong with their personal relationship, because he has not managed to spare her from that vision that seizes everything and everybody from the outside—as is indicated by his mocking cry, "words, words, words"—and because he can see nothing but opacity and lies in every manner of thinking and speaking, including those of young women. Even if one feels compelled to try other keys—oedipal motivations, for instance—for understanding the suspicion with which Hamlet persecutes Ophelia, it remains nonetheless true that this suspicion betrays, in its difference from the simple faith of Hamlet's father, an alienation, an isolation, a vertigo that the earlier, more united society could never have imagined and would not have tolerated. And it is, furthermore, in his ambiguous relation to his father, who represents, who is, in fact, the former world, that Hamlet's disgust most clearly appears. He does not want to doubt that he admires and even loves his father; but when he calls him the "old mole" or thinks he sees him in his nightgown the second time he appears, or lets himself be carried away by the thought of those sins which keep him in Purgatory—the reference to him as "gross" and "full of bread," for instance—aren't these simply more signs of Hamlet's inability to understand the ways of the world and the beings in it, as the old way of looking at life would have allowed him to?

This inability to recognize his father for what he truly is, although he will affirm his worth at every chance he gets, is doubtless one of the most painful of Hamlet's secrets and one of the unacknowledged elements with which he nourishes what is obviously his sense of remorse, and it explains a number of the most obscure aspects of the play, beginning with the other great obsession that structures it. There are certainly many reasons that explain Hamlet's rages against Gertrude—and once again I am not attempting any systematic analysis here—but it seems clear to me that the son accuses his mother so violently of betrayal because he himself—although he does not realize it—has betrayed the very person whom, he maintains, she should have kept without rival in her heart. He always insists that it is the majesty of the old Hamlet, his twofold greatness of man and prince, that have been insulted by the new marriage; he vehemently denounces Claudius's vices, especially as they show him to be unworthy of the role he has usurped; but the whole scene of the "two pictures," during which Hamlet tries to prove to Gertrude the grandeur of the one and the ignominy and even the ridiculousness of the other, only serves to show that rhetoric plays a large role in the emotion he tries to feel. Once again we are at the theater, and perhaps even more so during these moments of accusation and introspection than when the player recites those rather bombastic, if deeply felt, verses on the death of Queen Hecuba. Hamlet tries to live according to the values handed down to him from the past, but he can only do so on the level of "words, words, words," his obsession with the emptiness of which we now begin to better understand. He who, in order to wreak his vengeance, in order to restore the threatened order, in short, in order to proclaim meaning, feels it necessary to disguise himself for a time, which in fact becomes endless, is merely an actor on this level as well—so that his true double in the play is, alas, neither Laertes nor Fortinbras nor even Gertrude, who is guilty only of weakness—and Hamlet knows this, as does his father, who keeps reminding him of it—but rather the character who says one thing and thinks another, merely pretending to respect and observe values in which he certainly no longer believes: Claudius, the destroyer, the enemy. This is the true core of *Hamlet*, as well as the necessary consequence of that crisis in society of which the murder of the king is only the symbol. Those who appear now, and who can be seen to exist beyond the boundaries of the broken social order, are more deeply imbued with reality, more fully steeped in the denseness of life, than are their fellowmen, whose obedience to the categories of former times seems only backward and obtuse. They may live in anguish and confusion; their survival reactions may be cynical and ignominious—as is certainly the case with that opaque being, Claudius, for so long the shadow of his brother. He is an undeniably covetous man, as there have always been covetous men, but he is also one who has consciously transgressed the strictest social codes.

Throughout *Hamlet* we find a thousand signs of the nephews's fascination—sometimes bordering on the equivocal, it seems so affectionate—with his uncle. One senses that something attracts him in the very person he thinks he detests, without it being necessary to infer from this strange obsession, at least as its essential reason, some ambiguous extension of the complex algebra of the oedipal relations. I would say that Hamlet doesn't so much love as simply *understand* Claudius for what he is, and that he understands him more intimately than he can understand others, because it is his contemporary he is encountering, and his only contemporary in these changing times that have suddenly become a thundering storm, a sinking ship. With this man who is his adversary according to the reasoning of days gone by, and certainly his enemy according to values that are eternal, he feels the instinctive solidarity that binds together shipwrecked men.

II

In short, in *Hamlet* we see clearly, deeply, specifically the problematics of a consciousness awakening to a condition that was undreamed of and unimaginable only the day before: a world without structure, truths which henceforth are only partial, contradictory, in competition with one another—as many signs as one could wish, and soon far too many, but nothing that will resemble a sacred order or meaning. And it is from this perspective that we must try to examine the idea of "readiness," as Hamlet advances it, at a moment, it should be noted, that is late in the play—in the fifth act—when Hamlet has had the chance to measure the extent of a disaster that he experiences at first as an endless tangle of insoluble contradictions. And what about Claudius? Hamlet was so filled with the desire to kill him, and yet here he is still hesitating to do so, apparently resolute, as resolute as ever, but distracted in every situation by some new consideration—this time, for instance, by his interest in Laertes. And Ophelia? It is certain now that he did love her, the news of her suicide has given him absolute proof of it—he loved her, he says, more than forty thousand brothers, and more in any case than Laertes, whose grandiloquence is clearly open to criticism; and yet this strange love, poisoned by suspicion, disguised in insult, has only thrown her into despair and death. It is clear now that he is suffering deeply from an evil for which he can find no cure, and that he has lost all hope in his ability to arrest the collapse of meaning. Hamlet is acutely conscious of his own powerlessness as he gives expression to his deepest thoughts on the last day of his life in the presence of Horatio, who always seems to incite him to profound reflection and exigency.

What does Hamlet say to Horatio in this scene—preceded, it should be remembered, by their long meditation in the cemetery beside the skull of Yorick, the king's jester, who knew better than anyone the falseness of appearances? He says that even the fall of a sparrow is ruled by Providence, that "if it be now, 'tis not to come; if it be not to come, it will be now," and that if it be not now, let there be no doubt about it, "yet it will come." And as we do not know when this moment will occur, and never can, the important thing is to be ready. One might suppose that Hamlet is talking about death here, and in a way that does not seem in contradiction with traditional teaching, since the medieval mind loved to insist that God had the final decision about the fate of man's undertakings. Should we draw the conclusion that Hamlet—who has obviously thought a great deal during his trip to England, and after it as well—is in the process of rediscovering the truth of the ancient precepts and is referring, in any case, to those fundamental structures of being of which they were the expression? But Christianity confided to Providence only the final result of an act and not its preparation, which, on the contrary, it required to be subjected to careful consideration and brought within the bounds of established values. Hamlet, however, is taking advantage of what seems fatalistic in the traditional way of looking at things in order to dispense with the necessity of examining what he has been compelled to accept in a situation that could be decisive for him—the duel with a master swordsman, an encounter that could easily be refused, especially as it appears to be part of a trap. Why does he consent to risk his life before having brought to successful conclusion his grand scheme to reestablish justice? Neither the ethics nor the religion of the Middle Ages would have accepted this way of behaving, which seems to suggest that a prince is indifferent to his cause, a son to the wishes of his father.

However it may seem, therefore, Hamlet has not really adopted for himself an adage which in its true significance—"Heaven helps those who help themselves"—gave such apt expression to the old universe with its contrasting poles of transcendence and chance. If he has recourse to a traditional formula, it is to turn it toward aims of an entirely different nature, and this time authentically, totally, fatalistic. The "readiness" he proposes is not reliance on the will of God as the guarantor of our efforts, the protector of our meaning; it is rather cessation of what the God of former times expected of us: the fearless and unflagging exercise of our judgment in the world he created, the discrimination between good and evil. In place of the discernment that tries to organize and provide, and does so through awareness of values, Hamlet substitutes a welcoming of things as they come along, however disorderly and contradictory they may be, and the acceptance of chance: in a philosophy as pessimistic as this one, our acts seem as thoroughly devoid of a reason for being as the necessity that comes into play with them. Our condition is in nonmeaning, nothingness, and it is just as well to realize it at moments that seem moments of action, when normally our naïveté is set in motion. In a word, a single act still has some logic and is worthy of being carried out, and that is to take great pains to detach oneself from every illusion and to be ready to accept everything—everything, but first of all, and especially, death, the essence of all life—with irony and indifference.

Yet it cannot be denied that the Hamlet who proposes this surrender is also, as the whole scene will show, a man who is now far more alert than at other moments in the play, far more attentive, for example, than he once was to the ways in which others behave, even though his observation leads only to mocking and scorn. He can even be seen preparing himself for a sport that nothing in his past has allowed us to expect from him, a sport that demands a sharp eye and a swift hand—and also the encounter with the other, in that true and not entirely heartless intimacy which can exist in hand-to-hand combat. These characteristics, so unexpected in the one once covered by the inky cloak, are of course useful in paving the way for the denouement, which is to be effected through the battle of two sons who are, as Hamlet himself remarks, the image of one another; but they are so strikingly present that they also must be seen to play a role in the implicit characterization of the ethics that is developed, and so it would be a mistake to think that this *readiness*, which is a form of renunciation, is so in a passive or discouraged way. Doubtless because the conclusion reached by Hamlet has freed him from his earlier self-absorption, from his recriminations and his endless reverie, his new mode of being seems also to take on a body, a capacity for play, an interest, if perhaps a cruel one, for those things in the world he once had fled. This is now an all-embracing consciousness, an immediacy in the way the world is received that is already response, return: and this readiness is in truth so active, one can feel so intensely the need to bring together everything in the experience of the void, that one is tempted to compare it to other undertakings which, though they too seem pessimistic, are nonetheless of a spiritual nature and another form of the absolute. Is the readiness of Hamlet an Elizabethan equivalent of the Buddhist discipline, of the way in which the samurai, for instance, prepares himself—another swordsman at the end of another Middle Ages—to accept the moment of death without a shadow of resistance? A way of recovering positivity and plenitude in the very heart of an empty world?

But in the case of the Buddhist—be he warrior or monk—the critique of appearances, of the manifestations of illusion, is also, and primarily, brought to bear on the self, which has appeared to him, not without good reason, as the supreme form of illusion, whereas Hamlet's lucidity, however radical it may wish to be, is the reaction of a man who has considered himself the guardian of the absolute, who hasn't as yet resigned himself to the dislocation of a heritage that remains centered on the self. I see it therefore as the ultimate response of an unrelenting "personality," a kind of doleful, yet not entirely hopeless, meditation on the meaninglessness he himself has tried to demonstrate. Hamlet's readiness is not the Buddhist's effort to go beyond the very idea of meaning to attain to the plenitude of immediacy—a person's recognition that he or she has no more importance than the fleeting blossoms of the cherry tree; it is rather the degree zero of a meaning, an order, still vividly recalled, the fundamental structures of which, though lost, are still considered desirable, and the need for which is still secretly acknowledged by that very complexity of consciousness in which all the language that exists only for the purpose of hoping and organizing remains in reserve for the possibility of some future miracle. The new relation to the self of this king without a kingdom is therefore not a peaceful one; it is not the great burst of laughter that tears apart ancient woe. What should be seen, on the contrary, is a refinement of unvanquished suffering, its reduction to a single shrill note, almost inaudible and yet omnipresent, a form of irony not unlike that which Kierkegaard writes about, in which moments of gaiety or laughter are always chilled by nostalgia. Not the liberation but the celibacy of the soul—taken on as a last sign, a challenge full of desire, offered to the God who has withdrawn from his Word. An appeal, and in this sense a recognition of the existence of others, an indication that he who pretends to prefer solitude is in fact lying to himself—in all of which is prefigured, as evidenced by the enormous vogue of *Hamlet* throughout the entire nineteenth century, the dandyism of Delacroix and Baudelaire.

So I see the readiness that emerges in *Hamlet* as quite simply a negative strategy for the preservation of the soul, a technique useful at all times when humanity strives to recall what its hopes once were. And I believe, of course, that we should try to understand whether this state of mind applies only to the prince of Denmark and to a few others like him in Shakespeare's bountiful and polyphonic universe, or whether we should ascribe it, in one way or another, to Shakespeare himself and therefore consider it one of the possible "solutions" proposed by the poetry of the Elizabethan era for the great crisis in values it was beginning to analyze. It can easily be imagined as such: *Hamlet* is so obviously a personal play, and one can feel so intensely, in phrase after phrase of the protagonist, a poet's effort to stand in place of rhetorical conventions. But we must note that nothing has been undertaken definitively, even in the play itself, when Hamlet, at the very last moment, affirms and assumes his new philosophy. That he takes it seriously, that he truly would like to live it, can scarcely be doubted, since it is to Horatio, to whom he never lies, that he confides his deepest thoughts on the matter. But when he is mortally wounded an hour later, he offers his "dying voice" to Fortinbras—and beyond him to traditional values, or at least to the attitude that wills the preservation of their fiction. One may rightfully wonder whether "readiness" isn't for Shakespeare simply one phase of psychological insight and for Hamlet the whimsical stance that masks the even more disastrous reason that has led him to accept Laertes' strange challenge so lightly, and with it the possibility of dying.

III

Let us not forget that it is in *Lear,* not more than five or six years later, that one sees clearly designated that "ripeness" which Shakespeare seems to have wanted to place against the "readiness" of the earlier work.

The historical context of *Lear* is not without certain resemblances to the earlier play, for the work is set in an England at least as archaic as the Denmark of Hamlet's father—it is even a pagan world, closely watched over by its gods—and yet here, too, one discovers signs that seem to announce new modes of being. In *Lear* there also emerges a character who, one can sense from the outset, is incapable of recognizing that the world is an order, rich in meaning—Edmund, second son of the earl of Gloucester. A son, then, like the prince of Denmark, and one who, like Hamlet, has reasons for doubt about what will be his heritage. But the resemblance between Edmund and Hamlet ends there, for the painful plight of the son, which Hamlet has lived through with honesty and with the burning desire to do what is right, is now studied in one who is clearly evil, and with categories of thought that remain essentially medieval. At first sight, one might consider this certainly non-conformist personality modern, since he scoffs at astrological explanations, at the superstitions of those who surround him, and even at the values of common morality. But it should be observed that Edmund's speeches are accompanied by none of the indications in *Hamlet*—the actors, Wittenberg, the presence of Horatio, and so on—that serve as signposts to the modern era. What makes Edmund an outsider, far from being seen as symptomatic of crisis, is set very explicitly by Shakespeare in the context of one of the convictions advanced by the medieval understanding of man: if Edmund would usurp his brother's place, if he longs to see his father dead, if he thus shows how far he is from the most universal human feelings, it is because he is a bastard, born out of wedlock, himself the fruit of sin. And it is in complete agreement with traditional Christian teaching that *King Lear* asks us to understand that this sin, this adultery, is precisely the opportunity that evil, ever unvanquished, even if always repelled, has been waiting for—the chance to invade once again the order established by God, though in the end this order will emerge triumphant once more, thanks to the intervention of a few righteous souls. This being the case, if Edmund evokes nature as his one guiding principle, as the law to which his services are bound, one should not see in this a reflection of the Renaissance humanist for whom the study of empirical reality is unbiased activity of mind, but rather the revelation of the baseness of a soul, influenced by black magic—a soul that feels at home nowhere so much as where the commonest bestial urges reign. Edmund's actions do not disclose the ultimate crisis of sacred order but rather its inner weakness. And we know from the very outset of the action that he will perish—unmistakably, without a trace of uneasiness or regret, without a future in the new forms of consciousness—as soon as the forces of goodness he has caught off guard have reestablished their power.

Far from signifying, then, that Shakespeare's attention is focused on the problems of modernity as such, as was the case in *Hamlet*, the character of the son in *King Lear* serves to reinforce the notion that the old order remains the uncontested frame of reference in the play, the determining factor in the outcome of the drama, the truth that will be reaffirmed after a moment of crisis. And it is clearly for this reason that in the foreground of the play there emerges a figure missing in *Hamlet*, since neither Laertes nor Fortinbras ever attains truly spiritual stature: the figure of the child—girl or boy, since it is as true of Cordelia, third daughter of Lear, as of Edgar, firstborn son of Gloucester—whose purity and moral determination find the means of thwarting the traitors' schemes. In fact, even more than Cordelia, whose somewhat cool and arid virtuousness keeps at a certain distance from those violent, contradictory words, mingled with both love and hatred, through which the action of the play is developed and resolved, the agent of redemption for the imperiled group is Edgar, who, at the very moment when he might have yielded to despair or cynicism—hasn't he been falsely accused, attacked by his own brother, misjudged, without cause, by his father?—gives proof, on the contrary, of those reserves of compassion, of lucidity, of resolute understanding of the darkest depths of the souls of others, that can be found in anyone, even quite early in life and without special preparation. Struck in a completely unforeseeable way by what appears to be the purest form of evil, this still very young man, who only the day before was rich, pampered, assured of a future place among the most powerful of the land, chooses at once to plunge into the very depths of adversity, taking on the semblance of a beggar and the speech of a fool to shatter at the outset the too narrow framework of his own personal drama and to bring his inquiry to bear on all the injustices, all the miseries, all the forms of madness that afflict society. He understands instinctively—and here is clearly a sign that this world is still alive—that he will be able to achieve his salvation only by working for the salvation of others, each man needing as much as anyone else to free himself from his egotism, from his excesses, from his pride so that true exchange may begin once more.

In spite of everything, however, the hero of *King Lear* remains the one for whom the play is named—the old king—since unlike Edmund, who has been marked from the outset by the sin involved in his birth, and in contrast to Edgar, who emerges into his maturity through the crimes of another, Lear is thrown into his troubles by his own free act, and thus his punishment and his madness, his gradual discovery of those truths and realities he has neglected before, become a succession of events all the more deeply convincing and touching. Lear begins not with something rotten in the state, as did Hamlet, but rather with a mysterious sickness in the soul, in his case, pride. Lear admires himself, prefers himself; he is interested in others only to the extent that they are interested in him, and so he is blind to their own true being; he does not truly love others, in spite of what he may think: thus the ground is laid for the catastrophic act that will refuse to recognize what truly has value, that will deprive the righteous of their due, and that will spread disorder and sorrow everywhere and give the devil the chance he has been waiting for in the son born of adultery. Lear—even more than Gloucester, whose only sins are sins of the flesh—has relived, reactivated, man's original sin; and thus he represents, more than any other character in the play, our condition in its most radical form, which is imperfection, but also struggle, the will to self-mastery. When, on the basis of those values he has never denied but has understood so poorly and lived so little, he learns to recognize that his kingly self-assurance is pure pretension and his love a mere illusion, and when he learns what true love is, what happiness could be, we feel all the more deeply moved as his initial blindness belongs to all of us, more or less: he speaks to what is universal. And yet, even though he occupies the foreground from beginning to end of the play, Lear cannot and must not hold our attention simply because of what he is, or merely on the basis of his own particular individuality, since his spiritual progress comes precisely from his rediscovering the path toward others and thereafter forgetting himself in the fullness of this exchange. It is in the modern era, the era of Hamlet, that the individual—separated from everything and everybody, incapable of checking his solitude, and trying to remedy what is missing through the proliferation of his desires, his dreams, and his thoughts—will slowly assume that extraordinary prominence which ends in romanticism. In *King Lear*—as on the Gothic fresco, which is always more or less a *danse macabre*—no one has greater worth merely because of what sets him apart from others, however singular or extreme this difference might be. The soul, studied from the point of view of its free will, which is the same in everyone, is less the object of descriptions that note differences than it is the very stage of the action, and from the outset the only stage: and what appears in the play, what finds expression there, are the great key figures of society, such as the king and his fool, the powerful lord and the poor man, and those categories of common experience such as fortune or charity, or the deadly sins that Marlowe, in his *Doctor Faustus*, scarcely ten years earlier, had not hesitated to keep onstage. In short, behind this character, who is remarkable but whose uncommon aspects are above all signs of the extent of the dangers that menace us—and of the resources at our disposition—the true object of Shakespeare's attention, the true presence that emerges and risks being overwhelmed but triumphs in the end, is that life of the spirit to which Lear, and Edgar as well, and also to a certain extent Gloucester and even Albany, all bear witness, which is designated by the word *ripeness.*

Ripeness, maturation, the acceptance of death as in *Hamlet,* but no longer in this case because death would be the sign, par excellence, of the indifference of the world, of the lack of meaning—no, rather because acceptance of death could be the occasion for reaching a profound understanding of the real laws governing being, for freeing oneself from illusion, from vain pursuits, for opening oneself to a conception of Presence which, mirrored in our fundamental acts, will guarantee a living place to the individual in the evidence of All. We can only understand *King Lear* if we have learned to place this consideration in the foreground, if we have come to see that this is the thread that binds everything together, not only the young man with the old one whose soul is ravaged but intact, but the two of them with the Fool, for instance, who represents in medieval thought the outermost edge of our uncertain condition. And this consideration must be seen to dominate even in a context in which the forces of night seem so powerful, in which the Christian promise has not as yet resounded—although its structures are already there, since it is Shakespeare who is writing; we can therefore sense in them an indication of change, a reason for hope. Ripeness emerges in *Lear* as a potentiality for everyone, as the existential starting point from which the protagonists of this tragedy of false appearances begin to be something more than mere shadows; and from the Fool to Lear, from Edgar to his father, from Cordelia, from Kent, from Gloucester to their sovereign, even from an obscure servant to his lord when the latter has his eyes plucked out, it is what gives the only real substance to human exchange, which is otherwise reduced to concerns and desires that are only hypocrisy or illusion. This primacy accorded to the inner life of men, with the inevitable shaking of the foundations that comes with it, is what gives meaning to the most famous scene in *Lear,* in which we see Edgar, disguised as a fool, with the fool who is a fool by profession, and Lear, who is losing his mind, all raving together—or so it seems—beneath the stormy skies. Those blasting winds and bursts of lightning, that cracking of the cosmos, seem to suggest the collapse of meaning, the true state of a world we once had thought of as our home; but let us not forget that in that hovel, and under the semblance of solitude, misfortune, and weariness, the irrational powers that tend to reestablish truth are working more freely than ever they could in the castles of only a moment before. It is here that true reflection begins again, here that the idea of justice takes shape once more. The stormy night speaks to us of dawn. The brutality of the gods and of men, the fragility of life, are as nothing against a showing of instinctive solidarity that brings things together and provides comfort. And let us also remember that nothing of this sort appears in *Hamlet,* where, except for Horatio, who in fact withdraws from the action, and Ophelia, who, unable to be what she truly wants to be, becomes mad and kills herself, everything in the relationship between people is cynical, harsh, and joyless: recall, for instance, the way in which Hamlet himself gets rid of Rosencrantz and Guildenstern—"They are not near my conscience." It is not the universe of *Lear*—however bloody it may seem—that contains the greatest darkness. This "tragedy"—but in an entirely different sense from the Greek understanding of the term—is, in comparison to *Hamlet,* an act of faith. We meet in an arena of error, of crime, of dreadfully unjust death, in which even the very idea of heaven seems missing; and yet "the center holds," meaning manages to survive and even to take on new depth, assuring values, calling forth sacrifice and devotion, allowing for moral integrity, for dignity, and for a relation to the self that one might term full if not blissful. Here we learn that the structures of meaning are but a bridge of thread thrown over frightful depths; but these threads are made of steel.

IV

Ripeness, readiness—two irreducible attitudes. One, the quintessence of the world's order, whose unity we breathe; the other, the reverse side of that order, when one no longer sees anything in the grayness of the passing days but the incomprehensible weave.

And the most important question that one might raise about Shakespeare's entire work, it seems to me, is the significance that this absolutely fundamental opposition he has now formulated takes on for the playwright himself, in terms of the practical possibilities for the future of the mind and spirit. In other words, when he writes *King Lear* and speaks of *ripeness,* is it simply a question of trying to restore a past mode of being that our present condition dooms to failure, and perhaps even renders unthinkable, at least past a certain point—the only path for people living after the end of sacred tradition being the *readiness* conceived of by Hamlet, the Elizabethan intellectual? Or, taking into consideration the emotion and the lucidity that characterize the play—as if its author did in fact know precisely what he was talking about—

should we ask ourselves if Shakespeare doesn't, in one way or another, believe that the "maturation" of Edgar and Lear is still valid even for the present — the order, the system of evidence and value which is the necessary condition for this maturation having perhaps not so completely or definitively disappeared in his eyes, despite the crisis of modern times, as it seems to his most famous but scarcely his most representative character? An essential question, certainly, since it determines the ultimate meaning of the relation of a great poetic work to its historic moment. The answer to which must doubtless be sought in the other plays of Shakespeare, and in particular in those that come at the end, after *Hamlet* and the great tragedies.

We will find in them — at least this is my hypothesis — that despite the collapse of the "goodly frame" which the Christian Middle Ages had built, with heaven and earth around man, who was created by God, this poet of a harsher time felt that an order still remained in place, in nature and in us — a deep, universal order, the order of life, which, when understood, when recognized in its simple forms, when loved and accepted, could give new meaning through its unity and its sufficiency to our condition as exiles from the world of the Promise — just as grass springs up among the ruins. We will also find that Shakespeare understood how the function of poetry changed along with this recognition: it would no longer be merely the formulation of an obvious truth, already tested to the depths by others than the poet; rather, its task will be to remember, to hope, to search by itself, to make manifest what is hidden beneath the impoverished forms of everyday thinking, beneath the dissociations and alienations imposed by science and culture — and thus it will be an intervention, the assumption of a neglected responsibility, that "reinvention" of which Rimbaud will speak in his turn. Great thoughts that make for the infinite richness of *The Winter's Tale*, a play that is, in fact, solar and may be superimposed on *Hamlet* point by point — I will come back to this idea — like a developed photograph, zones of shadow becoming clear, the bright reality as opposed to its negative. The great vistas, too, that are dreamed of and explored in *The Tempest* — luminous double of *King Lear*. And grand opportunities, of course, for a resolute writer, which explains, retrospectively, what has always constituted the exceptional quality of Shakespeare's poetry — the first in Western literature to measure the extent of a disaster, and, above all, the first to seek to remedy it.

TRANSLATED BY JOHN NAUGHTON

CHAPTER THREE

"Art and Nature"

The Background of *The Winter's Tale*

AT A POINT IN *The Winter's Tale* where all its paths meet, Shakespeare seems to turn aside from the action to raise a philosophical issue, the relationship between art and nature.

Yet, had he wanted to give himself, or us, his audience, a few moments' respite after so many violent scenes, so much suffering and madness, he had only to draw on the hubbub and laughter, the music indeed, of a festival in the making. For it is at a seasonal celebration, a sheep-shearing festival on a prosperous farm, that Polixenes, king of Bohemia, has just arrived.

There are matters on Polixenes' mind, however, and on the minds of two young people who are also there, that either leave them little inclined to levity or have them latch onto the significance of this feast day with a gravity and wholeheartedness that would make a simple interlude of dance and folk song seem out of place. Furthermore, these preoccupations, along with this bustle and excitement, are expressed in a way that clearly asks us to reflect on a question similar to that of art and nature: the question of appearance and being, of illusion and the truth concealed by illusion, sometimes in a deliberate and unprincipled way.

The king of Bohemia, then, has just arrived at the farm in disguise, for he hopes in this way to catch out his son Prince Florizel, whom he suspects of wanting to marry a shepherdess. The latter—who, like her lover, is also the child of a king, though she is not yet aware of this—is likewise wearing fancy dress, as is Florizel, though in their case it is not to mislead anyone. Quite the contrary: in dressing her lover as a young shepherd and decking herself out in flowers like Flora come back to earth, she merely means to show, in these hours at the height of summer, that the essence of human life is divine and that "the great creating nature" must, somehow or other, have been innocent of original sin. The king and the shepherdess appear before us in disguise; they have taken some trouble over it, and we who are witnesses cannot help but think that their appearance must have required some form of art—even, in the case of the girl, a natural aptitude or talent, however honest and plain-spoken she might be, since Polixenes finds her extremely attractive. The problem of art and nature, at a point in the play that might seem surprising, crops up of itself, as it were. An Elizabethan audience—familiar with the problem, since this "paragon" haunted the Middle Ages and the Renaissance—could not fail to be reminded of it when it saw here, at the beginning of act 4, "the mistress of the feast" decked out like a figure from Botticelli, greeting the king concealed behind a false beard.

But it is not their disguises—one of which, moreover, no one has seen through at this point—that give the protagonists pause, but an observation one of them makes about flowers, in other words about realities in which essence and appearance might seem, unlike disguises, to be one. Perdita—such is the unusual name of this illusory shepherdess transformed into a no less illusory Flora—wants to bid courteous welcome to the unknown arrival and offers him rosemary and rue, which, she says, "keep / Seeming and savour all the winter long." The rue is also an allusion—and Perdita emphasizes this—to that Grace which has transformed the destiny of mankind, hitherto burdened with original sin. It is a pledge made to the visitor, therefore, that he too will receive this gift from heaven—provided, of course, he show an equally clear understanding of the symbolic significance of the other plant, rosemary. The important thing is to remember. Remember sin and divine forgiveness, says Perdita; remember to make yourself worthy of that forgiveness, just as we, at the farm, will remember your gracious visit.

Kind words, but Polixenes for his part—at least when he is in the presence, as here, of the beautiful young woman his son wishes to marry—is arguably less concerned for the fate of his soul than for the longings of his body; so much so, that he replies with distinct bitterness and in a somewhat brusque manner that these flowers, which are for winter and humble in appearance, are well suited to men of advanced years like himself. He shuts himself off from spiritual considerations and deep symbols, preferring to think only of his life among the good things of this world, in the evening of pleasures he soon will lose. At which point Perdita protests, somewhat mischievously but with all the more vehemence and conviction, that though there are undoubtedly, in these months of summer not yet past its prime, finer and more flattering flowers—carnations and gillyvors—these she cannot offer him. These flowers, she has heard, are so "pleasantly pied" only because art has collaborated with nature in making them.

This immediately calls forth a discussion that strikes us less by its novelty—the gist of it can be found in Montaigne and other thinkers of the period—than by its intensity and seriousness and by the speed and clarity with which it proceeds. On hearing what Perdita has so much at heart to affirm, Polixenes—who is somewhat taken aback, and now less put out than interested—retorts that art adds nothing to nature that it has not already taken from it, being nothing more in this case, as in many others, than a grafting of one plant onto another, in certain respects more satisfying: "The art itself is nature," he says, as Perdita herself acknowledges. And since this is so, why not resort to art to improve on what already is?

It is at this point, however, that Perdita puts off her reserve and this time around hands the king the simplest wildflowers imaginable, to which there can be no possible rejoinder—lavender, mint, savory, marjoram, marigolds, "flowers of middle summer . . . to men of middle age." She will no more grow gillyvors, she exclaims, than she would have Florizel desire her merely because she is dressed up in this way, or wish to make a mother of her merely for that reason. From a discussion hitherto composed largely of sensory considerations and more a question of aesthetics than of morality, she has moved onto a plane on which she herself is at stake as well as in turmoil; a plane on which an art that alters nature is also, she feels, a snare that evil—that spirit of evil which nature is spared—makes use of and can turn to its advantage.

And, indeed, nothing is easier for Shakespeare's contemporaries to understand than what Perdita is trying to say. At the beginning of the seventeenth century, the audience at the Globe, or even at court performances, has no doubt that God created the world. The world, in other words, is not a conglomeration of matter diversified by purely physical laws but a group of beings that, however humble in appearance, reflect and refract the divine presence and thus have what may be called an inner life and a potential symbolic significance. It follows from this momentous idea that appearances grafted onto reality by artificial means cannot but disfigure God's handiwork, cast out spirit from the natural order, and deprive the human being of this lesson in unity: in short, reenact—through a painted face, as it were—original sin, which was to no longer consider the self-evident sufficient in itself. The only course in life is to love God through his creatures, whose outward form, though it undoubtedly possesses beauty, does so by virtue of its inmost self, and of the divine unity that illuminates it from within. It is to will in each person or thing what this divine power has imprinted on it; in a young woman, for example, the child she will one day bear, which through its new life will make good—and herein lies the mystery of time, the gift of finitude when we have learned to accept it—the erosions constantly wrought by death in the great chain of being.

We must not interfere with the outward appearance of being, we must not even consider it in itself, independently of the lesson it bears; hence—and we can now return to this point—the uneasiness with which the medieval and, later, the Renaissance mind, and Perdita with them, viewed the artist's activities, especially those of the painter. In dwelling, as in the work of a portrait painter, say, on this or that aspect as though it were an end itself, do we not risk losing sight of the natural order, preferring instead a substanceless singularity that has been stripped, to the immediate advantage of the most outward passions, of the all-important idea that the key to salvation is incarnation in time, procreation, the "memory" of death, as Perdita would say? The artist who has forgotten this truth and who works, therefore, "in scorn of nature"—in scorn of time, that is to say, in scorn of the laws of being— can only give "lifeless life" to his picture, a breath as misleading as it is deadly: he is dangerously, perhaps culpably, akin to the magician. "There's magic in thy majesty," as another king in the play will shortly declare of a statue we would today describe simply as surprisingly lifelike. The artist can indeed perceive, can even elucidate, the symbols that are God's ciphers; he can express their "majesty"; but he also has the means to distract from them. Art, therefore, is at the very least a battlefield between faith and those "wicked powers" which dance attendance on the painter or the sculptor the better to ensure his downfall.

II

These, then, are the thoughts in the mind of Perdita, the young woman who, though she has dressed herself up, has preserved the symbolic overtones of what she has borrowed from the world of nature; these were the categories and convictions in the back of Shakespeare's mind when he wrote *The Winter's Tale*. And at this point in our encounter with the work—a work that is particularly rich in ambiguities, as we shall see—two avenues of thought seem possible to me.

On the one hand—and I shall pursue this line of thought for a moment—

we may recall that the anathema pronounced with so much passion by the lovely young queen of the feast, at a moment when everything seems to enfold her in innocent joy and commend her virtue, is uttered with equal force in other passages in Shakespeare's work; and that the very different contexts in these cases only add to the force of the reproach. Very early in Shakespeare's work, in *The Rape of Lucrece*, for example, the young woman whom Tarquin has just so cruelly abused realizes to her horror—to her remorse even, for she ought to have seen through it—that her guest has achieved his ends only by disguising them with a good deal of art; which means—and a painting is there to prove it, a painting that Lucrece is reduced to tearing apart with her nails—that a work based on appearances alone can do more than simply deprive its audience of the truth of life; it can also simulate virtue, at the risk of leading even the most virtuous souls astray. A little later, in the *Sonnets*, Shakespeare—or at least the person who speaks in the first person at the beginning of that book—upbraids an extremely handsome young man who does nothing but look at himself in the mirror, perfecting his beauty in the reflection and fixing its expression as a miniaturist would, instead of thinking about procreation. Romeo is likewise much given to daydreaming about things he has only dimly perceived (images, in other words), and there is every reason to believe that it is his propensity for illusion that brings about the disaster. Whatever was in the back of Shakespeare's mind when he was writing the discussion scene between Perdita and Polixenes—protagonists in a drama that has called for what they say—we can recognize in the words of the shepherdess contrasting art to nature an idea of art more or less constant throughout Shakespeare's work, and we can legitimately advance the hypothesis that it reflects his own convictions.

And this prompts us to ask why this great poet—who was, after all, an artist, at least when he was writing *Venus and Adonis* and many of the sonnets as well—had so poor an opinion of his own profession, and one so actively expressed. What we must remember, when pursuing this line of thought, is that at the time Shakespeare was writing his plays—in other words, at the end of the reign of Elizabeth I and the start of a new reign of even greater ostentation and luxury—the art favored in many courts in Europe had unquestionably become the kind of illusionism denounced by Perdita—and one far more shameless than she, in her youthful innocence, could ever realize. At Prague, for example, from which Polixenes, "king of Bohemia," may well have come with his talk of carnations and gillyvors, the court of Rudolf II—who himself dabbled in painting and was an important patron of the arts—had only recently admired a mannerism torn between religious feeling and a fascination for the beauties of the flesh, a dilemma that saved a style of painting designed merely to seduce from becoming overly realistic. Thanks to the teachings of Correggio, Giovanni da Bologna, and the Venetians, however, a more thoroughgoing verist art was now in the ascendant, an art which not only openly claimed to surpass nature but went about doing so in paintings that could hardly have been more erotic, and from which any idea of procreation was wholly absent. Painting in Prague was for pleasure, and for the passions that the pursuit of pleasure arouses. As for the symbolic aspects of the traditional worldview, the use made of them by Archimboldo, one of the leading figures of Prague art, is heavily ironic: to see this, you have only to consider the mounds of fruit and flowers out of which he creates faces to express the king or one of the princes. When Perdita is Flora, she brings out the symbolism of the flowers she hands out; if Rudolf II is Vertumnus, the god of the turning year, it is solely by virtue of the colors and forms—and no longer the meaning—of those same fruits and flowers.

In London, meanwhile, while the claim of art to vie with nature was less boldly inventive, it only needed limning—the art, widely practiced at the time, of the miniature portrait, a scaled-down image and therefore easily flattering, an instrument of seduction, the model that in Shakespeare's sonnets the all too handsome young man adopts for himself—for alarm to set in. It was felt especially by those who suspected the artist's activities of ungodliness; and did so all the more readily now that, as a result of the Reformation, the presence in churches of modern sculptures or paintings of a genuinely spiritual ambition and quality had dwindled dramatically. Art can easily give proof of its spiritual capacities. Even the most intense sensory perception is in no way incompatible with a symbolic reading of the world, since color itself, and form, have meaning and value in the overall economy of symbols. But there was no Van Eyck or Bellini for Shakespeare to remember, no Caravaggio at work under his very eyes.

In addition to this, as a man of the theater, Shakespeare could not fail to remember the still recent period when miracle plays recounting the life of the Savior or debating the destiny of a soul were openly symbolical or allegorical, and therefore unable to indulge in any kind of play on appearances. It is in the theater, in fact, that the opposition between a past seriousness—which was not wholly a thing of the past, however, since miracle plays were still being staged in the late sixteenth century at the feast of Whitsun—and new fields of inquiry, first and foremost in Shakespeare's comedies and court productions, might have seemed particularly alarming on the eve of Jacobean "masques" every bit as outlandish as Archimboldo's inventions. The author of *The Winter's Tale* had every reason, then, to feel uneasy about an activity of which his own work formed part. And there are good grounds for thinking—*Hamlet* suggests as much, as does *The Tempest*, each of which involves a reflection on the theater—that Shakespeare was keenly aware of his spiritual responsibilities in this century of rapid change. All of which makes much better sense of the discussion he has put at the heart of his play, at a time and place—a country festival—where only a few years earlier a miracle play might have been staged in which the figure of Perdita, who herself speaks of "whitsun-pastorals," might have found a place, as much on account of her costume as her speech. For Perdita to be accepted there, however, faith would have had to open itself, as Shakespeare so dearly wanted it to do, to the substantial quality of nature, to its beneficial—immediately beneficial—value, as much despised by the new fin-de-siècle Puritans as it had been by churchgoers of old. It was not from the standpoint of the Puritans, enemies of art who were equally contemptuous of the Mayday festival, with its dancing and simple joys, that Shakespeare was tempted to incriminate the theater.

III

Art and nature, art vying with nature: the debate between Perdita and Polixenes, then, is Shakespeare's way of setting down in words the doubts he feels—increasingly, perhaps, as the century draws to its close—when confronted with new forms of art, particularly in the theater. But to my mind there is another way of interpreting the discussion, which is to ask oneself whether it signifies this anxiety alone, having no bearing on the actions and characters of the other scenes in *The Winter's Tale;* or whether, on the contrary, the problem of art and nature does not reflect some larger tension at work throughout the play; a tension so crucial, perhaps, and so specifically active that it was only in this particular play and nowhere else in Shakespeare's work that the conflict between these two great principles could be made explicit.

I shall now deal with this other point of view—or, rather, I shall let it take possession of me, since it seems to force itself on us the moment the question has been raised, not least for the light it throws on the enigma of that other king, from Sicily this time, Leontes.

And in the history of the critical reception of the play, it is high time this was done, for at the very least Leontes has perplexed commentators. He is characterized by an act that is not only extreme, out of all proportion to the situation in which it occurs, but one that lacks any apparent or conceivable motive on the part of its perpetrator. All of a sudden, and in a manner utterly unforeseen by those close to him, Leontes is jealous of his wife, who is so obviously the incarnation of fidelity and love; accuses her of betraying him with his childhood friend, the king of Bohemia (whom we have just met at Florizel's betrothal); drives Polixenes from his court and insults and persecutes his wife. This succession of senseless acts brings suffering upon everyone around him, as well as upon himself. In no time at all, his wife has been condemned, his newborn daughter abandoned on some distant, deserted shore, and his beloved son destroyed by grief. The queen then dies; or so, at least, he is given to believe. As for himself, hardly has he ceased raging than he realizes his madness, repents of it, but has no choice but to withdraw with his sorrow into desperate solitude. An "infection" has taken hold of his mind, laying waste his soul—a soul said by all to be as loving as it was generous; there was not even that gradual poisoning that lends credibility to the not dissimilar misfortunes of Othello; and so we really are at a loss to understand what has happened.

There is no point imagining, for example, that Leontes is some kind of voluptuary who sees lust everywhere, since everything in the context opposes such a view; and while there are some grounds for detecting in him a latent homosexuality that has him use his wife to eroticize his own relationship with Polixenes—his playmate, as he remembers, in those childhood years when we are innocent of sin—this does not explain why his fantasy is so sudden, so frenzied, so destructive and self-destructive, for the repressed desire would overthrow his little drama. Furthermore, it is clear that Shakespeare himself wants to erase from the scene anything that might help us understand Leontes' behavior. It is the surprise, the stupor even, of those close to the king when confronted with his madness that Shakespeare is careful to underscore: none of them has the slightest clue what to do. And in drawing on Robert Greene's *Pandosto*, a tale written some twenty years earlier in which he found the plot and many of the elements of his play, Shakespeare has taken care to eliminate anything that would throw light on the "infection" that Leontes tells us has mysteriously taken hold of his mind; it astonishes him even as he stands there mesmerized by the acts and words of his wife and his friend. In reading Greene, the madness of Leontes must have struck Shakespeare, I imagine, as something other, potentially, than everyday jealousy; as the sign, perhaps, of an "affection"—another of the words used in the text—on a different plane from that of ordinary human passions; and one that certainly interested him, perhaps because he already had some notion of it but could do no more with it at that point than begin to dramatize it.

A scene involving other characters, other passions and actions, is precisely what it will become, and this leads me to believe that the meaning Shakespeare cannot yet explain to himself will be transposed symbolically, reflected and refracted, throughout the play. Who knows?—it may even be heard echoing through the discussion between Polixenes and Perdita.

IV

Let us return, then, to that discussion, the better to situate it now in the overall structure of *The Winter's Tale*. And let us begin by noting the position it occupies in the unfolding of the drama. It is not merely against the background of a traditional feast day and a medieval worldview that Shakespeare has placed this reflection on the truth of symbols and the fascinations of appearance; he has put it at the very center of the action, at that point in the play when the baneful consequences of Leontes' madness are about to be dispelled. The little boy who has died of sorrow will not rise from the dead, of course, but the daughter Leontes has lost will reappear, as will the queen herself, thought to be dead and presented as such in Greene's original text. Sixteen years, moreover, have passed, during which time Leontes has repented, and the abandoned child has grown up in the family that has taken her in, allowing the healing powers to do their work. And at this point, it is the arrival of the king of Bohemia at the home of the shepherdess—who is none other, of course, than Leontes' daughter—that will precipitate events. Polixenes loses his temper with Florizel, who runs off with his betrothed to Sicily, where Leontes will discover Perdita's true identity. Had Polixenes not been opposed to Florizel's marriage, had he not set his ostentatious court art against the self-evidence, the sheer force of conviction, of natural beauty and virtue, the wheels of divine providence would not have been set in motion, or at least not then.

Bearing in mind, then, that the discussion on art takes place at what is virtually the turning point of the play, when the world of sin—the word can properly be used to describe Leontes' act—is about to be dispelled by the light of Grace, we now notice that the wife who is under suspicion and condemned, the queen as beautiful and good as her daughter will prove to be, has been named Hermione by Shakespeare (who has replaced all of Greene's names with Florizels and Perditas that are clearly metaphorical), a name that explicitly means harmony, a happy balance between the different parts of existence or the world. Hermione has been the wife unjustly accused, but because of the name she bears she will reveal herself to be much more than that in the economy of the play: it is her task, as though with the blessing of heaven since birth, to make manifest the divine presence in the universe; and she performs this symbolic role by uniting conjugal love and love of God in her straightforward, peaceful approach to life. Hermione is love, and she is beauty untouched by artifice or "art." In the discussion with Polixenes she would have sided with Perdita and refused, with her natural good cheer, to grow carnations and gillyvors.

Alas, she who is proof that sensory existence is merely the threshold to a more profound order of being or harmony is the very person whom Leontes has judged on appearances, as they say—on certain aspects of her behavior which, though clearly of a piece, have fallen prey to Leontes' fantasies. What previously had been a spontaneous, happy unity has been broken down by this jealous husband into separate parts seen solely from without—disembodied mental representations from which the radiance of the divine presence has been extinguished, leaving the dreamer with nothing but the spectacle of a body, with its enigmatic gestures and remarks; in other words, with the kind of image that the more fleeting passions can do with as they see fit, as in those paintings at the Prague court that Perdita, had she followed Florizel to the home of a more hospitable Polixenes, would promptly have decided were merely daubing the beauty of the world with cosmetics.

Here, then, is what transpires in the light of Perdita's remarks on art and nature. In his jealousy and fascination with appearances that no longer reveal the truth of the object, Leontes has behaved like an artist, as Perdita understands that term and as does Shakespeare. In the presence of Hermione— that is to say, in the presence of nature in its divine essence—he has shown himself incapable of perceiving that profound harmony, that unifying light, which renders actions and appearances self-evident, in which trust is easy and joy pours forth of itself, as it were; he has even blinded himself to God. Hence the inevitability of fantasies and the turmoil of all who subscribe to them, for fantasies have no reality and no valid end; hence also, for those who follow that path, a terrible risk—that of hating what you no longer possess (which is what the devil, at one with such delusions, would like). Is Leontes a jealous husband, as everyday psychology would have it? Only because, deep down, he is an artist, the artist who has succumbed to the dangers which threaten all who must linger over appearances and may end up preferring them—and so sinning once again—to that divine essence from which nothing falls that does not continue glowing.

Leontes is an artist, he exemplifies the dangers of artistic creation. In a play of rare depth and ambition in this respect, Shakespeare has pointed up—whether consciously or not is of no importance, but consistently at any rate and, as we shall see, in a manner that reaches far into the structure of the play—a close kinship between the jealous man and the artist. The jealous man—our conception of whom, moreover, needs to be enlarged, for a sexual inquisition is not the only form of madness—is one of the shapes put on by the artist, taken in the broad sense of a gaze that focuses on the outward appearances of being and prefers or makes use of those appearances. Indeed, the creation of Leontes marks a considerable advance in our understanding of the soul and opens up all kinds of possibilities for further study, since the jealous man, a stock figure in the theater (Shakespeare had already portrayed one in *Othello,* but had done no more at that stage than take note of his misfortunes) will now enable Shakespeare to reflect on the problem—admittedly a very difficult one to pose or even to imagine—of the artist's conduct, of the risks he takes, of his errors and calamities.

And to reflect on this problem is precisely what Shakespeare has set out to do in the play, depriving Leontes' jealousy of any other form of explanation so as to maintain it on a level on which its significance is all the more profound, taking from or adding to Greene's play so as to extend and clarify what is basically a whole new field of inquiry. Without going so far as to ascribe all the events in *The Winter's Tale* to a unified and, above all, conscious symbolic scheme, which would be to fly in the face of all that is spontaneous or impulsive about Shakespeare's work, we may observe that throughout the play what might be called a "structure of intellection" has been built up, the purpose of which, almost consciously at times, is to bring out the relationship between art—in the archaic sense of that term, to which Shakespeare still subscribed—and existence, and to explore the sometimes disastrous consequences the one has on the other, along with the means and conditions for remedying those ills.

All kinds of events in the action of the play, as well as indications in the text, prove strikingly consistent. It would be going too far, no doubt, to see the death of the little Mamillius, the heir to the throne—a death brought about by the charge unjustly laid against Hermione—as equivalent, with respect to Leontes, to that lack of heirs with which Shakespeare, in the sonnets, seeks to frighten the handsome young man, who is all too narcissistic, all too enamored of the outward aspect of beauty, and whom he is forever telling that to abide by appearances is to be condemned to remain alone in the world in old age. Nevertheless, the analogy appears not wholly unfounded when we see Leontes deciding on a whim that the little daughter who has just been born—and who, for all his madness, he knows perfectly well is his child—will be thrown to the four winds on some deserted shore. There is an art, we remember, a form of creation—*iduméen*,[1] Mallarmé would have called it—for which birth by way of the flesh is indeed hateful. Since works of imagination borrow from the world only to dream up another, there are artists who want none of the agitation which, in the body of appearances they think of as reality, reveals other thoughts and ends than theirs. So much so, in fact, that an art which thinks to extract gold from the very dross of existence may nonetheless be described as the "winter" of life—which corresponds to the first three acts of *The Winter's Tale*. When Hermione asks her son to tell her a tale, "as merry as you will," Mamillius replies very firmly, "A sad tale's best for winter." Whereupon he prepares to tell the story—a mirror image of the events that lie in store—of a man who lives near a graveyard. The boy doesn't get very far, however, for Leontes comes rushing on stage, snatches him from the arms of Hermione, and grossly insults her.

As for the sufferings of Hermione, who is both an unhappy mother and a wounded wife, it is again not unreasonable to see them as one of the major recurring effects of artistic ambition, since the artist who sees only an appearance in woman risks no longer knowing her as an authentic, living presence; at which point, either he makes an ideal image of her and, by thus idolizing her, stifles her needs; or, turning the illusion inside out, he pours scorn on her actual ways of existing and thereby shifts onto the woman, or women in general, responsibility for the guilt he will most certainly feel at misrepresenting reality for the sake of a dream. This incrimination of another as the counterpart to the idolatry aroused by the selfsame person is the inmost cause of the jealousy supposedly felt by Leontes, that disguise worn by the artist which, in reality, is nothing more than a desire not to know that it is oneself, and not the other, who has betrayed and fails to love.

1. See p. 51, n. 1.

V

At the same time, *The Winter's Tale* reveals a force that can withstand the erosions of those who see only appearances; and it does so, moreover, on the very plane on which the logic of illusion might seem to have prevailed. After the first three acts have shown what such a logic can lead to, by examining it in a relationship between man and woman in which what one might call the "artistic" way of thinking is often uppermost, the fourth act presents us with a second meeting between the two protagonists of the human drama. This time, however, Florizel sees Perdita in the way that Leontes has ceased to see Hermione, or as he has never seen her perhaps: that is, as possessed of the beauty not of an image but of the whole being; in other words as a harmony in which appearances undoubtedly play a part, but revealed from within by the perception of a light suffusing them, bringing out their unity and depth, and making their suggestions into a presence, their charm into a being. Which is what Florizel is trying to say when he compares his young friend to an ocean wave, a luminous movement forever starting out afresh in the thick, green water. Florizel has only to perceive this quality of being in Perdita, has only to unleash its showing forth by instinctively consenting these same qualities in himself in the instant of pure, vital energy, let us call it vernal energy, that has built up within him for this purpose, and immediately in the economy of the world—at least, Shakespeare suggests as much—man and woman know one another, the foam of illusion is dispelled in the cosmic wave of their mutual trust, and art puts down its mask: they will be king and queen for as long as they exist. Surrendering to his "will"—his will-to-be—and turning it into a strength, loving and hence existing, Florizel moves with Perdita to the front of the feast-day stage, he as the Summer Lord, she as Flora.

In clear opposition, then, to that tragic moment in the first act when the marriage bond breaks down, Shakespeare has placed in the latter part of the play this second scene, in which love is reaffirmed—"that force which moves the stars," he might have written, echoing Dante. He has also explored the way in which love comes to pass in our lives, how, to attain absolute form, it must proceed dialectically via some chance event. It is an old and important notion, but one that needs to be stressed, since it, too, will have paved the way for that idea of art in life, of life in spite of art, which Shakespeare saw taking shape, I believe, as he advanced in his work. For the medieval mind, to love, to love Being through an individual being, was to consent to take one's place in that great chain of beings which is forever being eroded; it was to seek to repair that chain by a future birth, to situate oneself at a precise point in the chain. And since that point, before being revealed to us, is hidden somewhere in the maze of existence, we have first of all to recognize that chance is the path, that what we might decide to be chance—then continue on our way—may turn out to be the very incarnation of the absolute. Why do Perdita and Florizel know each other? Because a shepherd, quite by chance, happened to come across the little girl abandoned on the shore before the bear that would have devoured her did. And because Florizel's falcon, again quite by chance, happened to fly across to where the child, now a young woman, was tending her father's flock, some sixteen years later. Chance is the threshold of being.

Still, becoming aware of the crucial role played by chance—by fortune—in life is only the first step, for chance can be no less tragic than beneficial, as Perdita, fearing that "by some accident" her lover's father might also turn up on her lands and separate her from Florizel, is only too aware. It is important, then, that we try to understand how, in such cases, this step in the right direction can be made secure. The main function of act 4—and we are now in a position to see this—is not so much to acknowledge the fact of love, of its ability to recompose a reality that has broken down for want of it, but to understand that the same powers of chance that have furthered its cause can also turn against it, sorely testing it; hence the strength of character needed by someone who loves, to uphold that feeling in adversity. What happens when Perdita and Florizel appear together on stage dressed for the great mystery of the marriage vow that repairs being? Polixenes arrives, who could have sided with his son—and may have been within a hair's breadth of doing so at this crucial juncture—but instead decides against him, demanding , with a great show of anger, that he break off his betrothal to Perdita. To keep faith with the vow he has taken, Florizel draws on an energy that has nothing to do with chance this time round, an energy that will save him, will deliver him from the hazardous predicament in which he now finds himself by revealing itself to be of a different nature from the attitudes and qualities we normally meet with in life. Florizel immediately decides to renounce his heritage and flee abroad with Perdita to escape from his father's resentment. And to someone who wishes him well and seeks to offer him advice, he protests with great vehemence:

I am, and by my fancy: if my reason
Will thereto be obedient, I have reason;

> If not, my senses, better pleased with madness
> Do bid it welcome. . . .

"This is desperate," the friend in question observes, which is just plain good sense; and this time Florizel replies:

> So call it: but it does fulfil my vow;
> I needs must think it honesty . . . ,

which, if we draw out the meaning here presented in the form of an ellipsis, might be rendered as: "that is how it appears to you, but it's the only way I can honor my commitment while satisfying my desire." Florizel's "madness" will be the source both of the loyalty he shows in his conduct and of his happiness in life. It is reason, therefore, the utmost reason. To the contrast between art and nature, between the gaze that externalizes and the mind that apprehends the natural order, Shakespeare now adds another contrast, that between superficial reason and deep reason; and the idea emerges that only the latter, in situations that might be described as heroic, has any real chance of being effective.

Nor is that all. Shakespeare now takes this series of intuitions on which the play is built one step further by showing us, in a number of carefully structured scenes, what deep reason must do in order to become effective. The reader of *The Winter's Tale* is often puzzled by Autolycus, the rogue and peddler who, for his meager profits, wanders through the festival, whose air of mystery is assured, on a much higher spiritual plane, by Florizel and Perdita. Why, the reader wonders, does this undoubtedly entertaining figure, this rogue who seems so clever at taking in simpletons and selling perfumes and ribbons to their sweethearts, at telling tall stories and emptying people's pockets, at the same time have an aura of mystery about him, even in his most frivolous acts? He is like a little Mercury of the highroads, leaving a bit of light hanging from the bushes where he lies in wait for passersby.

Yet Autolycus is easy to explain. His rule in life is to take whatever opportunity offers, stealing what people leave lying about, hoodwinking simpletons who stray too far in their walks, then taking to the road once more, all the while singing his wonderful songs, in part melancholy, in part gay. He, too, trusts in chance. In his case, however, it is to profit from chance and not to challenge the nonbeing in it. In this respect, Autolycus is the exact opposite of someone who loves; he is the very antithesis of Florizel and, as such, may be compared to the artist as Shakespeare conceives of him, his passions likewise attached only to the surface of situations and things—except that the little brigand is less dangerous than the artist, since in the minds of his victims his tricks and ruses will soon be no more than a vaguely unpleasant memory. If anything, in making use of appearances that soon will be plainly shown to be a lie, Autolycus acts more like a revealer of eternal truths; and nature—who is his mother, too—certainly looks with indulgence on this wayward son. Does he not give the impression, moreover, of being born fully formed each spring, "in the sweet of the year," with the narcissus and the birdsong, and the "red blood" of youth, that he sings about?

Yet hardly has Prince Florizel left the stage with his great plan in his heart than Autolycus is back, this carefree soul living on the fringe of society and knowing nothing of the being of the world or the seriousness of life. And though we can be sure he does not love as Perdita and Florizel love, he reveals to us here, in a soliloquy about his day's work, about his many gains and his philosophy in life as a thief happy with his estate, that he also has it in him to think of something more: namely, of that steadfast lover and rebellious son whose plans he has overheard and whom he now wishes to aid in his endeavors. Autolycus is not really sure why he feels drawn to Florizel and tries to explain it away by his own fondness for the kind of trick he sees Florizel playing on his father. Still, he is needed, he will give him a hand. Shortly afterward it is again as a result of Autolycus's scheming that the old shepherd—the one who had taken Perdita into his home—finds himself on board the ship carrying the runaway couple off to Sicily and Leontes. The shepherd has about his person the letters and jewels that will enable the unhappy king to recognize his daughter. And so it is that, without knowing what he wants or what he is doing, Autolycus, the small-time dabbler in chance, becomes a deus ex machina in the denouement of this great drama of love initially defeated but finally triumphant.

In short, Florizel's decision, which seemed insane, is immediately furthered by chance. Chance comes as a godsend, as they say. And Shakespeare, we can be sure, would have taken this expression literally, for he wants us to understand that the schemings of Autolycus are not some cheap theatrical device designed to disentangle the intricacies of a tragicomedy, but part and parcel of the great mystery of being and the moment in the play at which the profoundest thoughts emerge. While in the case of Leontes everything breaks down as the result of his madness, to Florizel, in his different madness—in reality, the utmost reason—and to Perdita, everything is given: all that was needed for destiny to open its arms in welcome was for these two beings to trust in what is, despite the fact that the object of love, from Hermione to Perdita, has remained more or less unchanged, since the daughter, as we are shortly to learn, is the living image (a remarkable expression) of her mother. The eyes of love had only to release what exists from the fragmentations, the enigmas, and the daydreams that lie in store when all we see of reality is how it appears to us from the outside, and thus to close the path that leads to nothingness. And, to return to the discussion between Perdita and Polixenes, this also means that love, furthering the cause of nature, triumphs over art, which cuts us off from love—or, if this seems too optimistic, at least delivers art from its evil spirits, from evil. In its intuitive reworking of the rather substanceless text of Greene's *Pandosto*, *The Winter's Tale* now makes sense from start to finish. It has turned Greene's story into a series of propositions on the relationship between art and nature as Shakespeare understood these terms, as he worried over them, though still unable to grasp the crucial significance of this conflict in everyday life—even in the rantings of a jealous husband.

This clarification, this intuition, which turns out to be a constant preoccupation in Shakespeare's work, is confirmed, moreover—should any further confirmation be needed—by the otherwise all but incomprehensible episode of Hermione's statue, the bizarre manner in which the queen has chosen to come back to life.

We are now at the end, the very end, of the play. Perdita and Leontes have recognized each other and embraced amid laughter and tears; they have also been informed that, in a house nearby, a splendid statue of the queen is to be found, recently completed by a famous Italian artist. Yet even here we are somewhat surprised to learn that as they make their way to see the great portrait that will reveal the mother to the daughter, will recall the wife to the husband (as repentant now as he is nostalgic for the past), the two of them linger awhile, "not without much content / In many singularities," in the small museum adjoining the room in which the sculpture is to be found. Yet it is only too true that art has been the constant background to the action of the play whenever it has been set in Sicily; and that it is also part of the promise concerning Hermione's portrait made by Paulina, the queen's dear friend who commissioned the statue. This statue, she has said, is of "the greatest art." It took many years for Julio Romano, as the artist is called, to complete his work; we also know that "had he himself eternity and could put breath into his work, [he] would beguile Nature of her custom, so perfectly he is her ape." We recognize in these words the claim traditionally made by Renaissance painters—and by sculptors, as well—to do as well as life or even to improve upon it. At the same time, we are reminded of the limitations of their work: being merely apes and lacking speech, artists can imitate appearances but not the model's inner life or its relationship to God. There is a risk, then, that they will misuse these figures, since the soul is wanting that would shield them from the fantasies or illusions that the passions of the artist, or of the beholder, will project onto the work. For all that, the statue of Hermione is so lifelike, Paulina tells us, that one is tempted to speak to it.

And in the presence of the statue—a full-length portrait—Perdita and Leontes, and Polixenes and his son, do indeed forget that it is the work of an artist. Speechless, they cannot but marvel at the verisimilitude, the naturalness, the "life" that has been breathed into this extraordinary work; it seems to radiate light, that same light which, in Hermione, emanated from the depths of divine creation; and when Perdita wants to kneel before the sculpture, it is in order to draw its hand to her lips and secure its blessing. Is art capable, then—contrary to the suspicion that has weighed on it all through the play—of transcending the fragmented narratives of the senses? Of renewing, by imitating appearances one by one, that bond which makes them the symbol of the divine presence in life? Of endowing its all too suspect "magic" with the "majesty" of the natural order?

The hand that Perdita wants to hold in her own, however, is not the stone that the artist must employ but the hand of Hermione herself—Hermione who, contrary to what Leontes and everyone else had thought, is not dead after all. Paulina had nursed her in secret, then kept her in hiding for the day when, as an oracle had given her grounds to hope, the forsaken child would be known to be alive. This is why the queen can make her appearance today—and, first of all, in the guise of an artist's re-creation, for which there are good reasons. For what else was Leontes' suspicion, the cause of his suffering, if not that act of judging by externals which is always a risk in art, which has only appearances in mind, regardless of their roots in being— a beauty admired solely for the idea the disembodied imagination makes of it, an image rather than life? To be reunited with Leontes, Hermione has to remind him—if a reminder is needed, which it may well be—that no art can ever equal nature.

And what we are left with once the spell of art has lifted is woman—to whom, all things considered, art does a great injustice. Is this claiming too much? Given that Hermione's "resurrection" is the ultimate signifier in the epiphanic structure built up throughout the play, and bearing in mind the name she has been given, I don't think it far-fetched to suppose that Shakespeare, at this great moment, has taken on an important problem—and one that we should seek to clarify since Shakespeare himself has not done so, but without misrepresenting the play. In other words, now that art, on this great day, has deferred to nature and its delusions have been dispelled (the object of those delusions, in a world where man has the upper hand, as often as not being woman), this woman, at once idolized and reviled, jeopardized and held up as guilty—in a word, this victim—can claim her rightful place in life, stepping down like Hermione from the pedestal on which art had placed her in order that a music more lofty still—"music, awake her; strike!" cries Paulina when the statue is about to move—may echo in the mind: the very harmony of living nature, calling the world to her side and reconciling. The dignity of woman, her right to be herself not only on her wedding day (which Leontes was so fond of recalling) but throughout her life—such, I believe, is the final element in the "structure of intellection" of consciousness and the world underpinning *The Winter's Tale*.

VI

Is *The Winter's Tale*, then, a reconstruction, via the blows which society inflicts on it, of the truth of life—in its essence, which is love; in its most basic and arguably its only law, which is the trust between man and woman that makes good injustices; and in its habitation, "the great creative nature," that network of signs and symbols and emanation of the divine? Twelve years after *Hamlet*—in which Shakespeare had advanced the idea of a theater that mirrors society but could do no more than expose some of the more cynical or simpleminded misuses of appearance without ever resolving them or probing the depths of human existence (hence the failure of the "play within the play" and the distress of its author, the prince of Denmark, at his inability to articulate the intuition that haunts him and his failure to love Ophelia)—might we be hearing, in what is virtually Shakespeare's last "romance," a "positively charged" discourse in which the more immediate, symbolic, and epiphanic character of the medieval mystery plays serves to underwrite a religious feeling delivered from Puritanism, dolorism, and the sexualization of sin? It would be tempting to conclude as much.

To stop at this point, however, would be to overlook certain details in the play or, to be more precise, to fail to perceive, behind the body of thought inspired by Leontes' jealousy, the mind at work weighing up the relationship of that body of thought to society as it is and, I would venture, to the author himself. In other words, we must pay attention, in *The Winter's Tale*, to those details which complicate the picture—the beautiful painting—of man and woman restored to their natural radiance, to their nakedness, as it were, among the fruits and flowers.

One such detail, the importance of which, so far as I know, has not been fully grasped by critics, is the curious manner in which Shakespeare tells us how Leontes and Perdita are reunited at a moment that is crucial to the economy of the play, since it is the very moment when those healing forces that for sixteen years have secretly been coming together in the depths of being proclaim their truth; the moment, in short, when absence becomes presence.

It becomes presence but does so—and this is important to note—once again in absentia, for these moments of transformation and redemption do not take place onstage. We have seen with our own eyes, so to speak, Florizel and Perdita making their pledge, deciding to flee Polixenes, and setting out on the voyage that would lead them to Sicily; we have also seen them entering Leontes' home; and we have seen Leontes warming to the runaway couple. Why, then, are we not admitted to that moment in time, only a few instants later, when—Polixenes having now arrived and the shepherd having shown what he had found on the shore beside the newborn child—father and daughter suddenly recognize each other and are reunited amid tears of joy, their trials seemingly at an end? Granted, courtiers returning from this extraordinary, unexpected outcome keep us well informed, one after the other, of what is happening between these beings whose sufferings and hopes, by this point in the play, are those of all mankind. But the events they describe seem somehow remote from us, to be taking place in another world than on the front of this stage where they rush about talking, with only Autolycus to hear them, as though we, the audience, and we alone, were the ones they needed to address.

The relative disregard Shakespeare shows for so crucial a scene is certainly astonishing; so much so that he has sometimes been criticized for not presenting it directly. It has even been seen as a sign of his aging, of the waning of his genius, since the coming together of father and daughter, and of Leontes and his friend Polixenes, would have ensured, with little effort on Shakespeare's part, the emotional involvement of the entire audience. The meaning of this distancing is certainly more complex than that. For my part, I will simply note that while it clearly deprives the audience of the physical gestures and movements of the characters, and of a depth in the manifestation of their inmost being, it also signals something new in *The Winter's Tale,* for it invites us to consider this momentous event—which by its very nature demands our full participation and the suspension of our disbelief—as an image, the very essence of an image.

On the one hand, the event does indeed take place a long way off; we get a glimpse of the characters but hear nothing of the commotion; we no more communicate with them than if they were painted figures and end up fixing them in some dramatic pose, with a "casting up of eyes," a "holding up of hands," as the text of the *Tale* itself suggests; on the other hand, the people who speak to us of the scene, for all that they were present at it, seem themselves to have viewed it as a painting. Dwelling on what at the moment of their reunion must have been no more than a fleeting instant, and substituting that instant for the flood of exclamations and gestures, the first of these gentlemen says of Leontes and Perdita, and of the others present, that "there was speech in their dumbness, language in their very gesture," reducing them to what the eyes alone make out, rooting them to the spot; and even this is told in exactly those terms used in the Renaissance to explain how the painter vies with the poet in making his painting a wholly significant representation.

That we are given to understand what took place as though it were a painting is further underscored by the fact that the scene in question, and the significance of that scene, is marked in the gentleman's eyes by an ambiguity that was again much criticized in what is only a picture. Immediately after describing the protagonists as painted figures, the gentleman adds: "They looked as they had heard of a world ransomed, or one destroyed: a notable passion of wonder appeared in them; but the wisest beholder, that knew no more but seeing, could not say if the importance were joy or sorrow; but in the extremity of the one, it needs must be." If an intensity is manifest in this tableau of attitudes and gestures, it is perhaps because some motive in the design of the artist who willed it has intensity as well. The mute eloquence of painting, however, fails to express the inmost nature of spiritual events, the one that those participating would not have failed to see directly in the action as it unfolds in time—assuming, that is, that the scene actually took place, other than in a world of pictures.

It is from without, then, like a picture, that Shakespeare wants us to view this great scene in which the natural order, after long being held at bay, comes once more to the fore, is once again self-evidence, unity, speech. In the very scene in which we were preparing to receive a revelation and embrace its truth, he asks us to see no more than a story, a dream perhaps; and one which casts over the entire play—even over the sheep-shearing festival and Hermione's resurrection—a kind of shadow, albeit a luminous one in which a great many questions are reflected. Does Hermione cease being an image only in the context of a work that itself remains an image? Can the transcendence of nature over art be expressed only through the medium of a narrative—in other words, through art again? And is this tale, in which we thought to see the winter of being awakening to new life, nothing more than a "tale"? "How goes it now, sir?" asks the second gentlemen of another who arrives close on his heels; "This news which is called true is so like an old tale, that the verity of it is in strong suspicion." This uncertainty is also part of *The Winter's Tale*. We can, indeed we must, see it as part of the "structure of intellection" of the play; and we would be doing less than justice to the scope of the play, to the sheer force of uncertainty and restlessness at work in it, if we failed to ask ourselves, for example, to what degree art—which for all the invocations to, and celebrations of, "the great, creative nature" remains stubbornly present throughout the text of the play—does not likewise have a right to exist, a truth.

Yet Shakespeare, in writing about Perdita and Polixenes, had *Pericles* and *Cymbeline* still fresh in his memory and *The Tempest* already taking shape in his mind. And it is also in these other plays that we see his thoughts on reality and appearance, truth and illusion, the ultimate nature of art, and perhaps the need, at the end of an age of symbols, to think these things out anew, feeling their way forward. Let us leave art and nature, representation and presence, and *The Winter's Tale* at this point, when the idea an Elizabethan might have of their dialectical relationship is perhaps in the process of changing. To push on, we will need to broaden our investigation.

TRANSLATED BY MARK HUTCHINSON

CHAPTER FOUR

A Day in the Life of Prospero

HOW VACANT, at least so it seems, how vacant or how repressed, is Miranda's memory of things! The scene just a moment before was all howling winds, cracking masts and planks, sailors rushing about, curses and cries of terror from the passengers—a ship was going down in an enormous tempest, but now everything is calm once more. Prospero the magician is speaking with his daughter on the shore, wanting to know what she remembers, and when she answers, the impression she conveys is of depths as vast and as dark and empty as the ones that caused such fear a moment earlier for the sinking ship. "Be attentive," says Prospero. "Canst thou remember / A time before we came unto this cell?" He presses her: "By what? By any other house or person?" But Miranda can at best remember four or five women who tended her, and this but vaguely. In the "dark backward and abysm of time," as Prospero himself calls it, is there anything else she sees? No, there is nothing else. And so, with this introductory scene, where the few shadowy memories make the absence at the center of things seem only the darker, we come to learn that Miranda has no memory of her mother and seems neither surprised nor sad about it. Even the idea that mothers could exist seems never to have occurred to her.

Yet Prospero will tell her in passing that the mother she had, in other words his wife, was "a piece of virtue"—which, it should be said, is the only allusion he will make to her in the entire course of the play, an allusion that is, furthermore, an entirely conventional remark, lacking in any real contour—since virtue is what one expects of a noblewoman, and the best way not to be noticed, not to exist. Prospero immediately adds, "Thy father was Duke of Milan," and explains that Miranda was his only child, a princess, and heir to his own incomparable distinction. Could Prospero be glad that Miranda can remember nothing and does not miss her mother? Is Miranda meant to be a "child of an Idumaean night," [1] born into a world without women? We seem invited to think so, especially since Prospero's story of his arrival on the island, alone in a boat tossed by the waves with his still unconscious daughter there to spur him on, resembles nothing so much as a story of childbirth.

Miranda does not remember, and so the first three years of her life do not play their normal role, which is to keep alive forever in the child the memory of what a loving presence can give, something both infinite and simple; and thus we are made to fear that what has happened to Prospero's daughter over the subsequent twelve years—years of solitude on the island, years during which the father has been able to educate her solely on the basis of his own values—is exactly and uniquely what he wanted, theosophist that he is, contemplator of essences, shut off—or at least such is his wish—from the feelings and emotions of ordinary existence, which has its place in time. Miranda, educated? Hypnotized would be the better word, judging by the way the magician knows how to capture her attention, or even, when necessary, to put her to sleep. And submissive. When she rebels, timidly to be sure, an hour later, Prospero will exclaim: "What! I say; / My foot my tutor?" The foot has but one thing to do, and that is to go where thought wants it to go.

But let us leave the enigma of Miranda for a moment in order to reflect on another strange aspect of *The Tempest*. The existence à deux of father and daughter comes to an end when Prospero's magic causes a boat to sink near his island, or apparently to sink, a boat whose passengers, stunned and miserable but all perfectly safe and sound, wash up onto various beaches. Yet there is not a single woman to be found among these new arrivals. On the trip out, the royal vessel did in fact contain several women, a princess and her retinue, because the king of Naples was taking his daughter, Claribel, to Tunisia to marry her to the sovereign of that country and has left her there, somewhat against her will, at least at first. And at this critical moment of his daughter's life, he too has asked her to obey his will, as surely was common practice in the society of Shakespeare's time. Prospero has similar ideas, since we

---

1. See Stéphane Mallarmé, "Le Don du poème": "Je t'apporte l'enfant d'une nuit d'Idumée!" For Mallarmé, the "child of an Idumaean night" is the atemporal poem. Since the Idumaean child is not born of woman but emerges directly from man, it could be thought of as symbolizing what seeks to escape from chance and time. *Iduméen* thus suggests our desire to exist outside time, in denial of finitude.—Trans.

learn at once—so keen are his intentions—that he plans to marry Miranda to Ferdinand, heir to the throne of Naples, having made this decision, it goes without saying, without consulting his fifteen year-old daughter, whose knowledge of human beings extends no further than Prospero and his slave Caliban. For as well educated as she may appear to be—and Prospero insists that she has learned more than princes elsewhere in the world ever could have done—Miranda is destined to take her leave, with only her virtue as wealth, after the solemnity of marriage.

Moreover, does anyone in the play talk about either Ferdinand's mother or Claribel, the wife of the king of Naples? It is as though Claribel had never existed either. It is as though, in the world as it needs to be in order for Prospero to be about his business—who knows? perhaps even to exercise his powers—it were necessary that no woman exist except the heiress of his own thought. And yet there is one woman, and an important one, in *The Tempest*, Sycorax, the mother of Caliban, a slave "as disproportioned in his manners as in his shape" who was growing up when Prospero landed on the island. And this Sycrorax, who has already died, and fortunately so, was a horrible witch devoted to black magic and the accomplice, if not the mistress, of the devil. As the only mother in *The Tempest*, and the only woman in the play besides Miranda, she casts throughout an ominous shadow over the condition of women.

This should give us pause. We should reflect, first of all, on the special interest this play had in the nineteenth century, and on the supreme importance attached to the figure of Prospero, who was seen as a paragon of spiritual qualities, the very embodiment of the philosopher-poet—and on the boundless admiration for Miranda as well, of whom Coleridge said that she possessed all the "ideal beauties" that the greatest poet of all times and all lands could imagine. But a society is sure to show this kind of favor to a work whose dramatic situation has the same structures as the society. It may therefore be useful to reconsider some of the characteristic ways that the past has read the play.

These preliminary remarks on the relation of men to women—or, more generally, on our relation to *the other* in the course of life, when one loves, procreates, has joys and sorrows—are connected to another issue, which has received attention much more recently with regard to a problem posed, at least implicitly, by *The Tempest*, namely, the place that magic, Prospero's magic, occupies in the work, the role it plays and the meaning assigned to it by the author. It is an issue that Shakespeare may have wished to make the most prominent feature of the play, especially since Prospero is so obviously the central character from beginning to end; and the only one, besides Caliban, whose judgments and actions are made freely.

II

Magic is the major reference point of Shakespeare's last dramatic work. There can be no doubt of it, for Prospero refers to it constantly and is forever donning the cloak or waving the wand associated with magic—actions that might cause us to smile a little; but he also puts it to use, and with the efficacy it was commonly thought at the time to possess. The tempest in the first scene of the play is brought about by magic, and this action is clearly supernatural: for if the storm and shipwreck are only illusions created by the magician, which leave lives intact and garments without a blemish, the king of Naples and his son and his courtiers have nonetheless been transported to shore despite all the laws of nature.

Even though it has always been recognized that magic is one of the principal concerns in *The Tempest,* Prospero's relation to occultist thinking was long viewed as a peripheral matter and has become a central preoccupation only in the past forty years or so, thanks initially to the work of Frances A. Yates, D. P. Walker, Frank Kermode, and others who showed the importance, during the reigns of Elizabeth I and James I, of the kind of thought associated with the occult, with magic, which was both precise and quite widespread in circles Shakespeare would have known.

Certainly precise. It is not my intention here to relate the details of this occultist philosophy, which has often been discussed. For the interpretation I shall offer of *The Tempest,* however, it is useful to recall that, at its highest level, the research undertaken by the Hermeticists, Cabalists, and other adherents of "white" magic was indeed a quest for knowledge, pursued with rigor, even while it called into question the metaphysical structure of the universe, already scarcely credible for many, and criticized a number of outworn beliefs.

The structure of this way of thinking, inherited from medieval cosmology, involved an interlocking of the worlds of the elementary and the celestial or divine, with between them correspondences established through analogies thought to be self-evident. A legacy of Neoplatonism was the belief that spirits existed between heaven and earth that were immaterial, as human beings are not, but capable of helping humans in their ascent toward a superior form of reality to the extent that they could be compelled by the power inherent in the analogies just mentioned. And so it seemed natural, since God could only desire the salvation of his creatures, that these creatures would look for opportunities to elevate themselves by degrees to the lofty realm of the author of all things. This ascent of the soul was bound to reveal in the process those forces which God keeps hidden beneath appearances—such as the power of attraction in the magnet or the virtue of the meek—and these forces would provide instruction to such minds. It was thus simply a case of elaborating a knowledge as precise as possible—which explains the atmosphere of science, of "advanced" science, that predominates—that would allow for this work, which aimed at an intelligence of things that was both objective and internal, to begin.

This is "white" magic—"white" to underscore that its intention was opposed to that of black magic, which called upon spirits of a lower order than humans, those obedient to the devil and whose aim was the satisfaction only of carnal desires, presumed to be sinful. I should emphasize in passing—remembering Sycorax, whom I mentioned earlier—that neither the doctrine nor the practice of the magi sought to repopulate the spiritual world with feminine figures. Their thinking was based on analogies between various aspects, events, or things that thereby could be perceived only in their generality, and so it was fundamentally concerned solely with essences, divorced from time and place; it developed only by meditating upon these essences, on their structural relations, on their progressive unveiling of a divine reality in itself impersonal, which meant turning away even more from incarnate existence: for the return to highest heaven, therefore, no relationship whatsoever was needed with the other beings of this lower world, except perhaps through a common meditation. The Good, the Beautiful, according to the magus, present themselves only through denial of the mortal condition. This connection to eternal Platonism, despite the unusualness and singularity of the practices, is crucial, and I will return to it often.

Let us recall that this philosophical magic, this "natural philosophy," at once licit and occult, goes back to antiquity, and that Marsilio Ficino in Florence, and Giovanni Pico della Mirandola even more, rediscovered it or, rather, renewed it by drawing in their own way from the Kabbalah, which was taken to be a collection of the oral teachings of Moses; they drew, too, from the famous writings attributed to Hermes Trismegistus, the supposed contemporary of Moses, and from other sources as well—after which a few pioneers or followers, such as Reuchlin, Paracelsus, and Agrippa, prepared the way for its favorable reception in England during Shakespeare's time. This was one of its most important moments; theoreticians such as John Dee, to whom Frances Yates has given considerable attention, surely had considerable influence on the finer minds of the late sixteenth century, an influence that can be felt, for instance, in Spenser's poetry. Occultist thinking even tried to play a role in public affairs, for it could easily include dreams about what order to reestablish or to institute in society. When, after the success it had known during the reign of Elizabeth, occultism had a resurgence (though this time opposed vehemently) under James I, it was because it was supported by Henry, the prince of Wales, for whom there had been such high hopes but who died prematurely in 1612, and also by his sister, the new Elizabeth, the one who was to marry the Elector Palatine and to found, or so it was presumed, a utopia on earth in Bohemia.

During the festivities organized in connection with the engagement and the marriage of Elizabeth, in the winter of 1612–13, *The Tempest* was performed in revival. The play was especially appropriate for the occasion since it ends with the union of two princely families, and with its masque scene it mirrors one of the specific forms of entertainment enjoyed at the time at royal parties. So it seems legitimate to raise the question of Shakespeare's own relation to the occult and, more particularly, of the meaning he assigned to the figure of Prospero in this his final work, which might therefore be taken as the expression, at last made explicit, of his thought. Should we see in the magus of *The Tempest*, avid reader that he is of hermetic writings, a portrait of the magi of the time, perhaps someone like John Dee? And should we therefore imagine that Shakespeare takes the science and the religion of the magi seriously, even to the point of being willing to see in them a reflection of his own work as a creative artist—which would give the end of the play a positive meaning for him—the moment when Prospero comes to the front of the stage and takes leave of the audience, less as a character at the end of his role than as the actor who has played him and the author who has imagined him? Indeed, these two questions—is this a portrait? and, if so, should we take it as a simple character study, managed with all the necessary neutrality, or rather as a sign of Shakespeare's adherence to the kind of thinking he evokes?—are not necessarily the only ones that might be asked. For we might also hypothesize that Shakespeare, while closely observing the magus, has made him an object not of admiration but of criticism. Let me say from the outset that this last position is the one I have adopted and will try to make credible.

There is no doubt that Prospero is a magus in the sense that this word had in the most learned circles of Shakespeare's time, as many of his most characteristic traits clearly show, starting with his exceptional powers and his way of using them. Like the magi described by the classical exponents of occult practices—the ones whose books, which he brought with him onto the island, he constantly studies—Prospero has command over the spirits of the air, specifically Ariel, who is assisted by many other such sprites. With their help he is able to produce effects in nature or in human beings that are beyond comprehension. He is, furthermore, the opponent of the other form of magic, the one practiced by evil powers. The place where destiny has led him, with its springs and meadows, its deserted moors and its brambles, all of which are evoked without the slightest idealization—there is even a manure pit near Prospero's hut—can be seen as a fragment of reality as it might exist anywhere else, with all the species and forms of life that nature can produce, including those emanations of pure matter of which Caliban, the deformed son of Sycorax, has more than his share. And in this world, in the final analysis the one appropriate to the human condition, which must decide between good and evil, we see Prospero scornfully condemning the black magic once represented by Sycorax, who had tried to enslave the spirits of the air and even to corrupt Ariel, but had succeeded only in paralyzing their forces until the arrival of the exiled duke, who immediately freed Ariel and then made him his assistant.

Prospero is a magus then, but a magus of white magic, especially since his sole objective in exercising his powers has been what he calls "the bettering of my mind," in which we can recognize the spiritual ascent, the release of the soul, which every master of natural philosophy since Ficino and Pico della Mirandola had seen as the supreme goal. At first sight, Prospero might seem to be pursuing more ordinary ends on a purely earthly level. Through his magic, which draws his enemies to the island and places them under the power of his spells, he seeks to confound his adversaries, to expose his brother the usurper, and in this way to recover his dukedom—a perfectly banal political power—before returning to Milan to marry off his daughter. These are aims, in appearance at least, that lack grandeur. But the success of these objectives is merely a means of achieving a loftier goal, one of an undeniably spiritual nature, for as a result of these efforts, the society currently suffering under the rule of a traitor, who is the source of every problem, will be restored to that harmony which is the precondition for tranquillity of mind and for the supreme undertakings of the spirit. It was precisely because Milan was successfully attacked by evil beings—related, at least through their intentions, to black magic—that Prospero's own research was halted for twelve years and that he was forced to practice, on his almost completely deserted island, a magic one might call utilitarian; but now he sets his sights at a higher level on the ultimate goal, as can be seen in the promise he makes to Ariel at the outset of the play, which is also the beginning of the decisive day, to give him back his freedom when the day ends. The magician will give up his power once society has been restored to order; he will then concentrate on higher forms of knowledge and on his own inner liberation.

Seen in this light, Prospero is—or clearly seems—precisely what a magus was supposed to be as defined by thinkers such as John Dee, and it is certainly tempting to think that so developed and explicit a portrait is the sign of an identification on Shakespeare's part. This is the conclusion, in any case, that Frances Yates did not hesitate to draw. Prospero, she wrote, "is the climax of the long spiritual struggle in which Shakespeare and his contemporaries had been engaged. He . . . establishes white Cabala as legitimate." [2]

But it would be dangerous to think that Shakespeare's treatment of Prospero can have meaning only through the specific features of the magi it brings out, as would be the case in an historical or philosophical text, since these references are but one element, however central, in a play as complex as *The Tempest*, a work that is preeminently literary. And so it is important to call attention to those other elements in the play that tend to nuance the figure of the magus or to establish a sense of his limits. "I'll to my book," exclaims Prospero when he sees that Miranda and Fernando love each other, which favors his plan; and certainly this means that he will now be able, his mind at ease on this point, to search in his treatise on magic for the formulas that will help him with his other projects. But it also means that if the marriage takes place—the cornerstone of reestablished harmony—the magus will be able to devote himself to the fundamental practice of his art as never before, which is troubling because of the lack of interest in human affairs that his cry of relief portends. The disdain for relations with other people, seen as a precondition for the soul's ascent, is not evoked here for its significance and its value in spiritual pursuits; rather, it is perceived, somewhat ironically, as an aspect

---

2. Frances Yates, "Prospero: The Shakespearean Magus," in *The Occult Philosophy in the Elizabethan Age* (Routledge and Kegan Paul / Ark Paperbacks, 1983), 160.—Trans.

of what one already knows or senses are the ambiguities of a person. One might say that Shakespeare reveals here a reservation about Prospero's philosophy and the value of the project of "bettering." Indeed, with the marriage, "exit Miranda" seems likely. Prospero's return to his book is encouraged by a world become masculine once more. Isn't this what Shakespeare is showing?

But is there ever anyone in the play, man or woman, who really matters to Prospero? Is there anyone who truly possesses qualities that seem to us worthy of sympathy or love? I'm afraid there is not. It is clear that this dispossessed prince has nothing but aversion and disdain for his brother and for his accomplices, that he finds the king of Naples and his courtiers scarcely appealing, and that if he shows his esteem and even his affection for Gonzalo and kindness to his future son-in-law, it is only because the one has helped him at a moment of great peril and the other is the means he has chosen to successfully accomplish his plans. The magus is interested in Gonzalo—who obviously is not what Prospero has decided he is, as shown in many scenes by his witless, crude, and even sinister jokes and the shallowness of his thinking—and in Ferdinand only insofar as they represent aspects of what has been and remains essentially Prospero's relation to himself. And Shakespeare depicts neither them nor anyone else in the play in a sufficiently unconventional way to make them into true presences. The only character in *The Tempest* who has any reality, any proof of being, so to speak, and who can therefore arouse some interest, and who should, is Caliban, though it is clear that Prospero does not recognize this to be the case and does not want to know anything about him, until, perhaps, the last moments of the play. What counts for Prospero is not individuals but society, which, by the harmony it regains, could emerge as a reflection of heaven and thus help the sage to more fully devote himself to himself.

Prospero, in short, is a magus, but he thereby shows himself to be a person closed up in himself. It is not by chance that the word "closeness," meaning seclusion, is associated in his mind with the very idea of "bettering." His vocation is to free himself from relations with others, which could hold him back in the imperfection and contingency of ordinary existence, and to raise himself through "bettering," a kind of contemplation, to a perception of that cosmic harmony into which he would like to integrate himself as a form within a form: form being the way, through beauty, to the good. This is the qualification Shakespeare seeks to bring to his evocation of Prospero as magus. And if, with Frances Yates and others, we regard the author of *The Tem-*

pest as an adherent of occult thinking, as its exponent even, we need also to consider that he thus assumes—quite consciously, and with all its consequences—the idea of impersonality as an appropriate spiritual path.

IV

But we must remember that this same Shakespeare is the author of a number of works from which this conclusion cannot be drawn. If we consider only his last period, which begins in 1608 when he tackles an old tub of melodrama, the history of a prince from Tyre, and transforms it into poetry, what do we find that his pen has produced? Three plays—*Pericles, Cymbeline,* and, most important, *The Winter's Tale*—whose concerns and intuitions are so dissimilar from those of *The Tempest* that I do not understand why they are not more often contrasted to this play rather than being brought together, as is so often the case, in a single vision of "late Shakespeare."

Let us compare *The Winter's Tale* with *The Tempest.* These works obviously have points in common. In both, there is a father and a daughter. And after a very long period during which the action of the play seems to sleep but the prince is meditating—sixteen years in *The Winter's Tale,* twelve in *The Tempest*—there is a royal marriage with reconciliation between two kings, which will reestablish harmony in a society that has been sorely tried. There is also a tempest in both plays at a crucial moment of the action—the point of intersection between what is ending and what is about to begin—and this is probably no coincidence. But these similarities only make the differences more striking. We have seen Prospero detached from other people and even seeking his salvation in solitude. We know little, for instance, about who his wife was, for she has presumably been dead for some time, and neither she nor any other intimate female relation is included in the plans he makes for his life once he is back in Milan.

On the other hand, Leontes, the king in *The Winter's Tale,* thinks of nothing other than his wife. He loves her, very poorly, no doubt, but passionately; he loses his mind over her; he is the cause of Hermione's unhappiness but for that very reason of his own as well; he despairs; he buries himself in remorse and regret—and this is how the sixteen years will pass—but he ends up finding his wife again, winning her back, and devoting himself at least to the effort needed for real love. Woman, absent in *The Tempest,* where Miranda has been and will again become Prospero's docile pupil, is thus at the very heart of *The Winter's Tale;* all the more so in that the free, proud, and confident presence of Queen Hermione is complemented by the dazzling figure of Perdita, her daughter, of whom it certainly could not be said, as of Miranda, that she has forgotten the very idea that one could have a mother. The moment when Perdita is reunited with Hermione, from whom she too has been separated from birth, is one of the most moving in all of Shakespeare's drama.

But this fundamental disparity is not the only thing that distinguishes the two works. It is in the unfolding of the action—and in the kind of power that establishes this unfolding—that their difference is discernible in the most significant way. In *The Tempest,* the active forces are almost exclusively supernatural—powers controlled by Prospero thanks to his knowledge of the occult. It is possible, and I will come back to this point, that Miranda's love for Ferdinand, which is a power of a different sort, ends up influencing the behavior of her father in an entirely unforeseeable way, even though the union of these two young people has been planned and realized through magic, just like all the other events in the play. If, for example, Stephano and Trinculo, the two drunks who dream of taking Prospero's place, seem for a moment to elude the iron determinism that decides everything on the island, this is really nothing more than an illusion—hasn't Stephano, at the worst moment of the storm, been provided by Ariel with the cask whose wine will dazzle Caliban? From the outset their plans are perceived and monitored, as they will eventually be punished, by the eye that controls everything. Here, then, is a play in which feeling is an object of attention but almost never a cause. And if we exclude Prospero's spiritual aspiration and a certain *élan* in his daughter, emotion in the play is never more than ordinary, and at times downright ignoble: Ferdinand's love for Miranda, which is so easily distracted; the somewhat driveling loyalty of an honest old counselor; the guilty ambition and perfidy of Antonio and Sebastian; the base covetousness of Stephano, the common man—and, in these latter cases, plans for betrayal and murder. There is, moreover, no real sorrow in *The Tempest* to tear apart its protagonists. Prospero, as opposed to Leontes, Hermione, and Perdita, has lost nothing in his life except his power; he experiences pique and frustration but not suffering. And as for the shipwrecked king, who fears that his son may be dead, his unhappiness will bother him only for a short while like a bad dream in the long series of mirages and wonders that take place on the island.

It is as though the action in *The Tempest* were never rooted in a place of origin in lived experience, that is, in the feelings that people have for one another—hatred, jealousy, friendship, love, and the frustrations, joys, and sorrows that result from them. Magic is the deciding force in the play, the gravitational power that subsumes everything into a project that seeks to free itself of interpersonal relations. In *The Winter's Tale*, on the other hand, the causes acting through the situations and the characters are precisely the ones excluded from *The Tempest*, especially the power of love. It is true that we see it weakened in the early scenes, in the very place where it might have been thought to be strongest, that is, in the way that Leontes, king of Sicily, looks at Hermione, his wife. His manner of loving is perverse; he can only see appearances. Hermione, on the other hand, is capable of true love, pure love; and though the fascination she exercises over the imaginings of the king brings on disaster, the power of her love will transform a dead world into a place for living once more. The queen almost dies of grief but manages to hold herself together, in secret because of her bond to her daughter, who is supposed dead but whom she hopes beyond all hope to see once more; and when her daughter reappears, Hermione too can emerge from the shadows. As for Perdita, raised among the shepherds, she has shared with a young man a love so strongly felt that it quickly breaks the ice which, at Leontes' instigation, has frozen human relations.

In this reversal of action, we clearly see that in *The Winter's Tale* love is the cause of things, whereas in *The Tempest* it is magic. Perdita's betrothal to Florizel has been determined by feelings of the most spontaneous sort; and when this love is faced with the ill will of Florizel's father, the king of Bohemia, it is its absolute quality—the steadfastness resulting from the determination of these two young people and the fascination this determination has on people as different as Camillo, lord of Sicily, and Autolycus, the rogue—that creates the chain of events, which otherwise would have seemed inconceivable, that lead directly to Perdita's return to Sicily, to her recognition by a deeply moved father, and to the reappearance of Hermione. Love in *The Winter's Tale* is causal in that it cuts through situations that have prolonged the disorder of which those situations were the product.

The difference between the two works is therefore not a slight one—like a change of title on the bill at the Globe: at stake is a way of thinking about the ultimate nature of what is. Being in *The Tempest* is God, but experienced as an impersonal essence, a structure in which the magus aspires to participate—which tends to turn him away from the level of existence on which finitude and the fatal element of chance it entails are viewed as impediments to the full deployment of one's immortal form. The active force here is an aspiration toward the divine that seeks its realization through a restoration of society and the world by means of those analogies the magus can observe between elements whose nature is also impersonal. This philosopher of analogies, of essences, suggests to some that they too should free themselves from their place, from their entanglement in mortal time; to others, especially women, he prescribes thankless little tasks, useful to the preservation of order. This way of thinking is, of course, just more Platonism; nothing good happens in the sublunary realm; nothing is real in the *hic et nunc*.

And now, what of being, value, in *The Winter's Tale?* When we follow the look Florizel gives Perdita, we are bound to see that what his loving eyes perceive is specifically existence here and now, the kind of reality which, as Vigny says, "one will never see twice" on this earth.[3] And when we learn from the events that unfold that this look — this love — is what decides the future, sweeps away the misunderstandings, transfigures appearances, and thus renews social life, we may rightly conclude that the relation of one existence to another, a relation disdained by the magician of *The Tempest*, is in *The Winter's Tale* the act and the place of the real. In *The Winter's Tale* what is meditated on is mortal being; the truth is to have understood that the presence — be it only for one hour — of mortal beings is the only thing that matters. Even if such beings may seem to be shadows, nothingness itself, when we love them — at times with the passion that can mean procreation — we restore a foundation for being; we thus repair, through sexual union and in the midst of "the great creating nature," the breaks in the chain of lives on earth. Ontology of the human person as absolute: an intuition that may make use of the idea of a personal god, a god of love, or simply the reality of nature, when spring follows winter.

Between these two great works, therefore, separated in time by only a few months, there is a profound difference, an opposition, that seems irreducible. If it is true that *The Tempest* gives expression to the principles and methods of the occult philosophy of the elements, it is also true that only shortly before, Shakespeare had exemplified another way of thinking, an almost mystical understanding of life made incarnate in the world at its simplest and most natural. Has there been a sudden change of heart? one might ask. Does the description of Prospero the magician in 1611 mean that *The Tempest* not only is on the side of the magi but also is seeking to win others over to that

3. See Alfred de Vigny, "La Maison du Berger": "Aimez ce que jamais on ne verra deux fois."—Trans.

point of view? Or should we not rather conclude that this apparent change of heart is in fact based on an inadequate reading of the play, and that Shakespeare, having always in mind the thinking that animates *The Winter's Tale*, has merely given another way of looking at the world its chance in *The Tempest*, but not without indicating in the text of that work his reservations, if not his condemnation, which we have simply failed to notice? Let me say that it is this second way of seeing the play that seems to me the correct one, as I shall try to show. After which I will have yet one more question to raise: at the end of his career as a writer, why would Shakespeare need to make a fundamentally critical assessment of the figure of the magus?

v

Let us return to a close reading of *The Tempest*, in which we can observe what I consider to be the reservations, the very serious reservations, Shakespeare brings to his study of the magus: shadows in the picture of a Prospero who was supposed to have conformed flawlessly to the principles of occult philosophy and to have demonstrated thereby their validity.

The first point that seems significant to me, as I mentioned before, is Prospero's lack of interest in other people. As troubling as this detachment may seem to anyone who cannot accept the principles of natural philosophy, it surely must be seen as a logical consequence of this kind of thinking, and must be presented as such in the structure of *The Tempest* if Shakespeare means to make the play a defense and illustration of white magic. Shakespeare may or may not have viewed this detachment as a prerogative of the magi, but he clearly does not see it as a quality that Prospero can assume without difficulties. It is true, as I have said, that Prospero neither feels nor displays any emotion other than estrangement, disdain, and indifference toward everyone he knows, except for Miranda. But this does not mean that there are not at least two people in whom he takes a special interest, even while rebuffing them, an interest that truly preoccupies him, that even borders on obsession, and that makes one wonder about the nature of the detachment experienced by a magus.

The first of the two who torment him in this way is his brother Antonio, who twelve years earlier usurped his power in Milan. Every time Prospero speaks of him, or thinks of him when he is alone, we can sense the intensity of his indignation; his wound has not healed. He cannot find words harsh enough to describe Antonio. And it is remarkable that when he draws him into his trap so as to unmask him and to take his revenge upon him, he in fact imitates him: for the action he has undertaken reproduces in its substance and its aims the one his brother is guilty of. First he casts him ashore on the island, as had happened to himself as a result of his brother's crime; what is more serious is that he commits his own form of betrayal, for by deciding to marry his daughter to the heir to the crown of Naples, he will make Ferdinand, the Neapolitan, the master of Milan one day and thus subordinate his dukedom to him in an even more radical way than had been the case with Antonio, who had only paid tribute to the king. What a strange idea this marriage is! Has Prospero forgotten what he has taught Miranda, that Alonso, the king of Naples, has always been his "inveterate" enemy? Behind this almost incomprehensible plan, should we not sense a relation between Prospero and Antonio that is infinitely more intimate than his anger would have it? He actually admits to Miranda that he had loved him, loved him more than anyone except her, and had placed the day-to-day running of Milan in his hands with the greatest confidence in the world. Seeing Prospero copy his brother's behavior, literally enter into his skin to relive his crime, we can only conclude that Antonio is a part of him: the ordinary part, to be sure, the part he would have wanted to leave behind in order to become a magus and to ascend to God, but the part that continues to live in him, perhaps even to make demands—doesn't he seek to reign once more?—interfering with and thus hindering his goal of detachment. Is Prospero a magus? Doubtless he is, since he clearly has command over the elements. But he is always struggling with his old self, as though the books of magic spells were not enough to rid him of it.

The other presence Prospero never manages to chase from his mind is Caliban, that ill-favored being whose behavior is as wild as his appearance, the half-monster who is as unacceptable as can be imagined from the aesthetic perspective of a philosophy of form—the philosophy that equates the good with the beautiful—but who troubles Prospero visibly. Prospero had attempted, at one time, to diminish the problem through education, but gave up when Caliban tried to rape his daughter, and now he never misses an opportunity to heap sarcasm and abuse on him; he treats him with a cruelty that is as harsh as it is arbitrary. One senses that he would love to be done with him, would love to deny him once and for all his claim to humanity, but so much hostility, pursued with such insistence, shows all the more clearly that this "other," who is so decidedly other, obsesses him. Caliban too, and just as the disdainful magus has defined him, may be yet another part of Prospero himself: a nocturnal side of himself that he has never been able to educate, to convert to his spiritual ambitions, but that remains altogether active—which may shed light on aspects of his personality that the magician only shows in indirect ways, such as his lengthy discourse on chastity to Miranda and Ferdinand when they are engaged. For as loftily moralistic as he might wish to be, Prospero, as Shakespeare imagines him, is perhaps nothing more than a duality of body and mind that has not as yet been resolved.

There is little detachment, then, in Prospero, despite his claims to the contrary, and it is this inner battle that explains what must be seen as a major aspect of his character, though it is often minimized: the bad temper of this would-be sage, his fits of ill humor, his harshness, his aggressive authoritarianism—even Miranda has to pay the price, as we have seen—and his bouts of depression as well, those he will experience so obviously and so severely after interrupting the very festivities he has planned. Prospero speaks to the elements and knows how to cause tempests, but he is also the kind of man who keeps a manure pit, with its foul odor, close to his dwelling; and it is certain that he has not taught Miranda the love of flowers that so sustains Perdita. Despite his name, Prospero is, I think, a melancholic—melancholia being essentially the result of an inner contradiction—dreaming of a perfectly unified being-in-the-world, loving only this being, or thinking one does, and realizing one cannot or will not fully become this being. It is this rift, silently endured, that makes his relation to others not the serene freedom of the sage but, rather, distrust and impatient jealousy.

Prospero lives beneath this "black sun." Like the allegorical figure in Dürer's engraving *Melancholia,* he must often have been seated in the midst of his scattered instruments under the glow of an unmoving star. And thus we are better able to see that the tempest—which he willed because a "most auspicious" star seemed to present him with an opportunity for victory over his enemies, and over himself as well—not only takes place on the sea but also rages in the depths of his own being and—who knows?—may even grow more powerful as his views are subjected to unexpected events. He too adds, "I have done these things / That now give evidence against my soul," and will be able to tell himself at the end of a certain moment of this day: "O then began the tempest to my soul!" just like another prince in Shakespeare, who makes use of this obvious metaphor not only in *Richard III* but also to illuminate, with great flashes of lightning, the beginning of *Julius Caesar,* in which another melancholic mind soliloquizes.

What is more, the plan, so well prepared, clearly falls apart at a critical moment!

What does Prospero want? To put society back in order, which for him, as we have seen, means devaluing human finitude in deference to the great cosmic forms. Thus, simple human love will be banished from this order to the extent that it accords too much importance to mortal beings. In other words, though it would certainly be pleasant if Miranda's father could see that his daughter and Ferdinand were well suited and liked each other, he will get them married in any case, and Miranda must soon be reconciled to the idea of being nothing more than a mother.

The minute Miranda sees Ferdinand, however, she has feelings for him that Prospero views as much too intense, since he quickly appears irritated by them. "A thing divine!" Miranda exclaims at the sight of Ferdinand. At first, Prospero is pleased to have brought off his plan so well. "It goes on, I see / As my soul prompts it," he tells himself, and he even briefly undertakes to snub Ferdinand and drive him away—to appear inaccessible to him so that Miranda will not seem too easy a prey and hence without value to princely eyes that may already be somewhat jaded. But when Miranda takes Prospero's threats to Ferdinand seriously, when in turn Prospero sees her suffering from the humiliation he has imposed—in a very unpleasant way, since there is in fact a good deal of genuine ill will on his part—and when she then tries to moderate his behavior, Prospero turns against her in anger because she is disappointing his expectation. I have already made reference to his hostile remark, "What, I say, / My foot my tutor?" But he also adds, "One word more / Shall make me chide thee, if not hate thee." "Hate" is a strong word, and of course it can be viewed in the present case as not really meaning what it says, but it is not normally a word that Shakespeare uses lightly.

Later, when Miranda, driven irresistibly by love, goes to see Ferdinand, who is being held prisoner, and tells him her name despite her father's prohibition, Prospero, who is watching from afar, is moved. He reappears, however, only to make a moralizing speech in which he makes clear to them the only and absolute condition on which he can accept their marriage: respect for the prohibition against intimacy during the engagement period, which alone, according to Prospero, guarantees peace and fecundity in marriage. It is a sermon that Ferdinand listens to with only half an ear, and, as some readers have noticed, there are strange associations of thought in the answer he gives, which could be cause for alarm; but the masque is soon to follow, during which the lesson will be repeated.

Prospero has been touched, nonetheless, ever since the first meeting. "Poor worm, thou art infected!" he murmurs to himself when he sees Miranda trembling at the sight of Ferdinand laboring so hard at the tasks that have been assigned to him. What clearly motivates the action at this critical point is that Prospero has been surprised by the irruption into his plans of something unexpected, love of a sort unknown to him, alien to his philosophy and irreducible to the forces of magic; and despite his principles and his ideas for a better society he is able to feel some sympathy, even a strange happiness, when he sees that love coming to life in his daughter. "Fair encounter," he thinks to himself as he stands, unseen, a few steps away from the two young people. Prospero almost comes to accept an idea of life, an experience of the world, that has had no place in his thought. And this is very serious because his habitual way of thinking has not as yet been disavowed, so that he is now deeply disturbed at the very moment when he will need to muster all his magic forces to untangle the web of what is happening, or is being plotted, at other places on the island. So here he is troubled, distracted, and even, we discover, open to voices within him, to strange murmurings, which only a few hours earlier he would not have suspected.

VII

Shortly afterward we have the masque, a play within the play, which takes up a considerable amount of time, and I'm surprised that more has not been made of it. At parties during the Jacobean period especially, the masque was a form of entertainment with sumptuously costumed characters and music; and its playful aspect, its tongue-in-cheek solemnity, and the allegory it deployed to augur events to come in a favorable light—all this was destined to distract people from preoccupations that were troubling them on these occasions, which often were marriages, especially arranged marriages. The masque in *The Tempest*, it has been argued, is there because Shakespeare's play was revived for the wedding of Princess Elizabeth—a marriage, as I mentioned, to which much hope was attached—and at a time when Ben Jonson, Shakespeare's friend and great rival, was making a specialty of this kind of spectacle in ever more remarkable ways. But Shakespeare would not be Shakespeare if a court entertainment did not become something serious in his play.

And it does. At first sight, the masque—which, to honor the future union, is presented as a meeting between Ceres and Juno through the intervention of Iris, goddess of the rainbow—would seem to conform perfectly to the conventions of the genre: actually, it is more than normally didactic and allegorical, since we learn that Venus and her son Cupid, figures of sexuality, have just been shamefully banished from the ceremony in order that the precepts of the magus who has organized the spectacle may resound without contradiction. It is Prospero in fact who has thought up the subject of the masque and written the words for it, as he expressly tells Ariel when the latter is about to stage the work with his troupe of spirits. "Some vanity of mine Art": in other words, an illusion my magic is capable of creating, but also a slight thing my talent has the weakness to take pleasure in.

A slight thing? In fact the masque in *The Tempest* is scarcely less rich in meaning than the play itself. And to understand it we need to consider the specific features of this kind of *oeuvrette:* its relation to form and its way of evoking events while keeping them at a certain distance through stylistic decisions.

Form, in Prospero's masque, may seem conventional, traditional: his verses with their too emphatic rhymes, their rhythms lacking any subtlety—doggerel in fact—make clear from the outset that there is no attempt at great art here and that the august figures convoked by the allegory are nothing more than so much papier-mâché, surrounded by amusing mechanical stage effects. Juno, or even Ceres, must not be too believable; otherwise the audience might start to worry. And in the present case there is nothing to fear! When we hear Ceres bombastically exclaim,

Hail, many-coloured messenger, that ne'er
Dost disobey the wife of Jupiter,
Who, with thy saffron wings, upon my flow'rs
Diffusest honey drops, refreshing show'rs,

we recognize that the goddess's words are as droll as one could wish, even if they are adorned with traits of parody, contrary to the practice of most contemporary authors, and it is easy to discern in them double meanings of a frivolous and often rather dubious nature. Everywhere in the masque, and in the countermasque that follows, the evocation of the natural world and of beings, which could be rich in poetry and does in fact begin that way, is mishandled through the unbridled use of stereotypes and clichés; and these lend themselves naturally—with the help of the deliberate irreverence, the playful spirit—to allusions that are much less chaste than the "cold Nymphs" and the other Naiads are supposed to be—the ones Iris imprudently calls upon to join the "sunburn'd sicklemen" in "country footing."

Yes, it all seems very amusing, this "meeting of Ceres and Juno among the reapers and the nymphs." Yet when we think about it, doesn't Prospero's work seem a bit too risqué and inappropriate in the present circumstance, even if it is a masque? And don't the plays on words, on ideas, furtive but undoubtedly intended by Shakespeare, seem strangely like the associations and fantasies of the most ordinary kind of unconscious mind, and completely unexpected after the noble speech the magus makes only a few minutes before to the innocent and perfectly chaste Miranda? May the Platonic God forgive me, but seeing this Ceres and this Juno, uncertain in their rhymes, tottering, but laughing, on more or less iambic feet, I cannot but think of those satiric sketches performed at certain village festivals when men dress up as women. And since women are made fun of on these occasions, reduced to the level of the rawest sexuality yet inspiring a certain fear, a kind of anguished reverence, and since we also remember that although there are only female figures in the masque, the opposite is true in the play of which it is a part, where every character except Miranda is a man, we may well raise some questions here too.

I think that Shakespeare understood perfectly well that in real situations, such as court festivities, the strength of a masque resides in the effects it produces, regardless of how it came to be imagined or written; but when the masque is woven into the fabric of a drama in which a certain action is unfolding, it becomes an element that is meaningful in all its aspects, so that what we know about its genesis, the ambiguities we notice in its elaboration, will hold our attention at least as much as its surface qualities. And I conclude that the author of *The Tempest*, who wrote the masque but made Prospero himself responsible for it, had two things in mind when he did so, things that should not be missed.

In the first place, Shakespeare, who in the play examines a magus in a way that, as some have maintained, is both well informed and deliberate, shows us in the masque a work of Prospero's that is not part of his magic, which is conducted on a conscious level, but what one might call *écriture*, or writing that is a more complex mode of self-expression. In this way he makes us aware of ulterior motives, associations of thought that are as much a part of this practitioner of arcane science as his loftiest designs. And he shows us that however consciously Prospero believes he is dedicated to a metaphysics and a morality of the highest spiritual quality, one as free as possible from every contingency, the man he is in reality cannot be reduced to this kind of figure. In fact, a whole unconscious substratum extends far beyond such a figure; we may even say that it clashes with it, given its tendency toward totally profane and, sometimes, clearly sexual imaginings, and also, perhaps especially, given its fondness for games, its playful spirit—realities we would never have suspected beneath the criticism Prospero directs to his daughter or the scorn he heaps on the unfortunate Caliban. There is, in fact, much that is playful and amusing in the masque—a point to which I would like to return for a moment. It would seem that the musician who wanted to listen to nothing other than the music of the spheres has, with the greatest pleasure, given himself over to the suggestions of a librettist who could only have charmed the more modest Offenbach. And it should also be noted that just before the curtain goes up, Prospero—author and director of this entertainment—encourages his troupe to go forward with liveliness and spontaneity. What does he tell Ariel, the manager of the project? "Bring a corollary / Rather than want a spirit"—a nice play on words: "Appear, and pertly!"

Shakespeare reveals the "corollary": it is the part of the magus that exceeds what is apparent. But this is not all; and hardly has the masque been played, and the countermasque begun, than Shakespeare is able to make certain deductions and is about to show us much more, this time on the level of the action as it takes place in the play itself. What happens while the reapers and the nymphs indulge in the merriment of "country footing"? Prospero grows pale, and suddenly, brutally, he interrupts the performance. His troubled look surprises Ferdinand and Miranda: "Some passion," says Ferdinand, "works him strongly," and Miranda adds that she has never seen him "touch'd with anger so distemper'd." Why has Prospero's mood changed so abruptly? Is it because he has all at once remembered, as he says, that Caliban at that very moment is leading two conspirators toward him, who plan to knock a nail into his head? He had almost forgotten their scheme, and now it is high time to deal with it. But it is exceedingly doubtful that Prospero can have the slightest fear of the three drunks who have set out to locate his cell—where, moreover, he is not to be found—tramping unsteadily, their progress impeded by tricks played by Ariel, who is always in the know. If Caliban does play a role in what Prospero is feeling, it is for an entirely different reason.

The reason is that Prospero, in listening to the masque, which is his own work, has become aware of the background of his own being, which any reader can easily spot in this piece of writing. Is this a totally new discovery? Didn't Prospero sense it, and even wish for it, when, with the vertigo of one who is just beginning to understand what until then he has always hidden from himself, he asked Ariel, right after his severely moralizing speech to the young couple, to do the play with as much energy and unseemliness as possible? In any case, he now knows that he is not what he thought he was; that his spiritual concentration is unable to keep all that he desires, imagines, dreams, within its fine, noble structures; that his thinking will always descend to those aspects of life he thought he had refuted; that his ascent toward the "highest heaven" is therefore precarious; and that a lie may lurk in his innermost relation to himself, where he might have hoped to find salvation. This knowledge is enough to darken, to interrupt, what had been festive sounds and colors—and to make him think of Caliban, because this discovery of what psychoanalysts call the "id" makes a disconcerted Prospero recognize the existence of a Caliban in himself. That creature of base desires, the "misshapen slave" he has always judged so severely, even denigrating him more than was called for, is made in the same image as Prospero himself. And who is coming to knock a nail into his head—that is, to destroy the purely mental project of spiritual advancement—if not someone who is certainly not wandering about the island with two survivors from the ranks of the ship's menials, but rather the magus himself who is seeing himself in a new way?

Prospero's discovery is surely a shattering one; and that this is indeed his experience—and an event the development of the play will have to deal with—is borne out by the magus's state of obvious depression in the minutes that follow. In an effort to calm Ferdinand's uneasiness caused by the sight of his own anxiety, Prospero declares that those who have played in the masque and the countermasque are mere spirits and have melted into air—a fact that should not trouble him, since this is their nature, of which he has made use for his magic purposes. But he also maintains that the same fate awaits the most splendid palaces, the most sacred temples, the "cloud-capped tow'rs," and even the earth itself. The world as we imagine and construct it is but a dream. We are such stuff as dreams are made of, he says, and our little life nothing more than a lost moment in a vast sleep. Is this just a way of recalling what the magi teach, namely that one must rise above ordinary reality? Is it not rather a way of separating from them, since for the magi of Christian countries the earth has been created by God, and is therefore real, which is also true of natural phenomena and of our own lives? Indeed, what Prospero is now calling into doubt is that metaphysics which, together with the celestial structure of analogies and harmony, does postulate the reality of the material world, which exists at an inferior level but nonetheless most certainly exists. Like political power, represented by the "gorgeous palaces," like religions, represented by the "solemn temples," the project of white magic, which has been conveyed by that "insubstantial pageant," the masque, will have been nothing but illusion, one more dream, the kind of dream, in fact, that reveals to those who know how to read it the heavy burden it bears of ordinary fantasy, of human, all too human weakness. To one who has devoted himself to such a project there remain only weariness, mental turmoil, and old age. "Bear with my weakness. My old brain is troubled," Prospero says at the end of this speech on the nothingness of everything—a speech one can hardly imagine would make Ferdinand feel any more "cheerful."

The end of this scene is a decisive moment, or at least it could be—the moment when Prospero seems to encourage Miranda and Ferdinand to go off alone and seek repose in his cell, as if to wipe away his sermon on virtue, which he no longer feels justified in repeating. Is Prospero then about to change? It is not a question of giving up the first level of his magic powers, since Ariel is there to show him that he can still use this art, illusion or not. Neither is it a question of abandoning the idea of unmasking Sebastian, or of marrying his daughter to the prince of Naples, for why would he not pursue the kind of objective that even in a life without spiritualistic illusions he might have set for himself? But it does mean understanding that henceforth his loftiest and dearest ambition, the "bettering" of his mind, the elevation of his soul toward the divine, may no longer be appropriate as it is sure to come to nothing, for he has failed to connect with that part of himself which has just come to light. Far from having examined, judged, and sublimated it, Prospero has merely repressed this other side of himself until the moment when Miranda's love for Ferdinand, her artless and sincere spirit, the frankness of her feeling—the bursting forth, in short, of what is fullest and most direct in life on earth—caused him to remember certain of his own aspirations, certain regrets as well, and thus made the repression of his simple humanity intolerable, and impossible. And now that the truth has been made clear, will he still be able to think that by means of analogies he may one day partake of what is impersonal in the divine? Or must he now recognize that the body, desire, finitude, and chance are an irreducible obstacle to this kind of angelism—that they are in fact what must be recognized and lived if one is to participate in an authentic reality, if one is to achieve salvation as it should be, in both body and soul?

In a word, is Prospero about to experience an inner conversion that will flood *The Tempest* with the same kind of thought that fills *The Winter's Tale*? There is one sign that counters such an expectation—the speech that Prospero, dejected, addresses to Ferdinand and Miranda, to make them more "cheerful," he says, not without sarcasm perhaps, nor without pain. To say that everything is a dream, that there is nothing that is not merely an image, fleeting and insubstantial—is this to utter the truth? Is this to offer proof of the lucidity one owes oneself? This pessimistic view is certainly not shared by Perdita or by Hermione or, in *The Tempest*, by Miranda, who is delighted at the prospect of her future life. For a person who loves, the world exists. What one feels for someone or something other than oneself—for what is neither oneself nor the thought of oneself—extends its reality to everything around as a result of the hopes and fears that are a part of the interest one takes in the object of one's love. And is there the slightest reason for calling this faith into question, for not following the paths it traces into the substance of what the world offers, when it is from this faith and this faith alone that human society derives, with the horizons it has built for itself—the temples and palaces— which, when all is said and done, are illusions only for the person who has ceased to believe in his legitimacy as founder of a world, as surely he should? The mistake made by Prospero, the philosopher of the occult, had been to consider real only the impersonal structures he imagined in the various worlds; and now his mistake is to feel that there is nothing real beneath these forms once they have disappeared. In both cases, in fact, it is the same attitude, the same credo, disconcerted but intact, the same incapacity to perceive what truly is—and we may certainly fear that this man of such ambition, so deeply troubled at this moment, doubting the powers he might have hoped to have attained to on the level of angelic awareness, may yet be incapable of that inner transformation that would open a future for him in which he would be reconciled to his finitude.

We may well be concerned; and the events that follow will show, in any case, how difficult it will be for Prospero to persevere in the truth, which his contradictory relation to himself at once opens up to him and closes off from him. What happens now that he has become aware of that other being within him, and of the vanity of his pursuit of oneness and unity, now that he has proclaimed that everything is illusion, including his own being? From the perspective of his short-term plans, to punish his enemies, to marry off his daughter, the critical moment is at hand—"now does my project gather to a head," he observes—but here he need have no serious fears, for all the spells work and the spirits of the air obey, and so it is not mere magic, with its perfectly practical objectives, that is the problem, and the duke of Milan can already be seen on the threshold of his cell, ready to impose justice on the shipwrecked and bewildered villains. But what exactly is Prospero to do with his victory? Before succumbing to doubt, this hour of victory would have seemed perfectly simple to him, and his attitude obvious: the traitors would have been punished, the others obliged to adopt his views, and his power having thus been reestablished in a society once more restored to order, this prince-magus would then have been able to devote himself in a more intense and direct fashion to the second phase of his research: the disinterested contemplation of occult powers, used to this point only for limited aims.

But now? At the very moment when he is to appear all-powerful before the others, must it be that he can feel nothing but the emptiness of the hour he has desired for so long—the hope having vanished that this hour would initiate his ascent to the heaven of analogies and forms, the "gorgeous palaces," "solemn temples," and high towers of future power in Milan now all seeming equally illusory (and there can be no doubt he was thinking of Milan, which he saw also melting "into thin air," when he spoke a moment earlier of the nothingness of everything)? Worse still, must he now admit that he has to this point pursued only aims of the most ordinary sort, especially the desire for vengeance, spurred on by that "fury" which takes hold of him every time he thinks of his brother?

Prospero wonders what he is going to do with his victory. And this is when the thought of forgiveness quite naturally occurs to him, but in a way that will remain—and here is the whole meaning of the end of the play—withdrawn from that great possibility that *The Winter's Tale*, on the contrary, had sought to show was realizable. Withdrawn, and consequently without the power to see order reestablished in being, without the power to help life begin anew and flourish once more.

What happens at the beginning of act 5, when Prospero takes stock of the day's events? Ariel describes for him the wretched state of the king of Naples and his companions in misfortune, exhausted from the delusions and ordeals to which they have been exposed; he discretely suggests to Prospero that he should be moved to pity them. And there can scarcely be any doubt that Ariel, who is but a spirit of the air, ignorant of time and suffering, only advances this idea because, as he puts it a moment earlier, "Thy thoughts I cleave to," words that Shakespeare has surely considered deeply. Ariel is one with Prospero's thought; he hears it as it comes into being, and he sometimes anticipates it. The idea of pity, of compassion, therefore comes as such to Prospero himself, and it is obviously a sign of the awareness he has that the present situation offers him the possibility for self-transcendence, for if it no longer holds the promise of progress on the mystical level, it does afford an occasion for experience on the moral one. And although he has given no thought to it before—since it was only social order that mattered to him, not the fate of individuals—he now sees that his situation as victor has become a test. He can accept it as such, learn from it that forgiveness is more impor-tant than vengeance, practice "virtue," as he says, and once again feel greater than what I would call his unconscious self. Moreover, once he has made his decision to grant pardon, he resolves to abandon the powers that were his as magus, powers that can only incite him to idle dreaming and thus distract him from the one true path, which is the practice of virtue. Already that very morning he had agreed to give up Ariel, but in the way that one leaves be-hind the first rung on a ladder. What he is now rejecting is entirely different, and we can sense an element of condemnation in it. Scarcely has he told Ariel, with regard to the shipwrecked prisoners he has held captive, "release them, . . . their senses I'll restore," than he turns toward the universe whose occult forces he had sought to master and abjures with great solemnity that magic which clearly was only "rough," something material, since nothing true along the path toward the salvation of the soul was encouraged by it. He will use one last bit of this power to awaken those wandering on the island and to assure a peaceful sea this time for the ship's return, but nothing more, and Prospero breaks his staff and drowns his book "deeper than did ever plummet sound": so deep beneath the waters that no one will ever be able to recover its incitement to delusion and self-misunderstanding.

But what are pity and forgiveness, as Prospero understands them? Con-trol that he will be able to exercise over his impulses, and nothing more. When Ariel persuades him, the masque having reminded him of what in fact he now knows, that is, that he is merely a human being like all others, suffer-ing just as deeply from the same passions, he calls upon his reason to check his resentment, his "fury." Virtue is higher and more beautiful than ven-geance, it is the "rarer action": and reason and virtue in this context are no longer a part of the Platonic world of ideas but are, rather, a function of the will to mastery, which has to do with who one is, and has no other concern than with oneself.

In short, Prospero, though forgiving, has not been moved by a true feeling of sympathy for those he is about to pardon; still less has he been gripped by the great power of love that *The Winter's Tale* showed in bursts of life suddenly awakened in springtime; and so the world that the exiled duke has judged disordered and subject to blame will not be redeemed. What marks the last act of *The Tempest*, in which the very opposite, something wonderful, has so often been hoped for, is that after Prospero's revelations, after even the forgiveness he explicitly grants and the decisions he makes known, everything continues as before. The traitor Antonio, whom Prospero still detests—to call him brother "would even infect his mouth"—and his accomplice Sebastian show not the slightest remorse. The one keeps silent, the other murmurs that it is the devil who is speaking in Prospero, and what next we hear from them are their usual jokes, as crude as ever—behavior that this time is quite different from Caliban's. It should be noted, moreover, that Prospero himself knows only too well that nothing can be expected from them. Later, he promises himself, he will denounce the schemes that Antonio, whom he has pretended to pardon, and Sebastian, brother of the king, have also plotted against the latter. And there is no reason to depart from the first Folio edition of the play, which puts the verb in the present tense when Prospero tells Antonio that he is driven by ambition.

Vice is not dispelled; people are not changed, at least on this level. And on another, the one that can be seen as the positive aspect of Prospero's plans, the heart of his hopes—Miranda's engagement to Ferdinand with the consent of the king of Naples—will it not seem that society has been changed when this marriage at least can claim the right to harmonious accord? But it is precisely at this focal point of the whole play that Shakespeare gives us, and surely intentionally—he has staged it so well—a most disappointing sign. All the scores being settled, all the actors in the drama, or in any case the nobles, having come together, except for Miranda and Ferdinand, it is only appropriate that the lovers reappear, and Shakespeare's idea, which is a brilliant stroke, is to open in front of everyone, including the audience, the cell in which a moment earlier Prospero had urged the lovers to seek rest. The magus has all eyes turn toward what has been his dwelling, and with some solemnity he promises the old king, Ferdinand's father, "a wonder" that will please the king as much as he himself has been pleased to recover his dukedom. Upon which the curtain is raised—the words are fitting, since it is so clearly a theatrical situation before a courtly audience — and Ferdinand and Miranda are revealed in the place assigned to them by Prospero, it will be remembered, as a test of the seriousness of their love, that point upon which the young prince had insisted so strongly.

And, indeed, when Miranda and Ferdinand appear, they are behaving with perfect propriety, sitting across from each other and bent over a chessboard, and for a moment we may legitimately assume — knowing what a game of chess represented in medieval and then in Renaissance society: that is, an opportunity for courteous relations between knights and ladies, the acceptance, at least for a brief moment, at least symbolically, of equality, of fair play, in the struggle between the sexes — that Shakespeare this time is encouraging us to think optimistically. But what happens at the very moment when all eyes are directed toward the players? "Sweet lord, you play me false!" exclaims Miranda. "No, my dearest love, / I would not for the world," answers Ferdinand. And Miranda, in return: "Yes, for a score of kingdoms you should wrangle, / And I would call it fair play." Has Ferdinand cheated? Shakespeare does not allow us to know for certain. But what is certain is that Miranda, who an hour before had offered to become Ferdinand's servant if he chose not to love her, sees herself in the future, as she already does in the present, as the wife who will submit to the law, if not to the whims, of her husband; as someone who will matter less to him and to others than the ambitions of the manly power he exercises in the world of other men.

But let us now recall that this exchange takes place on a kind of stage; and let us also recall that there was already a theater within a theater in *Hamlet*, when the Prince of Denmark, author of a good deal of the work about to be played, had explicitly told his actors that the purpose of theater was to provide a form and image of society, to hold a mirror up to its truth. May we not conclude that with this chess game and the incident that disrupts it, Shakespeare has sought not to brighten the austere intensity of the last act with an amusing episode, but rather to show, in a way we might call archetypal, that the society Prospero had sought to restore to harmony and order emerges at the end of the day the same as it had been when the day began? And, in particular with the same absence of women, though even more complete, since before Ferdinand's arrival Miranda was a loving woman with her future still before her, whereas now she is about to go forth to a life of sacrifice and submission, just like Claribel. What does the "mirror" in *The Tempest* show? Not the murder of the king, as in *Hamlet*, but the symbolical murder of the queen.

In this twilight of *The Tempest* we are far from that other curtain that goes up at the end of *The Winter's Tale*, when Paulina shows Perdita and Leontes what appears to be a statue of Hermione but is in fact her living presence: the woman who comes back to life and thus restores to the world its unity and its harmony. The end of *The Tempest* is pessimistic, despite the congratulations, despite the preparations, made with seeming jubilation, for the voyage home on the ship that has also emerged from the illusion of shipwreck. Yet it should also be noted that this pessimism concerns only the specific action of the play and judges only the kind of renewal of society Prospero has sought to effect. And in the light of this failure, which is the magus's failure and his alone, the question we raised begins to find an answer. When he writes this, his last play, has Shakespeare sought to demonstrate, to glorify even, the powers of contemporary magi? With respect to the example he has chosen to represent, he clearly decides to underscore only the inconsistencies and the weaknesses, and to have his magus discover that he is full of illusions about himself by showing that at the end of the day this investigator of secret powers will not have known how to revitalize even to the slightest degree the relation of human beings to society and the world.

In the autumn of 1610, at the Globe theater—the Shakespearean center, par excellence—Ben Jonson, as has often been remarked, presented in *The Alchemist* a *social* critique of the proponents of occult science, amusing his audience with a tableau of the frauds perpetrated in their name or committed by some of their own members. Shakespeare, on the other hand, was the artist who sought to present the *metaphysical* critique of this problem of the era they shared by bringing his inquiry into the mind of the occultist himself and showing the illusion that acts initially on him, who thereby becomes his own victim. Shakespeare and Jonson were on friendly terms during this period when people took sides on important issues. But Shakespeare's thinking took place on a deeper level, and the conclusions he reached were not made as quickly or as severely as those of the satirist, his friend and rival. Analyzing and judging the magus, he did not condemn Prospero.

X

My reason for putting forward this claim and for suggesting, in extremis, that we take another look at Prospero, this time a more forgiving one? It's the unusual "epilogue" Shakespeare provided for this last of his plays—those twenty octosyllabic, rhyming lines, so different from the writing in the rest of the play, that he has placed in the mouth of the duke who is making ready to leave his island.

To recapitulate: Prospero has just given Ariel his freedom, the elf has vanished into the sky, and the magus himself withdraws from the entrance to his cell so that the king may enter it—but he has not yet left the stage. And to what we imagine must have been the surprise of members of the audience in 1611, he comes toward them and speaks to them directly from the front of the stage. To their surprise—for what can he have to say to them now that the die is cast?

The audience, however, and the readers of *The Tempest* must surely recall, now that the play is ending, that during the masque Prospero had begun to think about something that troubled him, that caused him to hesitate, but had no chance later on to make known how his thoughts developed. The only thing the audience has learned from these thoughts is that they have led him to abandon the practice of magic—the materialist magic, the "rough magic"—because it has not helped him to look higher, to seek in the lofty realm of the Idea the "bettering" of his soul. The audience may also have understood that Prospero then sought—in virtue that would henceforth be purely moral and based uniquely on reason—another, if somewhat less ambitious, solution to the problem of which he has just been made aware, namely, how to maintain in these new circumstances his hitherto unwavering self-esteem.

I would also like to recall that when Caliban reappears, covered as much with shame as with mud, his criminal intentions revealed, and expecting to be punished, Prospero not only forgives him without showing too much severity but also tells the brilliant assembly that this "thing of darkness" belongs to him, is even a part of him—the phrase is ambiguous, perhaps deliberately so, but is in any case surprising. And finally I would like to emphasize that almost the last words Prospero utters in the play are that once he has returned to Milan, his "every third thought"—after his daughter and her descendants, and the exercise of his power—will be his grave. Hearing these words, doesn't one suspect that precisely from the perspective of this ultimate sign, the sign of death, the sign of existence understood within the limits of time, of place, of chance that becomes destiny, Prospero has been reflecting a little—encountering for the first time in a long while society as it really is, as it can only be—and has nurtured a new experience, one he now would like to formulate?

How moving it is to learn in this last speech—which he delivers while standing at the front of the stage, turning his back to that island of illusions, gazing at all the eyes in the audience that are fixed on him through the same mirages—that the magus of only a few hours before, that arrogant, even brutal being who had not the slightest doubt about the legitimacy of his claims and the value of his science, is now able to accept himself for what he is and to recognize that he is the most ordinary of men, duke of Milan perhaps, but with no true possession other than the awareness he has of himself, which is, furthermore, precarious; and in danger of despair if he does not receive from others the sympathy that all through the day he himself has scarcely known how to offer. "Now my charms are all o'erthrown," he says, "And what strength I have's mine own, / Which is most faint." Then he asks to be relieved by "prayer"—a word which should be seen less as a reference to established religion than as the recognition of those regenerative powers of love and compassion evidenced in *The Winter's Tale*, but of which *The Tempest*, written just one year later, seemed to know nothing. "Pray for me," he seems to say, "Your prayer is all I have." I exist only through the regard you have for me and to the extent that I have regard for you. I am just a human being who only exists because of the way in which the absolute is shared between me and men and women like me, swept along, all of us, on the currents of death. Currents, eddies, depths that recall a tempest, nothingness itself, but which, when seen from the perspective of reciprocal giving, can become a calm sea as well. "Gentle breath of yours," says Prospero, must fill the sails of my new little boat as it sets out toward its supreme shore. These words are certainly moving. But they are something more.

They reveal that Shakespeare may very well have wanted to offer a critique of the contradictions inherent in the speculations of the magi, a denunciation of their abusive pretensions. He remained nonetheless capable of thinking—thanks to the sympathetic intuitions that never fail him—that all proud or immoderate people have the power, once their delusions have been mastered, to recognize that they are human beings like everyone else, but with all the great resources that reside in humanity. The moment that the unrealistic imaginings have run their course is also the moment when the person who has erred, and erred again, is in a position to discern and do what is truly important. This is an optimistic recognition, certainly, especially as it comes just after the moments that I find so dark in the fifth act. It may even be feared that Shakespeare has brought about this recognition too abruptly and deliberately, for how can one not be surprised to see Prospero pass so quickly from harsh forgiveness, from virtue based on reason, to that feeling of desolation that is expressed with such emotion in the epilogue? The recognition, it is true, must also be reassuring to Shakespeare, who at certain moments of his life may have wondered whether he himself was merely a spinner of dreams.

So I have come to the second question I wanted to take up, which is no longer whether or not Shakespeare gave credence to the figure of the magus, but rather why he became fascinated with one such figure at this point in his work and in his life.

And this seems an essential question to consider as we examine these last few minutes of *The Tempest*, since character and author are, for one brief moment on stage, a single, identical presence. Prospero asks the audience to release him from his "bands," which are the categories of thought that have kept him trapped in his own drama, but the "hands" that are going to free him from the idea he has had about himself are the ones that give their approval to Shakespeare for the play, and thus for his own thought, by clapping. When Prospero comes forward toward the audience, he already begins to reveal the reality of the actor who plays him and, beyond this actor, of the author who has determined the action of the play. Is this to suggest that there is, sadly, some of Prospero in Shakespeare? Or, on the other hand, and fortunately, some of Shakespeare in *The Tempest*? In any case, what is made clear is that there is a reciprocal connection between the writer and his creation that merits further reflection.

Why this link, which is so strong, so specific, between Prospero and Shakespeare? On one level, the answer is easy. For the Elizabethans a magus was essentially one who creates illusion; they did not truly believe that white magic was capable of acting on reality itself. And Prospero, as we have seen, has hardly departed from this restriction, since the shipwreck he has deluded Ferdinand and all the others into believing has not soiled a single garment or placed in danger a single life. Now if only appearance is at stake, the theater can create illusions as well as any Prospero can, and Shakespeare certainly has the right to feel, though not without irony, that there is magic in his art. And the irony is plainly visible precisely in the shipwreck scene of *The Tempest*. From the perspective of the exigencies of the play, the scene is unnecessary; nothing happens in it that is important to what follows; it even breaks up the unity of time and place that Shakespeare, for once, apparently wanted to observe. A few words of explanation in the following scene could have replaced the whole thing without any real loss. But it is important in this sense that putting a ship on stage, with howling winds, water crashing down, and flashes of lightning is a way of showing the resources the theater has at its disposal when it sets about to create an appearance of reality. And when it is learned that the supposed reality that has been evoked—this terrible tempest—was nothing but an illusion, a theatrical show created by Prospero, it may be that the dramatist in the Globe is sending his regards to the other one over there on the island.

But it is not only his own ability to create illusion, his own magic—superficial when all is said and done—that Shakespeare aims to compare to that of the magi; he is much greater than that; his is a mind that thinks deeply about things—especially about the virtues and dangers of the theater and the effect that theatrical illusions can have on the mind, his own to start with. This kind of make-believe is useful, even beneficial, he may have thought, and sometimes clearly appropriate. When Hamlet gives his advice to the actors, he tells them, as I have already recalled, that theater makes up situations and characters in order to hold a mirror up to society so that society may discover a truth that real life fails to recognize or hides from itself. Theater's illusion is truth. It tends to undo the self-delusion with which men and women cloak themselves in real life. Yet the author, in putting together his play, has nonetheless followed his own vision of society, of life, of the world, and his conception may very well be erroneous and hence cloud the mirror. Even in *The Winter's Tale*, where so much conviction is asserted with so much force, do we not sense toward the end of the play a bit of uneasiness on Shakespeare's part about the possibility of truly realizing what he shows, namely, that being is founded by the will of love—a truth of which many admirable scenes nevertheless seem the proof? The dramatist is an honest witness, but he may dream the truth he teaches. Far from having discerned the forces that truly govern the world, it is possible that he imagines others, and that by constructing his own scenes of temples, shipwrecks on the shores of Bohemia, children lost and found again, falcons leading princes to shepherdesses, he is merely luring his audience toward mirages, labyrinths in which they will lose their way.

But no one will get lost in my labyrinths, the magus asserts. Through the fake shipwrecks, fake losses of son, of father, fake feasts falsely given, and other tests in which illusion plays the leading role, the people that Prospero has taken on are effectively encouraged to recognize themselves, are forced to the truth about themselves—this at least is what the magus might contend. And this, in my opinion, is the reason why Shakespeare became interested in occult science after *The Winter's Tale*, and why he wrote *The Tempest*. These magi claim to possess the truth, to know how to attain to it and to encourage its pursuit through their control of appearances. Beneath what may sometimes seem a purely "theatrical" approach, do they in fact hold the true science in their power? And in this case, should not a conception of the analogy between things, Ideas, Numbers—in other words, a philosophy based on the impersonal, on disdain for the element of chance in mortal time—prevail over the intuitions and the fervor that rewrote *Pericles* and gave life to *The Winter's Tale*? Or could these theoreticians of white magic be merely stagers of certain aspects of the world that are exterior to the being of life, to its most profound existential truth? Shakespeare's fascination with the figure of Prospero is based on his desire, not to celebrate qualities of which he would have no doubt, but rather to judge these qualities from the perspective of his own research, which was leading him in other directions.

And so it is in this manner—at the innermost level—that, in my opinion, we need to read *The Tempest*. We need to see it as the project of an observer of society, Shakespeare, who takes his inspiration from a way of thinking, an ontology, a set of values, that are very different from those of the followers of the occult, the magi; and struck, perhaps, by this opposing way of thinking, Shakespeare may have wished to examine closely its claims by doing what a dramatist does, the one thing of which he is capable: putting on stage one of its representatives and, by letting him speak, reliving his experience from within in order to explore its limitations.

It is a project that presupposes, of course, that Shakespeare feels capable, at the most critical moments, of perceiving what someone like Prospero would not see; of being, at such moments, a better interpreter than Prospero of situations he will have known how to infer from the magus's needs and principles—and with sufficient force to convince. Certainly a difficult undertaking. Both deep reflection and acute psychological insight are needed. But as he attempts to probe deeply into another's mind, Shakespeare can draw support from what he has already discovered in his past work concerning the subtlest and most intimate stirrings in people's souls; he can build upon what he knows and has verified with respect to their inconsistencies, their fears, their weaknesses, even if it means noting his own at the same time. And in this he has surely succeeded, as could easily be shown at many points of the play. But I have already indicated some of the most decisive of these, in particular the recourse to the masque. And so I will limit myself, as I continue to reflect upon what Shakespeare has intended or implied, to a consideration of the two characters who, with the exception of Prospero, may be viewed as the most important in the play.

XII

The first is that enigmatic being whom the magus confines to a "hard rock," as far as possible from his cell, because he identifies him with the element of earth, that element which makes the liberation of the mind difficult. "Thou, earth, thou!" Prospero says to Caliban, with what would be contempt if the "thou" did not betray the fact that the "I" in these words that mean to wound is secretly on the alert, perhaps anxious.

And even on a first level of understanding, it is easy to recognize that the "savage and deformed slave" is one of the means by which Shakespeare has sought—very consciously, I believe—to put the magus to the test and force his limitations and his weaknesses to appear. What do we notice during the moments—whether comical, painful, or tragic—when Caliban is on stage? Nothing that justifies or supports Prospero's diatribes. There is no doubt that he is extremely ugly; even Stephano and Trinculo, the drunken butler and the jester—neither of whom is easily disgusted—call him a "monster" the minute they see him and are at first afraid of him. He is a loathsome being, vengeful, even worse—for his speech, which is often full of invective, abounds in expressions of lust and cowardice, and even cries of hatred and grisly ideas of murder. But these thoughts and fantasies can be understood, as the whole context shows, as expressions of the frustrations of the slave, his sense of the injustice perpetrated against him when his freedom was taken from him, his regret at having an education offered to him and then with-drawn; and so they show nothing that would suggest that there resides in him what Prospero accuses him of—that is, evil itself, the desire for evil, innate depravity: that obsession, that mysterious fatality that Shakespeare knew so well how to evoke whenever he wanted to, as with Iago, whose physical ap-pearance has nothing exceptional about it. In what he suffers, pretends, or dreams, in his naïveté as well, in his credulity, his fears, his humble pleasures, Caliban is merely a representative of ordinary humanity. He even shows on a number of occasions that he is capable of love. "Then I loved thee," he tells Prospero when he recalls the time when Prospero taught him language, taught him how to name things, which gave him great joy; and his most moving cry is when he says that despite this initial happiness, the only profit he will have had from learning to speak is now knowing how to curse. Shakespeare has conceived a Caliban who elicits sympathy, and at the same time he shows how harshly Prospero treats him and how much he misjudges him. And in this way Shakespeare clearly reveals the limitations of the magus's ability to understand other people.

But as he imagines Caliban, Shakespeare does not limit himself to what is seen by Prospero, who wears blinders—a vision, moreover, that is confirmed by enough other aspects of the play. It is important to note that there is a lot more to Caliban than the peculiarities of his physical presence or of his character. If we listen to him as seriously as we listen to Prospero or Ariel—as Shakespeare asks us to do, since he often has him express himself in verse, particularly in his soliloquies—we discover that his speech is not limited to the assertion of his rights or to his cries of pain, his howling. In all of it, the memory of what he was before Prospero came to the island shows through. What he evokes are moments of bright color where an adolescent can be seen, a witch's son perhaps, but also an orphan who has lived alone on the deserted island, feeding himself on sea-birds' eggs and wild berries, seeking out the fresh springs and shady hollows, wandering in every direction over a reality still virginal and as yet untouched—a reality he has no words to name. A happy life—one at least that does not see itself as susceptible to vilification, and one whose relation to the world is based entirely on an instinctive intimacy with the things of nature: a form of consciousness as it seeks to define itself, still unfinished but free to splash about in the light of origins before the chains of language with its abstractions close round about it. And in this way, too, Caliban takes on form and meaning in opposition to the magus. He represents a mode of being-in-the-world that might be called immediate, the very mode that Prospero repudiates. But he means more than this.

For let us now listen to the most beautiful lines in the play, along with those that are spoken at almost the same moment, in which Prospero exclaims that our thoughts are but dreams in the midst of a vast sleep. Caliban has just met Stephano, the shipwrecked butler, who has with him a wine that inspires and intoxicates the slave, who takes Stephano for a god. Caliban joins forces with him in a plot to kill Prospero—perhaps his least attractive moment in the play. But Stephano is frightened by a tune that Ariel—who, though invisible, is of course watching—plays on a tabor and pipe, and he feels lost in a strange world. Caliban, on the other hand, who seems to have been restored by the music to what is best in him, tells him that the island is full of melodious sounds. "Be not afeard," he says,

> the isle is full of noises,
> Sounds and sweet airs that give delight, and hurt not.
> Sometimes a thousand twangling instruments
> Will hum about mine ears; and sometimes voices
> That, if I then had wak'd after long sleep,
> Will make me sleep again; and then, in dreaming,
> The clouds methought would open, and show riches
> Ready to drop upon me, that, when I wak'd,
> I cried to dream again.

And we can only be troubled when we hear these lines, and we have to ask: what are these voices, these "riches"? What are these promises in the heavens that seem so like the "solemn temples," the "gorgeous palaces," and the towers evoked in Prospero's lines, they too placed among the clouds, with the same hazy, glittering, gently swaying appearance?

But let us not fail to note that the riches of Caliban's dream, were they to become blessings and beauties on earth, would need words to sustain them, words as well as the structures and other associations of language, and they would need them just as much as the temples and palaces that Prospero sees fading away. Other worlds cannot be imagined, even when only the shadows of forms are in play, unless they are imagined from the perspective of our world, through memories and desires that exist only by the grace of our greatest words. And so we must conclude that it is language, the powers and the potential richness of language, its music as well, that Caliban is dreaming of even before he knows the slightest word: which shows that the person who experiences immediacy can, at the very moment of his silent adherence, aspire toward speech as toward a second level—beauty, intensity, light that is differentiated but also one—of his intimacy with the world that envelopes him, and thus awaken to humanity, this bias of language, by imagining something like a heavenly earth—the mysterious place of burgeoning, of flowering, of transfigurations "unheard of"—a word I invest with all the meaning that Rimbaud gave it.[4]

In short, through Caliban's "dream," Shakespeare shows that nature de-

---

4. See Arthur Rimbaud, "Matinée d'ivresse: "Hourra pour l'oeuvre inouïe et pour le corps merveilleux, pour la première fois!"—Trans.

sires language, that it hopes through language to become an earth. Now at the very outset of the play, Shakespeare has Prospero's slave tell us that he felt this earth, this heaven, opening to him the day the magician who had come to his island began to teach him words—words that quickly enabled him to distinguish the sun and the moon and to see in a light, as though transformed, many of the things of the world dawning in distinct form. At the very moment that he released Ariel from the cloven pine in the rift of which he had been imprisoned, Prospero also seems to have set about freeing the young savage from his unawareness of himself with the great words of simple reality—those that make up for the ceaseless forgetting of the past, those that expand the horizon, those that let us hear the music rising from it.

Caliban makes clear in the lines I've cited—where the syntax is strange and the verb tenses seem to contradict one another to such a degree that past and present, reality and fantasy, seem to blend—that the dream he once felt was coming true is a dream he still has, that today as much as in those early years he longs to fall asleep to dream it once again. Why? Obviously because Prospero, who had seemed to open this earth of speech to him, did not do so, did not guide him along the way.

And it is precisely at this point in the relation between the two men that we can understand the deep meaning, the necessity, of Caliban's presence beside Prospero in the structure of *The Tempest,* and we can detect something of Shakespeare's final thinking about what a magus is and what he seems to provide but in fact stifles. Has Prospero really stopped teaching Caliban because he tried to rape Miranda and thus showed himself to be nothing more than a "thing of darkness," beyond redemption? Nothing but a clod of dirt, of simple, crude earth on which no teaching, no "nurture," will ever be able to imprint good effects? Isn't it rather that the way in which Prospero's words perceive reality, by considering simply the general aspects of things, their potential to fit into conceptual categories, constitutes a confiscation of speech: an abstraction that keeps distant from, and even denies, every true path that being-in-the-world seeks to open up. Prospero is incapable of helping Caliban because when he landed on the island, he knew even less than Caliban about the nature of what is: a finitude, identifiable and penetrable only in the categories of finitude. And because, until the transformation made evident in the epilogue, his only dream has been to escape from the earthly sphere, since he has been unable to understand the value, or even notice the path—though it is open in every spring one finds, in every berry one picks—of that incarnation whose light Caliban has dimly sensed.

Caliban therefore helps Shakespeare—and herein resides his significance in *The Tempest*—to uncover and designate the greatest of the dangers latent in Prospero's idea of the world and in his conception of life. Considered in its eventual relation to the instruction of young people, this philosophy is a poisonous "nurture," an erroneous teaching that suppresses the most specific intuitions and needs of mortal being and puts the student who has been misled at risk of misunderstanding the truth of existence here and now, whose luminous and open inner depth is "the great creating Nature," recalled in *The Winter's Tale*. The magus is a bad teacher, and all of society could be the victim. Nor will the figure of Ariel, portrayed a little above the ground in laughing colors at various moments of the play, soften Shakespeare's judgment in this respect.

XIII

Thanks to a few marvelously seductive songs, Ariel, that spirit of the air, is normally seen as the expression of an almost mystical experience, in which one is in the closest proximity to the acts performed beneath the level of language by those creatures one meets in the nature that surrounds us, and thus seeks to partake of their immersion in the All, and of its unity, of the infinite, intrinsic happiness that is a part of it. "Where the bee sucks, there suck I," sings Ariel; in the same way, he flowers with the cowslip—although it might be better to say that he flowers at the very heart of the cowslip's flowering—and he sleeps in the owl's cry and flies in the flight of the bat. These seem to be moments freed from any awareness of time or place, from any memory or worry, moments of pure presence to the world in the ecstasy of a "now," an "altogether now," without beginning or end or limit: in short, this would be to live, as Rimbaud said, "a golden spark of the light, *nature*." [5] But it doubtless only appears to be thus for Ariel, at least at the moment when he knows, through conscious speech, that he is dealing with the bee or the cowslip. For this happiness in immediacy risks being impeded by the weight that is imposed on the desire for an absolutely "free freedom" by words, which, because they name, keep things at a distance. To call the bee by its name means

---

5. See Arthur Rimbaud, "Délires II: Alchimie du verbe," in *Une Saison en enfer:* "Enfin, ô bonheur, ô raison, j'écartai du ciel l'azur, qui est noir, et je vécus, étincelle d'or de la lumière, *nature*."—Trans.

running the risk of being retained in the idea one has of it, rather than living its full and pure presence.

In Ariel's case, moreover, this alienation is aggravated, even at his moments of swiftest soaring in the light, of most joyous drinking of the air before him, by Prospero's orders that he accomplish certain tasks—orders made in words, which therefore require a knowledge of words, demanding the use of essentially verbal categories, which are forms of blindness to many aspects of the world in evidence before us. At one moment Ariel is asked to set fire to the ship that is passing by, then to save its passengers and put its crew to sleep; at other times he is asked to create first one kind of mirage intended to fill one of the shipwrecked with remorse, then another meant to amuse two young people who are becoming engaged. And in each case it is deep within the intricacies of language—deeper than five fathoms!—that he will have to dive in order to enter into his master's thinking, though at the risk, as we saw in the case of the masque, of making a number of unconscious fantasies his own. An obvious consequence is that the captive spirit may very well yield to Prospero's orders without necessarily feeling one with them. He has feeling, even affection, for the man who has taken his freedom from him. But his only goal is to regain his freedom.

This raises a problem, and a major one, in the organization of the play. What meaning has Shakespeare given to the relation between Prospero and the spirit of the air whom the magus has subjected to his rule—to his speech—thus altering, or differing, what might have kept Ariel in the intimacy of the life of the world? Listening to Ariel's song, we can only surmise that Shakespeare is fully aware of the specific nature of this need to be in the midst of the One, a need that aims, like the Eastern mystic, to exclude every mediating form of thought, which would set in opposition a kind of intuitive Buddhism or Taoism in Ariel and the entrapment in essences and ideas that characterizes the latent Neoplatonism of the philosophies of the occult. And so we are tempted to conclude that the elf, who is explicitly presented as a rebel, as one who longs to return to his original state of "let it be," is what allows Shakespeare to inscribe in *The Tempest* yet another way of indicating the alienation he sees as inherent in Prospero's values and convictions. In this view, Ariel is fundamentally different from his master, which is confirmed by the fact that Prospero often tells Ariel that he is not unaware of this difference and promises him that he will soon recover it fully. In short, Ariel, like Caliban—though via another aspect of the relation to the world, an aspect that needs to be more fully understood—might be regarded as one of the elements of Shakespeare's critique of the magician, in accordance with what I have indicated as the intention of the work or, in any case, the way it has come together.

But the relation between Ariel and Prospero cannot be so simply defined. For on the one hand, we must not forget what has already been said, namely, that Ariel's desire to be present to presence—that absolute that should be lived without words—is nonetheless experienced by him, at least at moments when he speaks, as specifically linguistic, since he names the bee and the bat. Terms that are just as Prospero likes to use them: as carriers of an idea, let us say, of the bee, which captures the idea in its essence. However much Ariel desires immediacy, he remains, when he speaks, in that which generalizes and mediates. And thus his desire, his expression of desire, has similarities to what one might call dreaming. He sings in the song of the bird, he tells us, but the song of the bird does not know itself as something that sings.

On the other hand, it should be noted that this song of Ariel's, this manifesto of his truth as spirit of the air, is not sung in the play at a moment when Ariel is alone with himself, which we, as spectators, could take as a sign of his autonomy in being, but rather at the moment when—in the rush of events, as Prospero gets ready to appear in majesty before the king of Naples and his retinue—he is helping his master to dress in a manner appropriate to so great an occasion, going so far as to look for Prospero's old rapier. It is at this moment, when he is turning around him, when he is so close to him, that the gentle servant hums, "Where the bee sucks, there suck I." And Prospero listens to him with great pleasure. "Why that's my dainty Ariel! I shall miss thee," he tells him.

What does this feeling of sadness mean? Shouldn't we remember that from the very beginning of the play Ariel has claimed, and has shown, that he is one with Prospero' thoughts, that he even anticipates them, delving so deep in them that, as I mentioned, he uncovers the magus's unconscious? And shouldn't we notice as well that Prospero, from the outset, continually demonstrates what his words "I shall miss thee" express, that is, that he loves Ariel, that Ariel's way of being pleases him, that he is sad at being unable to keep him near him forever? And from all this, isn't it reasonable to conclude that, contrary to Caliban's dream, Ariel's song is not so much a thought foreign to Prospero, a thought of which he would be incapable, as it is something primarily within the magus's own mind at this moment when he is so carefully preparing himself for his final test.

This is, in any case, what I believe; for Shakespeare intuitively knew how to recognize an essential aspect in the relation to the world of beings who, like Prospero, are determined by general ideas and by the aspiration to impersonal structures with which they hope to create a reality they imagine as superior in the realm of the intelligible. These minds—who are people, too, for as long as the period of imperfection lasts—seek to establish analogies through the perception of the essence in each thing; they leave outside their consideration a whole store of other perceivable reality, which they have determined is nothingness while recognizing nonetheless that to discard it means giving up a number of moments that could have been pleasurable. From the life they have given up they therefore retain both a feeling of frustration and a nostalgia that dreaming will need to compensate for; but only as dreaming can, that is, with the help of representations—of what has been rejected—that remain on the same level of generalization as the search for the "highest heaven," which has seemed too arid. The bee is encountered during a carefree walk in the heat of summer, not to introduce the analogy between the hive and a heavenly Jerusalem; but the bee is still the bee in itself, since it is seen in a word and so remains forever the same eternal bee at every moment on a path where time, place, chance, and other categories of a life fully lived do not play the role that is so supremely necessary for the approach of presence. In short, it is not through attachment to the particular object, whose countless dimensions might truly connect to situations of incarnate life, that the twofold and contradictory need—to abolish the immediate, but also to regret it—of these friends of the Idea, who are prey to such nostalgia for the simple earth, has sought satisfaction. That need has required abstraction itself, whose effects their impossible aim seeks to offset, and it is certainly not this way of dreaming that seriously undermines the particular vocation of a magus.

Ariel, in short, is Prospero's dream, a dream he cherishes, while still having to believe it is only a dream. A shadow of immediacy, a faint memory of a lost plenitude, but kept just short of a truer kind of experience by the dreamer's refusal to separate himself from what in words is their fatal tendency toward abstraction—and destined therefore to become that pointless, carefree song Prospero sometimes wants the Ariel within him to sing; that Ariel he usually takes as the instrument of his endeavors as magus. If Prospero should succeed in the evening of this day, as he had hoped, in freeing himself from his regrets about the ordinary world, from his imperfection, if he should succeed in devoting himself entirely to his "bettering," Ariel would vanish from his master's thoughts, would return to true immediacy— but by ceasing to be Ariel and by becoming once more the unawareness of self that dwells within the bee that does not know itself as a bee. If, on the contrary, Prospero begins to have doubts about his spiritual capacity, as he does at the end of the masque, Ariel too troubles him; when he comes near, he brings confusion to the plans that were formed in the morning, and yet he sings with still more seductiveness and power while his master thinks about what he has been and what he must be. And when Prospero has truly changed, when he is ready to say those words in the epilogue, Ariel will disappear, this time forever, into the gentle air. But in any case, he will have been only one aspect of the relation to self in a human mind, in all human minds—which, be it said in passing, is entirely in agreement with Shakespeare's thought and with what might be called the fundamental anthropocentrism of his conception of the theater. Even the witches in *Macbeth* are only the hallucinations of a potential murderer.

Ariel is Prospero's dream: the supreme means the magus will have had, through this imaginary approach to immediacy, to divert his mind from finitude. But he is more than this, and as I finish this reading of the play, I would like to recall a scene whose astonishing beauty is neither comprehended nor explained by what I have said thus far. It is the moment when Ferdinand appears with Ariel, who is invisible and is "playing and singing." From the point of view of the action—of the motivations and the multiple ambiguities—this is one of the most important moments of the play, for it will allow Miranda as well as Prospero their first look at this shipwrecked character. But this is not why the scene strikes the spectator or the reader so strongly. Just after the altercation between Prospero and Caliban, which is so harsh and bitter, almost brutal, what is surprising about this scene is the atmosphere of enchantment, of mysterious sweetness, that suddenly fills the play with its light. Here is what Ferdinand murmurs as he walks, enchanted, along the shore:

Where should this music be? I' th' air or th' earth?
It sounds no more; and sure it waits upon
Some god o' th' island. Sitting on a bank,
Weeping again the King my father's wrack,
This music crept by me upon the waters.

These words are but glimmerings, reflections, stirrings of a water lost in pools of shadow. A moment before, Ferdinand was in a state of prostration, but music that floated toward him over the waters has revived him, has swept him along, and how can we be surprised since Ariel sings,

> Come unto these yellow sands,
>   And then take hands.
> Curtsied when you have and kissed,
>   The wild waves whist,

—words that are an infinitely gracious and lighthearted invitation announcing and promising a world freed from every worry, from every memory. On the threshold of an unknown reality, a voice that is all transparency, all miraculous innocence, suggests that other ways of living exist, that they are but two steps away, up there on those banks of sand and mist, that the island on which a group of people have been shipwrecked will soon be seen to be not death but deliverance.

What is this voice, what is this other illusion of the island, which is certainly bewitching? The voice is Ariel's, and since in Ariel's speech it is Prospero who thinks, acts and even dreams—at least in all the cases I have so far considered—it is tempting to think that the "yellow sands," the calm sea, the dance, all this obvious unreality, the whole invitation to what is more than the world, is once again the magus's dream, invading the action at this point and making him look at those who have arrived on the island in a new way, for a moment at least with more benevolence. But it is difficult to hold this position. It is only too obvious that Prospero, whether acting or dreaming, is concerned solely with the ambitions or the illusions that have to do with his relation to himself and to himself alone. He is not one to ask people to take hands and curtsey to one another. The idea of a heavenly community in the light over there, down by the waves that have suddenly grown calm, cannot come from him.

And in this case, who else can it come from if not from Shakespeare himself? Shakespeare has used Ariel as a device in the play that will allow him to catch a magus in the process of dreaming—dreaming in contradiction to what he thinks are his aims—but who has gotten caught in his own trap and who, imagining something so beautiful, cannot refrain from investing it with the very words of his desire, which is for a more trusting and youthful humanity, for a "perfect and rediscovered measure," as in Rimbaud's "Génie," and as in *The Winter's Tale*. Let me repeat that Shakespeare writes *The Tem-*

pest in order to examine, criticize, and reject a way of thinking, an ontology, that contradicts the earlier work. He moves forward from point to point in his severe examination of Prospero along the path that will reaffirm the intuition that has been threatened by the practitioners of occult science, and these are profound acts of the intellect. But at moments like this, Shakespeare outstrips his own progress and springs in a single bound of imagination to the extreme point of his desire.

From the point of view of the research he is conducting, this certainly means taking a risk. For it cannot be denied that Ariel's poem charms us and leaves us unwilling to forget its light, which stays in our minds during the acts that follow, softening with its gentle rays and its reflections the critical examination of the magus in the play, which is a careful consideration of thoughts and acts, while on the other hand fringing with its magic everything in the scenes of enchantment and illusion—scenes that Ariel has produced—which suggests the supernatural. And this explains, moreover, why the play has so often been interpreted over the centuries—down to Frances Yates and even by critics of today—as the reflection of an accommodating attitude toward this otherworldliness, if not as a defense of the magi, whereas it is in fact a denunciation of the illusion they practice, primarily on themselves. What drives an author to blur what he is saying in this way? Is it the thought that every attempt at poetry, however enamored of honest thinking it may be, still delights in beautiful images? The fear that there can be no poem that is not torn between truth and beauty? Must we conclude that Shakespeare too has had to recognize this ambiguity in his own works?

But let us not forget, as we conclude, that Ariel's beautiful song "Come unto these yellow sands" is addressed to Ferdinand, who only a few moments earlier was prostrate on the shore, overcome with melancholy. And let us also not forget that Prospero—who himself is more than just a melancholic in appearance—might have felt some compassion for this young man, who is the same age Prospero was when he discovered his books of magic. He who is now almost an old man, shouldn't he know what is at stake at these moments on the threshold of adult life? Shouldn't he know how easy it is to fall into a despair that can lead to dangerous choices of the kind he himself made at that age and that in just a few hours he will have repudiated?

But Prospero is still full of pride in his magic and will therefore offer only the most ordinary kind of destiny to Ferdinand, even if it is on the throne of Naples, since this destiny is the marriage, symbolized by the dreary chess match, that will relegate Miranda to a life of obedience and her husband to the misery of giving orders, which is almost worse. Ferdinand will attend to the good order of society from which the spiritual elite imagines it will be able to derive benefit at the expense of these servants. He will have no claim to the Idea, but neither—given the grayness that surrounds him—will he be able to become, with respect to others, the Florizel he might have become had Prospero not chosen him for the realization of his own aims. No, it is no longer toward the "yellow sands" that Ferdinand will henceforth be able to venture. Soon he will no longer be able even to hear the song that now tells him of them.

This being so, we can now see that through this other song of Ariel's, Shakespeare, who does have the gift of sympathy, has sought to formulate, with an emotion that becomes great poetry, what might have cried out in Ferdinand's life, as in every life—what might have cried out and saved, had words been able to free themselves, at least a little, from the entrapments of the intelligible—had they known how to give themselves to the music that is always latent in them so as to recognize the absolute, not in the bee that escapes them but in the simple acts they organize for the everyday life of beings who are busy building a world. A dream once again, this transmutation of finitude into light: the very dream that Shakespeare may have feared *The Winter's Tale* amounted to. But a dream that this time is ahead of life and not in contradiction with it; a dream it is difficult not to dream when the "airy spirit" that gives it expression appears in the guise—at once laughing and serious—of the adolescent.

This appearance, the youthfulness that Ariel assumes, the life that seems so naturally destined for the earth and not for the heavens is obviously one of the latent issues of *The Tempest,* and one of the main reasons for Shakespeare's fascination with the magic Prospero believed in for so long.

TRANSLATED BY JOHN NAUGHTON

CHAPTER FIVE

Brutus, or Appointment at Philippi

PEOPLE HAVE often noticed links between *Julius Caesar* and *Hamlet*, works that were written and performed just a few months apart; and they have likewise observed that Shakespeare himself invites the comparison. Just as Hamlet is about to offer the court the "Mousetrap," that "play within a play" destined to hold out a mirror to the old king's murderer so that he may recognize his guilt, Polonius, the Lord Chamberlain, declares that he too once dabbled in theater and performed the role of Caesar in a play in which Brutus killed him. When he wrote this, Shakespeare must have been thinking of the actor in his troupe who was going to play Polonius and had played Caesar in his previous work. The allusion would have reminded the Globe audience of the earlier play, but it also gives us to understand that Shakespeare, in thinking about *Hamlet,* was by no means forgetting his Roman play. Beneath the comic guise of Polonius—as we shall see, Caesar too was capable of empty discourse—Caesar's ghost was silhouetted in the *chiaroscuro* of Elsinore as it had been in Brutus's tent on Brutus's last night.

And this is surely something of a surprise, for the moment in which the Danish prince concentrates within the witch-mirror of his theatrical machination all the shimmer and ruse, all the make-believe, teeming around him—and within him, as well—is hardly reminiscent, at first sight, of what was being acted out in Rome in those supposedly lucid and realistic minds that Shakespeare has set before us. *Julius Caesar* seems to stem from a quite different idea of language. Unlike *Hamlet,* with its tangled mass of implied meaning, reticence, sarcastic wordplay, even slips of the tongue, in which the unconscious is forever surfacing, *Julius Caesar* deals in forthright exchanges of publicly shared notions and values—ones that may become decisive in that "Roman" space which, according to a whole tradition in Shakespeare's time, constituted the very theater of an intellect in control of its means as at no other moment in history.

Reading Plutarch for example, it was certainly easy to become aware of "continual factions, tumults, and massacres," as the title of a Roman history written by a contemporary of Shakespeare's put it, and thus to understand that at the end of the republic, at the time of Caesar and Augustus, human deeds could be as disordered, violent, and tenebrous as in Elizabethan England. But another reading of Rome was possible, and was promulgated in English schools, one that admired Roman law, Cicero's eloquence, and the philosophy of the Stoics, and that recognized Augustus as the first sovereign chosen by Providence, thus giving exemplary value to a few great figures who, in Rome, seemed to embody moral rigor and clear judgment. "Roman" is what might be reduced to the intelligible and hence controllable part of existence; to solely that reason which has detached itself from the "passions," as Brutus says of Caesar himself, of whom he is nonetheless highly suspicious. And, for his part, why might the former pupil of Stratford Grammar School not have thought, or dreamed, along these lines, since he chose as hero of his tragedy a Caesar whose sharpness of mind was as manifest in the development of law as upon the battlefields, and a Brutus guided by high principles to the apparent exclusion of any lower motivation? Far from being, as is *Hamlet,* a sequence of soundings cast into the unthought and the unknown, *Julius Caesar* might quite naturally be seen as a study of action in which thought, even divided within itself, is "clear and distinct"—the author himself having aspired to thoroughly master certain great ideas, by nature public and by vocation universal.

There is, moreover, no lack of repartee and soliloquy in *Julius Caesar,* which would seem to confirm this way of reading the play, given the references simply to ideas, and given the style as well, a style often distinguished from that of the other plays, even the Roman ones, for its relative simplicity, its abstract vocabulary, and its reduced imagery and wordplay. An exception with regard to the latter occurs in the very first scene, where we meet commoners (who, however, quickly disappear) who are "tongue-tied." There is no obscenity, which is assuredly a unique case in Shakespeare. Overall, there is a general reduction of signifiers to the advantage of stable signifieds, rationally articulated with all the gravitas of a classicism whose assumed task would be the perfect coincidence of signification and form.

Even so, a French reader, especially one who has sought to translate *Julius*

Caesar, may very well not accept without some skepticism this judgment of the play's supposed limpidity; and may also be surprised to hear these same critics, who deem the work easy to understand, nonetheless argue over its meaning, taking positions that are more radically opposed than for any of Shakespeare's other tragedies, with the exception of *Hamlet.* Anyone who has read even a few of these countless works of exegesis has come across a Caesar who is by turns admirable, ridiculous, determined, and demoralized; a Cassius who could be a rogue or the personification of virtue; and interpretations of Brutus's actions and intentions in even greater contradiction despite the grounding of each such reading upon undeniable textual elements. Whether critics approach the play from the largely unfruitful—but constantly adopted—angle of character psychology, or from the perspective of the great thoughts set forth by Brutus or Antony, or via the moral or political problems these characters supposedly help Shakespeare expose if not resolve, the same fog of surface propositions is in evidence precisely when a supposedly clear form should allow both coherent and convergent analyses.

"Roman" simplicity may therefore be an undeniable aspect of *Julius Caesar,* but merely, we may fear, as one of the elements at work in the play, and certainly not as the path leading to its meaning. It is better not to give in to this lure but rather to hypothesize, as the only other interpretative possibility, that this language of the explicit, with its seemingly impersonal concepts, its action that appears to be thought debating with itself, is in fact but the raw material of an endeavor having its intuitions and intention at another level, perpendicular to this surface, and not only its intention but also, probably, its coherence, for we should not fall into the trap of arguing—as critics of *Julius Caesar* often do when frustrated in their attempts to understand the play— that Shakespeare, interested above all in stage effects, is concerned primarily to lend his characters the feelings and motivations which, from one scene to the next, and even at the expense of contradiction, might give to each the greatest possible charge of dramatic intensity. In fact, Shakespeare could only have shown this kind of opportunism if he had believed that his audience was as forgetful of the moment just elapsed as are the common people Mark Antony manipulates; and to think him capable of this would be not only to make light of the obvious seriousness of his other plays, but also to misjudge the quality of the Elizabethan public, shaped by morality and mystery plays and great historical chronicles—all of them interrogations of a coherence which, for such a public, was essentially that of the divine word.

So let us consider that *Julius Caesar* has its truth not in the explicitness it offers, nor in its homogeneity with the principles and notions to which its protagonists refer, but in something beneath their discourse, a density of language and action in which symbols rather than concepts bear the meaning, and whose depth is revealed in contradictions and not in demonstrations. Let us listen and pay attention to clues, even where attention seems owed to statements and high deeds. And to this end, let us first of all look closely at two introductory inscriptions, two sentences that have generally gone unheeded.

The first occurs in act 2, scene 1, when Brutus, soliloquizing, is reasoning in an apparently logical fashion that does not completely convince us. He is in his garden, well before daylight, beneath a sky that has been ravaged by an enormous storm, and he calls out to his personal servant Lucius, who is sleeping—a circumstance that is clearly noted, whose significance we shall later understand. He calls to Lucius to light a "taper," a candle perhaps, or small oil lamp, in his study: "Get me a taper in my study, Lucius, / When it is lighted, come and call me here." After which the servant returns and tells him, "The taper burneth in your closet sir." In the meantime, however, Lucius has found a note, which Brutus reads. Then some people arrive, the conspirators, and we hear nothing more of the taper, which will continue to burn away in a night of high winds, lightning, and meteors—apparitions, too, as many Romans believed, and portents—until daylight fills the room.

Is this a meaningless detail? Yet it comes to mind once more, and this time late on in the play, in act 4, scene 3, and far away from Brutus's house when, with Caesar dead and Antony and Octavius in power in Rome, Brutus and Cassius are at the other end of the empire, in command of armies but clearly on the defensive and haunted by a premonition of disaster. An argument has just broken out between the two generals, followed by a reconciliation which, while increasing our esteem for them, allows us to gauge the inner turmoil experienced by Brutus, who has just learned, moreover, that his wife Portia, who had stayed behind in Rome, has lost her mind and committed suicide. And it is Lucius, who has followed him to this far-flung land, whom Brutus asks for "a bowl of wine" to share with Cassius in a spirit of emotional communion, the same Brutus who earlier refused to be bound to his friends by oath on the grounds that reason alone should suffice to hold them to the common cause. "I cannot drink too much of Brutus' love," Cassius will say.

Now Lucius has also brought along a "taper," for darkness is descending, and after Cassius has withdrawn, Brutus—having had Lucius play a little music for him, and having spoken to the boy, who is falling asleep, with affection and compassion, gently taking the instrument from him—picks up a book but seems to have trouble focusing on it. "How ill this taper burns!" he observes. Then suddenly he exclaims: "Ha! Who comes here?" as Caesar's ghost appears in the half-light and gives him appointment at Philippi, where final combat will ensue.

What is this "taper," which doubtless gave scant light to the place in Brutus' thoughts to which he would not go, back in act 2? Of what self-relationship within Brutus—or, who knows, within any human being—is the taper emblematic, or initiatory? The unfolding of *Julius Caesar*, until this night in act 4, may perhaps have been nothing so much as the gradual emergence of this question, and the sketching out of an answer to it.

II

Let us return to the great monologue in the second act, when Brutus is reflecting upon the action he should undertake and appealing to logic's resources.

In truth, it is high time in *Julius Caesar* that some modicum of reason be heard, for up to this point the play has fairly consistently lacked it. And it is not just because of the storm, during which some have seen lions and lionesses wandering about in the streets of Rome, and soldiers of fire clashing together in the sky—visions that may merely reveal the superstition of certain witnesses. For right from the first scene we find it odd that the plebeians who have put on their finery to celebrate Caesar should disperse in complete silence—or even disappear into thin air—the moment a tribune has admonished them. The tribune himself feels some uneasiness in their regard: "See, whe'er their basest metal be not mov'd; / They vanish tongue-tied in their guiltiness," he cries out after them, amazed that what he deemed to be an argument calling for discussion and response—didn't they love Pompeii, won by Caesar?—has had an almost magical effect: "tongue-tied" is exactly the effect produced by a spell. The plebeians are indeed the "basest metal," the lead of alchemy, dangerously present beneath gilded glittering; and are not the tribunes, who, we shall soon learn, have also been "put to silence," merely a part of the same ebb and flow of incoherent social matter? This expository scene, then, is speaking not only of the political situation in Rome but of what is or is not, of experiences that can hardly be put into words and confuse rather than assist the discourse that might determine the action.

Once again we have the impression of fundamental unreality at the heart of facts proclaiming themselves as real when, in the very next scene, Caesar, surrounded by courtiers and friends, adorned with the attributes of supreme power, moves forward among the crowd that now has gathered again. For the time being it matters little what he is saying or will say later. The essential thing is that he is speaking forcefully, referring to himself not as "I" but as "he," which suggests the historical, immediately self-sufficient quality of his presence and his power; as Antony says, in his first words in the play, "When Caesar says, 'do this,' it is performed." But at this very moment, from the midst of the throng, invisibly and yet "shriller than all the music," a voice cries out, "Caesar," which suddenly decenters the entire scene, all the more disturbingly as what has been uttered is a threat, and an obscure one at that: "Beware the Ides of March!" The very center of the world, its gold, is thus enveloped in strangeness and darkness. And the fact that the soothsayer emerges from the crowd and is judged by Caesar to be a dreamer does not lessen the fear we feel, a fear beyond our failing reason and soon to be increased by yet another decentering, another presence of the unknown, of nonbeing at the heart of being: Caesar will fall down, foaming at the mouth, in a fit of epilepsy. Deeply troubled moments, then, after which the first act finishes with the storm breaking out, an event that at this point hardly surprises us. We have already intuited that the order of the world can be shaken like "a thing unfirm," like a door off its hinges. And in these circumstances we expect all the more from what Brutus is about to say, for he too is Rome's gold, but this time, we are told, by virtue of his thought, the logical rectitude of which ought to reveal itself as the sole being, unassailable by nonbeing.

In the ensuing monologue in the garden, however, does logic really drive Brutus's thought? What does he say when solicited by Caesar's enemies? "It must be by his death!" These are his first words. We may assume that these words are the conclusion of careful reflection, reasoning having occurred in the preceding hours, and that the statement of the theorem will be followed by its rigorous demonstration. But the demonstration does not follow, or in any case brings on no analysis of Roman politics. A principle has taken precedence over any consideration of this nature: there is a space in the mind in which such analyses may take place, assuming that those making them confine themselves to the exercise of thought, in simple coincidence with the categories and values of the thinking that is supposed to deploy the being of the state and allow freedom of conscience; but on the other hand there is the human being, unpredictable, uncontrollable, and, it seems, destined to desire and act wrongly, since Brutus terms such a being "a serpent's egg." This is so even in the case of Caesar, whom Brutus has always seen, he has to admit, submit his personal inclinations to reason. Even though Caesar accedes to absolute power and is little inclined to wrongdoing, he will only be able—"tis a common proof," the common experience—to give free rein, in such circumstances, to typical malevolence. It thus follows that, desirous of power, he must die.

Brutus's reasoning is therefore reduced to the statement of a principle. And I shall not claim that this principle is absurd, least of all on an Elizabethan stage and in an age which, as much as any other, saw power corrupt those exercising it. It remains evident, however, that the decision to act on this principle was hastily reached. Why would it be required that a man so worthy, so reasonable according to Brutus's own confession, be put to death before his reasoned argument is even solicited? Why would Brutus, who will soon express his trust—in the name of reason, precisely—in any and all of Cassius's friends, the conspirators, whom he barely knows, not verify whether Caesar is truly lost to the republican cause he has served fairly well in the past? From the first act it becomes clear that Caesar, who already possesses all powers, is surrounded by flatterers, some of whom are his enemies, like the disagreeable Decius Brutus, one of the conspirators. People deceive him, they want him to make errors of judgment; the crown that is offered him, which admittedly he much desires, is perhaps a partial effect of this troubled atmosphere, saturated with toadying and thick with traps, that is weakening his aging lucidity. In judging him, why not give consideration, at least momentarily, to such unfavorable circumstances? Why not attempt, one very last time, to help him?

Brutus, especially, should help him, for he admires and loves Caesar—"Yet I love him well," he has already said—and is loved by Caesar in return, as Mark Antony will emphasize in his Forum speech. How his life will darken and be filled with regret immediately after the murder! Caesar hid his face in his cloak when he saw that Brutus too was stabbing him; his blood had rushed forth, as if he had hoped Brutus was coming to him with very different intentions in mind—perhaps to speak bluntly with him as he ought to have done. In fact, rather than following Brutus in his dubious train of thought, we need to perceive in *Julius Caesar* the unoccupied space of an encounter that might have allowed for the resumption of the only exchange guaranteeing the proper working of political society: Brutus speaking as he will do later with Cassius, in another moment of stormy explanation, but one that will lay to rest any misunderstandings, Caesar listening and understanding, words overriding weapons. Let us emphasize that had this encounter taken place in reality, had this duty of a friend been understood and assumed, had its outcome been a happy one, the face of the world might perhaps have been changed, since first and foremost the civil war Caesar's death brought about would have been avoided. And along with Shakespeare himself, I believe, we think of the confrontation Brutus thus refused, and we regret the missing scene. And this explains our discomfort, which once again comes not so much from what is said by one of the protagonists as from what is hidden beneath what he is saying.

In the present case, however, it is easier to recognize what is at play beneath words—those of the tribunes and then of Caesar or Brutus—that share a "Roman" quality associated with the loci of power. In Brutus's meditation, in fact, it is clear that what he sees as significant, what he offers in contrast to the uncertainties the Roman state would experience with a single man in charge, is a whole range of ideas—such as liberty, justice—or principles and values each with its universalizing orientation and, consequently, a certain atemporality, to the extent that one sticks to the plane upon which each is defined and thought out. And as Brutus accepts absolutely no discussion with others as to the application of all of this, out of fear of the "serpent" he imagines to exist in even the best of human beings, we may suspect that he is frightened simply by people's ordinary existence disguised as malice and limited as it can be by its means and by time—finitude, in short—whereas he likes to confine himself to this supposed universality, this atemporality, which he sees and contemplates as law. For him, great principles are less a way of managing society and the nation than of dreaming his own salvation at moments when these principles distract him from the thought of death. To accuse human finitude of being evil, to attempt to rid oneself of it by discrediting it, is a time-hallowed device that appears in various forms.

And what is outlined in this way, beyond the particular circumstance that shows us Brutus thinking about Caesar, is the kind of thought that rejects an ideally open use of notions, principles, and values in which one is just as prepared to learn from the experience of others as to distrust one's own views, and substitutes a process of a metaphysical sort: that is, the refusal of empirical experience; the extraction of essences from this experience, which are then set in opposition to it; the articulation and interweaving of these essences in a structure deemed to be the sole reality. In this project, the freedom sought after by a man like Brutus will be merely the right to lay down the burden of finitude. And naturally he will have to refuse to hear anyone who prefers not to play this game and who, in the field of intelligible essences, would therefore maintain the palpable presence of an existence—in other words, the finitude that has been shunned. A refusal to hear him, perhaps even the desire, and then the decision, to destroy him—even when this means destroying along with him, without realizing it, the living being one is oneself, despite the dreaming that thought gives rise to. Brutus, we shall see, is certainly "with himself at war," is his own enemy, to the point of accepting suicide when the pure mind in him has been obliged to acknowledge the reality of the other. And, as in Hamlet's famous soliloquy, Brutus's speech too considers the choice between "to be" and "not to be," albeit less lucidly. For a good while longer, Brutus will, in effect, see himself in the position of being, and will assert his claim "to be." Whereas Hamlet has already stopped believing in ideas that only seem to reflect being.

III

In short, in Brutus's thinking—and this was the cause of our discomfort—we have seen a metaphysical dream at work, a dream that, in Mallarmé's terms, agrees only to "circumstances eternal" and seeks to "abolish chance." In place of what seemed a political situation—Should Caesar be killed immediately or not?—a kind of intellectual questioning has been substituted, which shows that Shakespeare is simply pursuing in this new situation his great inquiry into illusion, delusion, make-believe. He has now discovered that these ruses and maneuverings not only exist in ordinary human circumstances—where, with a bit of what is called psychology, they can easily be detected in the dream of a Romeo or the naïveté of a Tartuffe—but also affect what seems to be the most primordial, most radical relationship, that of the thinking subject to his or her own thought, a relationship that this time is barely psychological, if only because the misunderstandings about life that stem from it profoundly distort human behavior. Shakespeare has switched levels, probably as a result of the long study of English history he has now completed in his chronicles, the last play of which, *Henry V,* has only just been produced. And so we can expect him also to change the scope of his ambition, even his humor in the broadest sense of the word. Ordinary make-believe, "pretence"—as it used to be called—is readily and often comic. There is no dishonesty in writing *A Midsummer-Night's Dream,* which is at times so full of joy, before or after a drama as dark as *Romeo and Juliet;* or in having fun with Falstaff even when Prince Hal is already dreaming of his coming regal responsibilities, against a backdrop of violence. But metaphysical pretence is always tragic. Breaking with reality as such, absolutizing one aspect of this reality at the expense of all others, is bound to lead to the most radical, as well as the least discernable, of those conflicts that never can be resolved; it is a civil war of the mind and, in the name of ideology, the cause of all other wars throughout history. The result—which will lead us to the tragedies—is a great deal of necessary and constant intensity, since what is at stake is the recognition of this pretence in the soul, and its unmasking.

If we doubt that this project has already been undertaken, and consciously so, in *Julius Caesar*, we need only pay attention, as I now shall, to the events in the play and particularly to Brutus's behavior.

It is not only Brutus's reasoning that conveys metaphysical "pretence," the negation of finitude, but also his way of harmonizing his acts with his thought. "It must be by his death," he has determined; Caesar must be killed. And he will indeed kill him, but he will also have sought to do it by way of notions and in a manner deemed so essential according to his logic that he does not hesitate to sacrifice the precautions that would ensure the success of the enterprise. For example, it would be wise to kill Mark Antony also, Caesar's dangerous friend, as Cassius realizes. Not at all, Brutus tells him. To kill Antony would be to slash away at Caesar's limbs after cutting off his head:

> Let's be sacrificers, but not butchers, Caius, . . .
> Let's carve him as a dish fit for the gods,
> Not hew him as a carcass fit for hounds.

The main thing is to have this murder coincide with the ritual forms of sacrifice.

Why? Because sacrifice as it takes place on the altar, beneath the priest's blade, brings about a transmutation of the sacrificed body into a transcendent reality; and it thus follows that if the murder of one man can protect the state from a singular threat, then sacrifice, if accomplished in due form, will manage, via the transmutation of Caesar, to strengthen Rome in its very being. Finitude, that affirmation of self to which Caesar has given himself—since he wants to place himself above the law—is what must be addressed specifically. That is the evil spirit, the evil genius, that ought to be cut out from the body thus returned to harmlessness.

> We all stand up against the spirit of Caesar,
> And in the spirit of men there is no blood.
> O, that we then could come by Caesar's spirit
> And not dismember Caesar!

says Brutus. And it is highly significant that he has also said, as we recall, "Let's carve him, . . . not hew him," for to slice cleanly into the body is to return it to intelligibility, to have existence evaporate by way of one of those realities felt to be pure structure and that Brutus identifies with the divine; and it is also to ensure the redemption of the murderers themselves, to ensure that they are no longer "butchers"—but truly "sacrificers." Let us note in passing how embarrassed Brutus was, prior to the project, by the means to be deployed! A conspiracy may have been required, but that is exactly what he hates most.

> Let 'em enter
> They are the faction. O conspiracy,
> Sham'st thou to show thy dangerous brow by night,
> When evils are most free? O, then by day
> Where wilt thou find a cavern dark enough
> To mask thy monstrous visage?

What he hates is the gathering of persons of varying motives, who are hardly known and perhaps insincere, that a plot may well involve; and he was even opposed to the oath the conspirators wanted to take—which would certainly have arisen from the same base of murkiness—preferring to dreamily imagine that reason alone can steel and sufficiently bind them: a long speech—twenty-seven lines—which the others listen to while thinking rather of how to handle Cicero or Mark Antony. The plot viscerally offends the man who wishes to be the sacrificial priest. What he anticipates from sacrifice is a kind of redemption of the impure motivations suspected in Cassius and the others.

If Caesar were to be sacrificed, not killed, if his death were to be experienced by the Romans as a reminder of the transcendent power of law, then Rome could be saved: Rome, which henceforth may appear to us, in the economy of the play, as yet another proof of Shakespeare's lucidity. As I have noted, what at first sight might appear as the reference which, in harmony with an entire tradition, would have lent rationality and transparency to a "political" tragedy can now easily be recognized as something quite different: the collective ruse employed by the self-deluding mind, and thus less a coherent reality than an assemblage of truncated perspectives. At the center of things, and despite the apparent sincerity of the citizens—"I am a Roman, thou art a Roman, a valiant son of Rome"—there is much bragging in the conspirators' words, almost as intense as the bragging in Caesar's, which are more naïve and more openly anxious. And everywhere we encounter a fog of false judgments, plans of action that are sometimes well founded, as in the case of Cassius, but then not followed up; fatal mistakes over people's loyalty, and finally, most important, intuitions seeking to surface but unrecognized and repressed because they are expressed in dreams, forebodings, and symbols that reason, anguished and congealing, is no longer in a position to understand. "Alas, thou hast misconstrued every thing": a remark valid not only with respect to a mistake made by Cassius in the final battle, but for all those who in Rome itself are trying to behave like Romans. Nonbeing is everywhere in the presumed place of being. It is Rome too that we see falling as if in an epileptic fit.

And outside, all around this fortress of metaphysical chimera, there is in fact some reality, but a reality whose precise destiny, blindly rising up like a great rolling wave, lies in the destruction of the Roman edifice, which is nothing but appearance. The anxiety we felt, with Shakespeare's help, in the very first scene is now explained: "tongue-tied" for a moment through the effect of reason's words magically applied, the Roman commoners, that mob of plebeians on whom the powerful disdainfully turn their backs—Casca considers them "stinking"—are there, rebuffed but irrepressible, and will soon bring about through the play, as much as in the actual history of the Western world, a sudden and great change in fortune.

One thing is certain: reality. The reality that is not in Idea but in human beings as they exist can never be done away with, despite sacrificial endeavors, and before very long its truth and its necessity will dawn. As soon as Shakespeare has established Brutus's metaphysical design, he proceeds to reveal first the hint and then the bursting forth of the reality of our psychic depths that Brutus had sought to repress. And this is first revealed in Brutus himself, who is suddenly brought to that inner space where it is no longer the intellect speaking but the unconscious. Caesar's murderer wanted, as he himself said, to make his act of murder a sacrificial ritual. But as soon as the blood has begun to flow, he cries out:

Stoop, Romans, stoop,
And let us bathe our hands in Caesar's blood
Up to the elbows, and besmear our swords.

Thus he calls for truly savage behavior—"these butchers," Mark Antony will say—which scarcely resembles that of a priest at the altar. No longer is it a question of "carving" Caesar's body, but of "hew[ing] him." And the reason for this hubris is obviously the fascination exercised by what is repressed over the consciousness that represses—blood being the major sign, the epiphany, of finitude. Brutus is here thrust back into reality as it is—irrational, violent—by the very excessiveness of the act he has sought to counter it with. And henceforth, despite all his efforts, he will be quite unable to forget, and the tortured body of Caesar will haunt his dreams and urge him on to death.

As for Rome, what is repressed arises too from its depths: witness the events precipitated by Caesar's death. Scarcely is the murder known than the commoners become alarmed; something within them is awakened—an expectation that some meaning will emerge from these excessive acts they instinctively perceive as mysterious. And after Brutus has revealed his motives and set forth his principles at the Forum, Mark Antony will not find it difficult, showing the plebeians the blood-drenched cloak torn apart by the daggers, to replace the judgment made of Caesar with the flagrancy of the murderous deed, and to call for vengeance. The commoners, moreover, are hardly concerned with the thought, so important to Brutus, of "liv[ing] all free men," for when have they ever benefited, poor and exploited as they are, from the things that allow a person to feel free? On the contrary, the people have lived through unhappiness, the wrath of extortions for which the guilty will not be punished, the frustration of having to submit to historical fact without being in a position to understand it, the need to break the law they have had no means of making their own; all of which creates the wave that begins to rise. The plebeians will simply dedicate themselves to disorder— and here we sense yet another consequence, and the worst, of the metaphysical arrogation. Never destined for sublimation by means of some true law, they will instinctively destroy before yielding to the authority of someone capable of flattering them and appealing to their instincts. Brutus and Cassius are quickly forced to flee. Civil war begins. These are the evils, this is the chaotic future for some time to come, that Mark Antony, though barely "Roman" himself, predicts as he stands before the body of Caesar.

That Shakespeare knew perfectly well he was not writing a political tragedy—if these two words can be brought together—but rather a study of the soul eternally torn between the intelligible and existence, between concept and presence, is finally shown by his decision, borrowing from Roman history through Plutarch, to deploy, and to nourish with every means of reflection and poetry he possessed, those speeches of Brutus and Mark Antony— in the Forum before those very commoners—that Plutarch had barely mentioned. Through this decision he reveals that he intends to penetrate that space in which, by means of speech and perhaps in spite of words, thought is born to itself and may become that closed form in which Brutus sought refuge. Taking advantage of the signs and symbolic meanings that at this point in his recomposing of the action have offered themselves to his pen, and having moreover put in place a groundwork of anticipation—"men may construe things after their fashion," Cicero had said; they may delude themselves or delude others—Shakespeare now wants to observe directly, and at its very source, the functioning of a language which has thus shown its ability to close itself off from the very reality it institutes, but which at times, too, may very well not fall into this trap, may no longer be "tongue-tied" in the face of the metaphysical dream. This is often a space of eloquence, since eloquence is the use of *verba* that remain at a distance from *res;* a space marked out by rhetoric, an accessible space in the case at hand, since the Romans who have eagerly come to listen are addressed first by Brutus, who wishes to be merely the abstract articulator of essences, and after him by Mark Antony, a contradictor who has something more in mind—even if he cannot fully assume what would give it value since he lacks the necessary virtue and moral rigor.

IV

In short, can a person attain to some reality when speaking and forming thought? In response to this question, Brutus, stepping up to the "public chair," is the first to offer his testimony; and we could already imagine this testimony, though not in the striking form given to it by Shakespeare, who reveals, if need there be, his perfect mastery of the problem. Brutus speaks, and let us note that he speaks in prose, the only occasion he does so in *Julius Caesar.* Why prose, since his purpose, as is clear from what he says, is not to reach out to the commoners? Is it not because verse has a characteristic that would interfere with the Brutus that Shakespeare is constructing at the very moment when Caesar's sacrificer is trying to coincide with the person he would like to be in the timelessness of Idea? Verse, in effect, is time. Used in tragedy because it has no patience with the everyday, with what is inessential, and thus readily sets its sights higher than ordinary necessity, verse is nonetheless a form of language which, because of prosody and its irresistible march forward, moves constantly from what is past to what is to come— ventures forth, that is, in the flow of time. Tragedy is not like the sonnet, whose overall form had previously attenuated for Shakespeare the direct experience of time moving on, sweeping everything away. And under these conditions, even if someone like Brutus is expressing himself in verse, he is still caught up in the language that is an experience of time, either when he is planning to take action, though clumsily, or when he is thinking things through and consequently aiming for the absoluteness of Idea but all the same hesitating, wrestling with himself, making his decision—caught up, therefore, in the flow of time, despite his impatience. So how could verse be chosen when, with Caesar lying dead, finitude supposedly exorcised, and Rome gathered to hear news of it all, one is suddenly in a position to explain the absolute? Inscriptions on monuments are not in verse, nor are legal texts.

This, then, is the source of the astonishing speech, which, in its brevity that negates time's flow but equally in the multidirectional space of its monumental prose, will construct, through symmetries and symmetries within symmetries, a form everywhere closed in upon itself and thus separated from those who are listening—just as a geometrical figure in its purity, whether circle or sphere, may be closed off and separated from existence. "Hear me for my cause, and be silent, that you may hear," Brutus declares at the outset, and to guarantee this silence, while pretending to want exchange ("I pause for a reply," he will say at one moment), he asks question after question, though all are but the sad *erotemata* of rhetorical teaching: questions ("Who is here so base that would be a bondman?") the answers to which can only be those suggested by the questioner. Who is here so base? "None, none," the citizens answer Brutus. But who will really have answered, being questioned in this manner? No one, of course.

No one! Brutus is persuaded he has offended nobody. But what he has really attempted to do is to abolish everyone in a speech that amounts to a superb machine for suppressing one's interlocutor and also, it should be observed, for dissuading the very person giving the speech from the slightest impulse to act and from any self-involvement in true societal life—as the last words of his address will show. Brutus has hardly finished holding forth, promising his own death should his country wish it, when he adds: "Let me depart alone," whereupon he does in fact withdraw, as if, despite the mounting risks that will soon force him to flee, his mind were elsewhere. The final words of his speech are the last Brutus will have uttered publicly in Rome. It is clear he has no desire to be among human beings as they exist, even when he is planning to guarantee what he calls their freedom; he merely proposes, out of hostility toward life, to bear witness to a superior reality and to do so by means of an act inaccessible to most, an act which, in this lowly world, is doomed to be a failure to all but a select few for whom it will have special meaning, the way an inscription on a tombstone does or the a statue of a great man. Brutus does not ask for approval, which would keep him in the run of events; he merely expects that kind of vague reverence that societies grant those who have carried out in seemingly disinterested fashion what their conscience dictated. What Brutus desires is a statue alongside those of the mythical Romans of the earliest, idealizable days of the republic, one of his ancestors being among such men—and he will get one, moreover, judging by Antony's words over his body on the evening of the final battle: he was, his stubborn adversary solemnly says, "the noblest Roman of them all."

This is Brutus's speech, and this is the relationship of a man to himself that the speech finally allows to emerge from the complex of signs that "Roman" language had let us perceive right from the beginning of *Julius Caesar;* and in this way Shakespeare, conceiving and then writing the speech, was able to verify, not without some anxiety perhaps in the handling of such a dangerous subject, that language, backed up by centuries of rhetorical experimentation, may very easily become a tomb for the presence of other people. Brutus, moreover, is not the only cipher in the play's economy, as we have already sensed. At the moment of Caesar's death we began to perceive more clearly a figure previously overshadowed by Caesar, namely Mark Antony, who had appeared up to that point to be merely Caesar's near-silent confidant and a stranger to the political preoccupations that carry weight on this kind of stage. Antony did not seem the sort of man who would count among the true citizens of Rome or even among those the latter might fear, since on the one hand he lent himself too readily to habits Brutus would disdainfully have termed superstitious—like running naked through the city at the Feast of Lupercal and touching sterile women as he went by to free them of their ill fortune; while on the other hand he indulged far too commonly in low pleasures, "wildness and much company," as Brutus says sternly. At best, Antony might be an opportunist, and Brutus felt—and this is strange and worth thinking about—that once Caesar was dead, Antony himself might very well die of melancholy, such melancholy, we are led to understand, being lack of appetite for action.

But this same Antony, having raced to the Capitol, nevertheless utters, in front of Caesar's remains and with real courage, the first words in the play that are stamped with emotion, aside from the admonishments made a little earlier to Brutus by his wife, Portia, though in conventional Elizabethan times such admonishments might have been taken merely as the expression of a woman's way of being. Antony's emotion is the sign of a manifestly sincere affection; and it precedes a sequence of events whose conception allows one to admire Shakespeare's psychology. The death of Caesar and the sight of his corpse had been a shock for his murderer; we saw Brutus fascinated, but only for a fleeting moment of odd and painful intoxication, and it became immediately apparent he would derive neither energy nor lucidity from the death. This epiphany of finitude he essentially must repress, and if it is soon bolstered by the evidence of other violence stemming from the initial one, if it sweeps like a wave through the social chasm, Brutus will be unable and unwilling to deal with it. Mark Antony, by contrast, realizes right away that he has the capacity for such survival, for such instinctive acts, such spontaneous intelligence. Stirred by the violence of the murder, but equally enlightened by it, reminded by grief and by the tragedy of the event of the reality of the forces that make and unmake the world, he feels by way of response a lucidity rising up within him, which becomes prophetic, as events will quickly confirm. What will ensue from the coup d'état perpetrated by Brutus, less against a man than against reality as such, is disorder, further and greater violence, injustice, as though blood were going to flow for a very long time from the body of society pierced by the dagger of abstraction.

Immediately after this prediction, which shows him to be susceptible to pity and a conception of the good, Mark Antony understands that what he himself implicitly is—"wildness," but spent simply in pleasures—is capable of merging with the great swelling wave. His insight beyond all illusions thus becomes a cynicism that will allow him to act more quickly and clearly than the conspirators, who are merely blind theory. Almost immediately after Caesar's murder, Antony puts into place those tactics and strategies that will prove to be the right ones; and he is successful because he correctly perceives that Brutus, only fitfully active, is the melancholy one, not he himself, but also, more importantly, because he instinctively realizes that the emotion he is feeling and his desire for revenge are what will similarly take hold of the commoners and have them serve his purpose. They too are a blind force—but as matter is, not ideology—and he will thus be able to handle them as surely as we shall soon see he can handle that other instinct-driven creature, his horse. In short, Shakespeare has now brought into full evidence, on the eve of Caesar's funeral, a figure capable of taking up the challenge that Idea has thrown down to the world. And it is with this new perspective that we await the speech Brutus was rash enough to allow Antony to make at the Forum, over the ravaged body. We now understand that Shakespeare himself will confirm whether or not the language that denies life should yield only to a cynical language that allows the anger of men to become the agent and plaything of the death instinct.

So there is a great silence within us, as readers of the work, when Mark Antony appears at the "public chair" to face some still hostile clamoring from the people. And soon there is much in his speech that will respond to our expectations, on levels at which we shall glimpse the hazards as well as the powers of human speech. What do we hear? First, a discourse which, while aiming to seize control of the state, will pretend merely to wish for revenge, and very skillfully succeeds in convincing the people of the unjustness of the murder by using certain oratorical techniques different from Brutus's—their two rhetorical styles may easily be contrasted—but just as much given to denial of being in others, which continues, in our view, to incriminate eloquence. "I am no orator, as Brutus is," Antony says, but to speak in this way is merely oratorical technique. And Antony does not disdain *erotemata*, the false dialogue of rhetorical questions, any more than Brutus does. "Was this ambition?" he cries out, when he knows the crowd can only answer no! no! no! Whereas Brutus spoke the way one writes on marble, Antony seems to be looking at his audience, calling them to witness. And the commoners are naïve and easily handled, a force masterfully subdued; their feelings quickly become a mere instrument, which Antony, with a mixture of satisfaction and irony, recognizes as being henceforth under his control: "You have forgot the will I told you of," he reminds the crowd, holding them back just as they are about to surge forth at his own instigation to kill Brutus and wreak widespread destruction. The negation of others practiced by Brutus is followed, in Antony's speech, by another invalidation, a very similar one, and one just as easily guaranteed by the artifice of language. And this point does not augur well for the salutary potential of this language.

v

But Antony's irony, to which I referred a moment ago, seems bitter to me. And there isn't a reader of this famous tirade who has not felt, following its successive movements (to use a musical analogy), an emotion going far beyond the interest in its rhetorical skills, even though these are bound up in it right to the end. What happens when Antony begins to address a crowd still very prejudiced against him, and gradually shifts its thinking in his favor, finally sending everyone screaming after Caesar's murderers? In effect, beneath the orator's tricks, beneath the carefully thought-out calculations of the animal trainer who has stepped into the cage, there is something much simpler than these rhetorical devices: a contrast is laid out. On the one hand, from beginning to end, there are statements of general ideas: Brutus is honorable, ambition is a fault, Caesar was generous, fortune is changeable, and so on—and this is thought, functioning like ordinary thought. But on the other hand, and all thought is suspended here, there is also is an invitation to become conscious of the fact that a human being was, and is no more—to become conscious, in other words, of an absolute, that of existence in its time and place, in this case dramatized, revealed, through the violence of a murder and, in this present moment and right here, through the ascent to the "pulpit" of a man who was a very close friend of the deceased. Here, now: that is what Mark Antony says over and over. "*Here* come I to speak"; "my heart is in the coffin *there* with Caesar"; "now lies he *there*"; "*here's* a parchment"; "look *in this* place"; "look you *here*"; and, finally, "*here* is himself, as you see" (my italics). Those who are thus called upon to see, with their entire soul, first form a "ring" or circle around the body, the circle being the primary form assumed in the visible dimension by any epiphany of the transcendent. Contrast itself is certainly a rhetorical device that helps the orator emphasize one idea at the expense of another in order to persuade; but in the present case it is not the contrast between two ideas that is being marked out, but the one between the workings of the concept and a reality that is clearly much more—and so we might be led to think that a melting of the mind's iciness could follow. In other words, the presence denied by Brutus returns—and is not this presence capable, despite Antony's cynical plan and the rhetorical means he too employs, of thrusting upon us its manifest reality, which would tear apart the fabric of these speeches, undo ideology, call for compassion and love, and gather together those divided by abstraction? Is not some sudden shift of an existential if not a poetic nature about to occur, rather than the simple reversal of the political situation Mark Antony had in view?

Almost immediately as we listen to this speech, we may, we must, ask ourselves such questions; and this—hence the emotion I have spoken of—is an occasion for hope for the first time in a tragedy that until now has seemed so bleak; for a moment, at least, a transmutation seems to be coming about, and exactly where it has to occur first, within Mark Antony. Let us listen to the following five lines, which are among the most beautiful in Shakespeare:

If you have tears, prepare to shed them now,
You all do know this mantle. I remember
The first time ever Caesar put it on;
'Twas on a summer's evening in his tent,
That day he overcame the Nervii,

says the orator slowly, reflectively; and we should realize that these words, simple on the surface, in fact constitute a movement forward of the mind to frontiers that could well be a threshold. Why? First, because these words help us to see what a human being was, in a moment of intimacy. They evoke the battle won, in its very locus, almost its hour, reminding us of Caesar's capability and his courage. A calling up of summer, itself a metaphor for the years he was in the prime of life as well as at the height of his fame. And yet, at the same time, an evocation of evening, even of the cloak, which we now understand to have been new on that day of victory, showing a great mind in the enjoyment of the simple and all the more human pleasure of christening a lovely piece of clothing among friends, true friends. Caesar is there, before us, there as a presence. And a thought comes to us, a hope. Such evocations are only words, it is true, words that generalize, words that once again serve Mark Antony's rhetorical purpose. But isn't it just as true that because of the presence of Caesar's dead body, and because of Antony's affection for Caesar, which allows him to relive in its happiness and intimacy a moment of a year gone by, this absoluteness of a person's being will irrigate Antony's words even though they are what encourages us to believe in it and will ensure that those great notions—summer, evening, victory, clothing—which build a world and produce meaning in it may henceforth keep alive, despite their near fatal abstractness, the light of presence? Words that would be as much being in its immediacy as the idea that dissipates such immediacy? Words and a world in which all persons and all things might see preserved the infiniteness of their individual reality, a reality so easily denied in ordinary discourse by the ideology of a Brutus or the cynicism of a Mark Antony? Words and a world in which the relations between human beings, between things, might remain within the bosom of life's unity, might quite naturally be music—and might extinguish in the Roman plebeians the desire for revenge, which is but the unhappy substitute for the absence of this music? Were the mind truly to dwell upon the poetry of Marc Antony's words, the world would be saved! And Caesar's death, which Brutus wanted to be a sacrifice, would truly be that, in effect: carrying by the radiance of its absoluteness the unity of being—the divine—into all circumstances of human life.

Alas, scarcely has Antony called to memory his summer evening friend and the new cloak than he adds sharply, "Look, in this place ran Cassius' dagger through." And pointing with these words to the tortured body, to naked violence, to a presence, this time one of nonmeaning, absence, absoluteness beyond words—"poor, poor dumb mouths" he says—he thus returns language to its night and allows disorder, briefly contained, to unleash itself upon Rome and the world. He might have gone in the direction of verbalized presence, a presence mediated by words preserving its light and differentiating its music, but he tears himself away from such a temptation, such a dream, and his language and that of others around him will be nothing more than a short-term ruse riding upon disaster or the clash of blind forces—as the following scene, thanks to Shakespeare's lucidity, will clearly show. The crowd has barely surged forth through the city with rocks and fire when a spokesman for language, for its richest and most insightful elements, its civilizing vocation—a poet—appears on the scene, called from his home by the obscure intuition that his life is coming to an end. And the rioters rush up, throwing themselves upon him with the anguish of action no longer aware of its motivation, killing him because his name is Cinna, the name of one of the conspirators. They realize it is mere coincidence, but that makes no difference. Henceforth magic takes over from logic in the mounting chaos, and metonymy serves its cause. "It is no matter, his name's Cinna; pluck but his name out of his heart." There is little wordplay in *Julius Caesar,* as we have noted, but what is used in this instance is frightful, for it reveals the murderous thrust of the conspirators' daggers into the very depths of language.

This is an obviously pessimistic fact to establish at the close of act 3, but we should not conclude that Shakespeare has thereby brought to an end the questioning of the power of words that I suggested he had undertaken in the scene with its two public speeches. Some things, certainly, have come about—through the very use of language, in fact—that confirm our worst fears: Brutus has declined human exchange, and in the resulting void Antony has unleashed a storm. But there are other indications that stir different thoughts. First, listening to Antony's speech we were struck when he paused, however briefly, to dwell on his memory of the summer evening in Caesar's camp: wasn't this evidence of a still unknown part of his being, of behavioral motivations other than pure ambition? I have said that the irony he uses when speaking to the plebeians he scorns is bitter. Ironic too—it seems to me now—and no less bitter is the "honorable" he applies to Brutus and his friends in order to protect himself, or so it first appeared, from the crowd's animosity. A useful precaution, true enough, but the words "they are honorable men" that he keeps repeating, and his pleasure, once he is in control of things, in taking apart the formula that had allowed him to edge toward such control, is inadequate to explain them: the words point to an obsession, which gradually becomes clearer. Antony is a creature of wild, basic desires, unscrupulous in his eagerness to grab what he covets; but he loved Caesar, as we realized, and his affection and admiration for a man of greater self-discipline and lucidity clearly contained an element of expectation, a desire that Caesar, returning his love, might help him to grow and mature. Unfortunately, Brutus was the one Caesar loved, the one from whom he expected affection and closeness. While he complimented Antony on his love of theater and his ability to sleep well, he respected Brutus as a man of virtue and honor.

"An honorable man"! We can quite naturally recognize in these three frequently repeated words the reason behind their irony, since it is the same Brutus who assassinates the friend who had shown confidence in him. Caesar was expecting Brutus to come see him, and he dreamed of that visit even as he was dying if we are to believe Antony, who has torn himself away from the happy memory of that summer evening only to picture Caesar's blood surging forth from the gates of his body, believing that Brutus—"Caesar's angel"—was coming as a friend. The man of honor was a traitor; irony toward him is therefore permissible, except that it reveals, in addition, that Antony has long been jealous of the preference Caesar granted that other son, Brutus, and that his struggle for power, even if it takes a civil war, will also satisfy a need for vengeful prosecution. And this shows him to be capable of much mental agitation beneath his seemingly cold exterior; and consequently at risk, should another passion seize hold of him, of losing some of his present clear-sightedness.

Shakespeare, of course, did not have to discover, as we must, this emotion hidden in Antony's words, since he is the author of the play. We can simply imagine that he came to perceive it while his uncertain intuition was being guided by his pen. But what seems probable, and this is the second lesson he seems to have drawn from this great scene—the other being the death of the poet Cinna—is that he gave some thought, always in the context of the power and the potential of language, to this passion as well, to these conflicting feelings, and this time optimistically. For even where Antony's speech may seem merely abstract and self-centered, a sense of mourning can be felt in it, and a frustration arising from the depths of his being, subsiding, and re-emerging—which means that there remains in his language a point of shifting toward the infinite, toward what is positive in life. Even an Antony can at times show himself capable of attaining to presence through the vehemence of words, as a society must do in order to assume meaning; we need only to listen more closely to him, and to others, to understand better what is happening within them at such moments, and what is being lost but might still survive. And here we have rediscovered a major raison d'être of theater. Shakespeare has brought Antony to the stage without offering just another form of make-believe in the place of "Roman" ideology. As he did in the great chronicles of the history of England, which he had recently completed, Shakespeare continues to recognize that human beings are capable of some form of love even at the moment of their greatest derangement. And so he now sets out simply to study the human being, with the new means supplied by the revelation in Brutus that to the many forms of ordinary self-delusion—those dictated by vanity and naïveté—may be added one of even greater power: the one that takes, or seeks to take, the mind's representations, the idea, for reality itself.

A new means? Yes, for we should not think that for a dramatic author of the stature of Shakespeare this renewed interest in human adventure, in people's excesses, in their madness, will be restricted, as the new work is undertaken, to yet more portrayals of great figures who take up the entire stage. Perhaps at times, before writing his *Julius Caesar,* Shakespeare had been tempted to proceed in this way, following the example of Marlowe, whom he much admired; but it is precisely from this point of view that we might observe the degree to which Shakespeare marks himself off from his rival, surpassing him in certain decisive dimensions. In other words, Tamburlaine is the whole of that bas-relief *Tamburlaine;* but Antony, however complex he may be, is not all there is to *Julius Caesar,* in which other telling elements, other dimensions and figures, especially the figure of Brutus, hold in reserve, in the secret depths of their reciprocal relations, more remote features and problems, which Brutus's passion—his metaphysical "pretence"—can begin to shed light on.

VI

One thing is sure, at all events: after placing Antony in the forefront of his third act, Shakespeare returns to Brutus, and to Brutus almost alone, for the final two. And as these two acts are of minimal use from a suspense point of view, given that the die is cast on the public scene, the author of *Julius Caesar* must have felt that other levels remained latently available whereby his meditation might be developed on a more interior stage.

Moreover, changes come about in the decor and in the writing, implying that attention is being focused on this new stage. All at once, after a last glance at Rome showing Antony and Octavius determining to share the empire between them, the action has shifted to a distant, mountainous region as foreign to the play's spectators as to Brutus and Cassius, who wander through it — a fine metaphor for self-awareness wrapped in its familiar darkness. And the proud succinctness of the earlier articulations of Caesar's murderers, articulations judged to be all Roman virtue and clarity, has given way, although those men now command two armies, to rambling, disorderly speech and implicit preoccupations that they either thrust aside or evade, while in their minds and hearts renunciations as well as maturings, of which they are hardly aware, seem to develop and unfold. Their priorities have changed. What concerns them is less the salvation of Rome than the future of their friendship, Brutus noticing that Cassius is being cold toward him, Cassius, crying out in pain soon afterward and reproaching Brutus for the same reason. Both are manifestly nervous, disturbed. Their philosophy no longer suffices.

This is confirmed, or rather explored, by their great argument scene, the occasion of a violent explosion in Brutus, indeed of utter unreason. "Go show your slaves how choleric you are!" he cries out to Cassius, who has been a little touchy over an accusation he felt to be unfair and who now listens to Brutus in amazement and dismay. In this clear display of bad faith it is easy to see that Brutus merely seeks to deflect an accusation he now continuously directs toward himself; and its nature is already revealed, or very nearly so. Brutus accuses Cassius of having accepted considerations when it is his task to entrust responsibilities — of having "itching palms," hands that suffer from an itching only money can soothe; and in this Brutus is seeking to forget that his own hands were burning from stabbing a friend at a time when they ought to have been held out toward him. In brief, Shakespeare has taken up his interrogation of Brutus at the point where Antony left it: when Antony was imagining Caesar at the moment of his death dreaming that Brutus had come knocking at his door. "*Et tu, Brute,* then fall Caesar!" Caesar had then groaned, words certainly not easy to forget for anybody who has struck home. Brutus has killed his best friend, killed him at a time when Caesar, grown older, weaker, was making ever more declarations of infallibility and immovable firmness only out of anguish—a clear sign of his need for help. And now we learn that a hundred senators are dead in the aftermath of the assassination, "Cicero being one"; and, the cruelest consequence of all, Portia herself, the wife left behind in Rome, has lost her mind despite her desire to remain strong, and has committed suicide in frightful fashion, swallowing hot coals. Brutus in act 4 is no longer a Roman living by his secure beliefs and a constancy offered by his stoic philosophy. He feels guilt and is prey to remorse, to the point of taking but a distracted interest in the campaign waged against him by Antony and Octavius, whose armies are nonetheless approaching.

And soon he will draw the most radical conclusion from his judgment of himself. Night has come, Cassius has withdrawn after a reconciliation restoring one friend to Brutus yet depriving Brutus of an object to satisfy his need for accusation, and so Caesar's murderer is now alone with Lucius, his young slave, who plays him a little music before falling asleep. Brutus tries to read for a while, but sleep catches up with him too, sleep meaning dreams, and we know very well at this point that Brutus now has only bad dreams. "How ill this taper burns!" he exclaims, though it is his sight that is blurring over, and Caesar's ghost, or so he thinks, is there before him, calling him to an appointment at Philippi, where battle is to be fought. Thereupon Brutus, forbidden by his philosophy to commit suicide, immediately determines to hasten the action and engage at daybreak in the combat he can no longer doubt will lead to his downfall. "Volumnius," he confides next day to one of his intimates, "The ghost of Caesar has appear'd to me. . . . I know my hour is come." Remorse has become the determination to expiate his crime, and the whole of act 5, the narrative of the great and often confused fray, seems to have been played out beforehand. Errors here, there, and everywhere, acts that fail, fateful illusions: the battle of Philippi is but a metaphor of inner destinies dominating human behaviors.

Brutus, in other words, has been vanquished, and above all by his own actions; by way of compensation, his persona in *Julius Caesar* has been humanized, less buried in abstractness than it was before. Yet there is more than this notion of remorse in Shakespeare's new approach to him; I should go so far as to say that the deepest interest of the play remains to be discovered, though it still resides in this great scene, two elements of which must now have our attention.

The first is that "the monstrous apparition" that freezes Brutus's blood is Caesar's ghost only because that is how Brutus wants it. "Art thou some god, some angel, or some devil?" he first cries out, and the ghost answers, "Thy evil spirit, Brutus," before disappearing when Brutus has "taken heart." The apparition is not that of a dead man seeking revenge, but the condensation—quite explicitly—of an aspect of Brutus's psychic being; reminding him of his fault, it coldly articulates the reason for it: his inclination to shut himself up in great abstract ideas out of aversion to actual existence. To the idea we have of Brutus, the ghost's words add a dimension of inner destiny, which, we should observe, is explained neither by the fundamental elements of the play, which are political and moral, nor even by Shakespeare's intuitions with regard to metaphysical delusion. Why is Brutus "with himself at war" and relentlessly pursued by an "evil spirit"? Should this predisposition, deeply rooted though it may be in the dialectics of his thought, be deemed nothing more than an oddity of character, traceable to some genetic infirmity?

But let us pay heed to another element toward the end of act 5, a detail not normally picked up, though it should be since Shakespeare's intuition has given it prominence. I shall begin by quoting a whole exchange, for every word has weight; and I shall first recall that Lucius, the young slave, appeared as early as the second act—when Brutus was deep in thought in his garden, beneath the stormy sky—as the object of some mildly gentle consideration on the part of his master. When Brutus called for him and he was not prompt in responding, for he was sleeping, Brutus exclaimed, "Lucius, I say! / I would it were my fault to sleep so soundly." But his impatience lacked all anger, and he seemed to truly care about Lucius's sleep, for a moment later he said to him, "Get you to bed again, it is not day." And now, in act 5, when he is alone for the night, with Lucius close by, the same caring reappears, even more solicitous. Brutus notices that the young boy "speaks drowsily," sleepily. And he adds, "Poor knave, I blame thee not; thou art o'erwatched," after which comes a moment of affectionate intimacy, which I believe we should think through:

BRUTUS:
Look, Lucius, here's the book I sought for so;
I put it in the pocket of my gown.

LUCIUS:
I was sure your lordship did not give it to me.

BRUTUS:

Bear with me, good boy, I am much forgetful.
Canst thou hold up thy heavy eyes awhile,
And touch thy instrument a strain or two?

LUCIUS:

Ay, my lord, an't please you.

BRUTUS:

It does, my boy.
I trouble thee too much, but thou art willing.

LUCIUS:

It is my duty, sir.

BRUTUS:

I should not urge thy duty past thy might;
I know young bloods look for a time of rest.

LUCIUS:

I have slept, my lord, already.

BRUTUS:

It was well done, and thou shalt sleep again.
I will not hold thee long. If I do live
I will be good to thee.
[music, and a song]
This is a sleepy tune; O murd'rous slumber!
Layest thou thy leaden mace upon my boy,
That plays thee music? Gentle knave, good night;
I will not do thee so much wrong to wake thee.

It is an exchange that ends with Brutus gently withdrawing the musical instrument from the sleeping child's hands and offering another "good boy,
good night" in which I feel I can already hear the "good night, sweet prince"
that in *Hamlet* marks the onset of another sleep. By theatrical standards, this
has been a quite lengthy conversation.

Clearly, the exchange reveals first of all that Brutus, in the same scene that
exposes the fatality oppressing him, his difficulty in loving, is also someone
capable of true affection, in a way Rimbaud might have called "delicate and
mysterious"—capable of loving or at very least wanting to love. Which

comes as a surprise as we watch this suddenly more enigmatic tragedy, and raises a question at almost the very moment when, the action drawing to an end, the elements of meaning ought to be on the point of closing in on that perhaps unfathomable but simple reality that is thought to characterize the tragic. What, then, is acting itself out in this Brutus who seemed to incarnate rejection of humanity, seeing it as nothing but "a serpent's egg"? Why is he both the one who rejects and the one who loves? Isn't there something irrepressible weighing heavily upon his judgments and his acts, something we should try to understand?

VII

We ask ourselves these questions, in the darkness shrouding the stage, just hours before Brutus and Cassius are reduced by the fate of arms to that mere trace of a human being that is one's public persona. But we must also realize, and it is high time to do so, that for understanding such enigmas as well as other elements in this work, means were available to the play's first spectators that are not available to us, and these means could even have been related to their sure beliefs. The Globe audience is indeed Elizabethan consciousness, its conception of the world being as radically different from our own as it was from that of the Romans at the time of Caesar. At the center of everything and even at its source, there is for Shakespeare's contemporaries a personal God, in whose presence there exists a single, vast sphere of other presences held together by the love each ceaselessly devotes to that God—human society merely echoing this same act of devotion toward its own kings, elected representatives of God. With such categories, the Elizabethan spectator is bound to understand *Julius Caesar* differently from the uninitiated modern reader; and we need to take account of this kind of reception, for despite the profoundly personal and obviously broader and more demanding side of Shakespeare's great intuitive genius, this reception is part of the raw material he is working with.

Hence, for example, his conception of Caesar, which has caused such surprise, as I was suggesting at the beginning of this study. When the spectator of Shakespeare's time sees the Caesar of his play so strongly desiring the crown, he can only judge his ambition according to the great light he perceives as residing in the king as he knows him, the modern king, intended by God; and not, moreover, without being prejudiced in his favor, for since Augustine the church was given to believe that Caesar, the root cause of Augustus's becoming emperor in Christ's day, had been destined by Providence to prepare pontifical Rome and serve as a model for sovereigns to come—such as Elizabeth, for example, who was fully aware of the fact. But the same Elizabethan spectator cannot forget that Caesar nevertheless lived before the era of Grace, in a society without experience of God; he therefore cannot be king in the only full and valid sense of the word. It follows that such a spectator will understand Caesar's hesitations—in our eyes, signs of faint-heartedness or cunning—as foreknowledge of an essentially supernatural impediment. Whatever his desire or his "will" may be, neither provides Caesar with that mysterious assurance that allows a Christian king, however mediocre—though his very foibles point to his humanness through which God once more becomes incarnate—to know he is fully entitled to and worthy of his people's veneration.

Similarly, Elizabethan spectators will feel they understand Brutus, and in a fashion not our own. On the one hand, they cannot fail to remember, faced with a prince's murderer, that regicide is an attack upon God, that such an assassin is a man seeking to exile himself from universal love and is consequently the instrument of the devil and destined to end up in darkest hell—in accordance, moreover, with Dante's judgment of Caesar as a man chosen by Providence: Brutus, and even Cassius, God's adversaries, are shown crushed in the lowest circle of hell by the jaws of the devil himself. On the other hand, and more naturally, Elizabethans could judge that Caesar predates Grace and that Brutus had no need to love him the way a Christian king is loved, which frees Brutus of any supreme guilt, absolves him of his act of suicide, a crime of similar nature—and even allows for an understanding of him which, in fact, makes a good deal of sense. Brutus, whose time precedes that of the new Law, has not had the advantage of love's revelation. To love one's king, one's neighbor, with that intensity and depth that ever since Christ we call love, was not an option refused, but one not available to him. And rather than being astonished by his rejection of life, we must understand his internal dividedness as a fatal destiny, one that bore down on pre-Christian antiquity, and perceive it, like Caesar's ambition, as a sign of nostalgia for some other being-in-the-world, indeed an obscure expectation of it.

I wager that at least a few minds in the audience at the Globe were thinking of a book other than the manual of stoic philosophy when Brutus, ravaged by guilt, said to Lucius, "Look, Lucius, here's the book I sought for so." More particularly, I believe that many were moved by his concern for the child and his sleep, and could easily find meaning there. In fact, I have not yet related the entirety of this exchange. And I recall the end of it, when Brutus says to the ghost, "Why, I shall see thee at Philippi then," speaking coolly, it appears, but unable to repress a great cry coming from the depths of his being, since he hurriedly calls for Lucius and asks him a very strange question, "Didst thou dream, Lucius, that thou so criedst out?" To which Lucius answers that he has no knowledge of having cried out, though Brutus insists, "Yes, that thou didst." Why would Lucius have cried out in his sleep? Because, Shakespeare's contemporary will think, the prepubescent child is still somewhat incapable of feeling the heartbreak and corruption that has weighed down upon the human condition since the Fall, and weighed even more heavily in the centuries preceding Grace—all of which turns his innocent sleep into a participation in the being of the world as it exists, undisturbed, in the high regions of heaven. While sleeping, the young child can attain to the music that allows us to glimpse unity—and Brutus may assume that the sleeping Lucius is playing this music, unless his instrument slips from his hands and breaks. In such an event, certainly, the evil spirit, which is nothing more than sin's hold over the as yet unredeemed human condition, will seize upon the grown adolescent and cause him to cry out in horror, like Brutus himself at the close of his childhood, Brutus who barely sleeps any more.

Brutus, the Elizabethan may think, identifies with the child because he makes him think of his own childhood, a time when he did not yet know "the doctrine of ill-doing, nor dream'd / That any did," as Polixenes says in *The Winter's Tale;* or else because his capacity for love, paralyzed yet whole, shows itself strong enough to attach itself to someone still possessing something of the light of being—a feeling that can only gain Brutus the sympathy of an audience remembering that Christ, summoning people to himself, asked that they be like "little children." "The strings, my lord, are false," Lucius cries out upon awakening, because his fingers, when he had fallen asleep, had lost control of them. Brutus knows that with respect to himself all is discordant in a much more fundamental way; he knew this even from the time when, for his own misfortune and Caesar's, he was playing on the unresonate chords of a logic become its own absolute. And he is thinking, at this already terminal moment of his life, about the mysterious way in which sin and the horror of being may strike down in similar fashion upon a child's innocence.

In short, in the eyes of his contemporary spectators, whom Shakespeare knew well, Brutus could easily and logically represent humanity before the era of Grace, when, stirred by obscure yearnings, human beings declined the facileness of pleasure-seekers and cynics, without however being capable of realizing their own dream, and were forced rather—through a fate half shaken off, yet, alas, falling back all the more heavily upon them—into "strange and sad errors," in the words of Rimbaud, to whom my mind keeps returning as I think about the conclusion of *Julius Caesar*. Brutus is someone Elizabethans could both understand and vaguely condemn; someone they could love. To have revealed Brutus's inner life in all its pain and therefore at its most profoundly engaging level meant that Shakespeare had given the second part of his work the turn that justified it. A turn not at the level of action, as in ordinary theater, but in the gaze cast upon that action.

VIII

But was Shakespeare himself just that ordinary spectator for whom *Julius Caesar* might be merely an hour's reflection on an ancient world happily no longer with us? And, consequently, do we have at our disposal all that is needed to bring about a synthesis of the work's meaning? To believe so would be to forget that the tragedy was written in 1599, at the end of an extraordinary century as well as at the ominous and disturbing close of the long, still bizarre reign of Elizabeth; to fail to appreciate, too, that what follows *Julius Caesar* without any break, and even with certain memories of the one persisting in the writing of the other, is the great undertaking of *Hamlet*—in which the prince of a Denmark that this time is modern, though still enveloped in medieval superstitions, clearly indicates that the theocosmic structure, the jewel of the Christian tradition, no longer offers in his view either meaning or value. Shakespeare, as we know today, the contemporary of Galileo and Harvey, and a reader of Montaigne, was concerned about the "new ripplings" that were disturbing the arrival of the new century—and announcing a new world age. And wasn't the coming change precisely what was about to unsettle that capacity for love his own time still believed it possessed? The love of God, the ability to give oneself over to such love, to become pure presence in divine presence—certainly this is what the religion that first spoke specifically of these things never stopped teaching, and this is what a revelation impressing upon the soul a faith in incarnation had made firm and solid. But there was also the network of avenues leading from God to his creature in the universe and leading back to him, avenues that can only be made up of symbols, symbolic decipherings of the world's components, because all reality must, as the object of God's love, bear God's presence, be presence in turn, and be perceived as such—which endows it with value in every particle of its manifestation and privileges its appearance—to be understood henceforth through its analogy with other appearances, as opposed to any slicing into its matter, as in the operations of modern science. In order to love, in order to perceive presence where it is, in God or in one's neighbor, one must have symbolic thought, and concepts close off this avenue. Hence the anxiety felt by some, we may imagine, at a time when the presence of bodies becomes biology, and that of the heavens a modern astronomy seeing nothing more than matter in stars that once were divine torches. Henceforth, it is in the very structure of the world and not just in those souls predating the era of Grace, that the strings are out of order, if not simple mirages.

And we should have no doubt that one of those most alarmed was Shakespeare himself; for he placed a stormy night in *Julius Caesar* on the eve of the Ides of March, a night whose wonders, it should be noted, offered no clear indication, allowed for no interpretation, because in fact—the experience belongs less to the Romans than to the writer of the play—such wonders are merely the disorder of symbols, the proof that the existing system of signs laden with meaning, "all the sway of earth," is being shaken by a terrible upheaval. "Shakes like a thing unfirm," Shakespeare writes, and he makes explicit reference to this night in *Julius Caesar*—yet another link between the two plays—at the very opening of *Hamlet*. "Disasters in the sun," Horatio will say. There is no better way to indicate succinctly the collapse of a theocentric symbolic order created and needed by Christianity. And the fact that the capacity for love is affected by this is clearly the hypothesis at work in *Hamlet*, where we know that "the time is out of joint," that "something is rotten" in the kingdom—that there will perhaps be no other value to guide future conduct than a "readiness" welcoming anything that may come about with the same pessimistic equanimity.

This then is *Hamlet*, but it is also, and already, *Julius Caesar*, not only because of the stormy night, but also by virtue of a question that now becomes visible in the fabric of the play, woven through as it is with values and references belonging to the ancient world. The fact that love's structure—a God, a king, one's fellow man, the very soul of a person seen as a spark of divine fire—which Christianity claimed to have discovered, finds itself robbed of its forms and loci via the disintegration of a theocentric cosmos; the fact that this decisive encouragement to rely on aspirations long stifled by the cruel centuries before Christ is losing its strength of conviction with the dwindling of symbolic thought; the fact that this lifting of the contradictions of life long thought to be absolute is now showing itself to be merely the illusion of a moment of history—for all these reasons, is it not natural to fear that what was believed to be the wretchedness of the ancient world might prove to be the destiny of future human beings? Should one not fear that Brutus, for example, torn between hatred and love of life, might no longer have to be recognized as simply the victim of fate prior to the new and absolute alliance, but as a human being in his or her ongoing condition—each one of us, suddenly present on the stage? The question at the heart of *Julius Caesar,* the anguish that rose up like a cry in Shakespeare as he read Plutarch and discovered that he too might have been slumbering with the centuries-long sleep of medieval Christianity, was to think that love, which doubtless exists and is truly a spark in our souls, may in the future no longer be self-empowered. A terrible fear, to be sure, and one fully appreciated by this great witness of society after his English chronicles; a fear that conjured up endless disorder in future reigns—"domestic fury and fierce civil strife"—which he himself described through the prophetic voice of Antony. A fear, moreover, that was not absurd. "The dogs of war," as we know, continue to tear hope to pieces. It is true they did so no less in the centuries of theocosmic order.

And it is a fear, in the final analysis, that explains the turn Shakespeare's work takes, leaving *Julius Caesar* for *Hamlet,* and an evocation of the English wars—storms, and at times darkness, though lit by the presence of charismatic kings—for a glimpse of another universe, this time in the depths of the psyche, where royalty, in a Claudius or a Macbeth, is but one representation among others, inciting ambition, fostering an increase in rapaciousness and violence; where nonetheless the mysterious realities of the strength of conviction of a glance or a bright face, as well as remorse, heroic devotion, and serene affection, still hold good. A hypothesis dominates this new period of writing and determines its method. If the era of those symbols supposedly able to speak the world's truth is indeed coming to a close, we must look elsewhere than in this outer arena for situations that will allow us to recover what conceptual thought is losing, that is, the immediate and full presence of events and beings, the only possible way of living life in its becoming; and we must therefore explore the self's relation to itself, a relation in which such presence is the only reality, no doubt with laws constraining it but perhaps with something to give rise to hope, beneath that fate that seems so inexorable.

In short, with the dying of that great light which once gave shape to external reality as the sun lights up the earth, we must think of that small flame, that "taper," which Brutus, in his perplexity and anguish, had asked Lucius to light in his study but then had forgotten about. It is this small flame, however, still burning feebly but all the more able to pierce the shadows and draw the mind to what lurks within them—it is this flame that finally opened the mind's eye to the sleeping child. And from its constant presence in a tragedy in which a great insight takes shape, we may deduce that Shakespeare had created it from the moment the night storm broke, shattering all cosmic symbolism—had created it as a symbol of a new type, and as the threshold of the path to follow.

I X

Shakespeare, moreover, is not the only one to take in hand, at the end of the Renaissance, this small light, the one illuminating the only stage on which humanity, henceforth alone in the universe, may hope to find itself in meaningful circumstance. It is the same light that exactly at the same time and for the same reasons is lit by another of the great witnesses to the disintegration of the heavens, one just as desirous of reinventing love as is the author of *Julius Caesar:* the painter Caravaggio. The luminism that will predominate at certain moments in Shakespearean theater and the chiaroscuro of *The Calling of St. Matthew* are of the same essence: a confrontation with what surges out of the darkness of biological reality, either to "mak[e the] blood cold," as with Brutus, or to encourage that complete acceptance of things as they truly are that modern thought is in need of.

Significant at this point in our reading of *Julius Caesar* is what the "taper" has left in the shadows, in the tent where Brutus keeps vigil—though our eyes, growing accustomed to the darkness, can now make out certain shapes. For here, at the very least, is an important additional problem for Shakespeare to meditate upon, one that will offer in *Hamlet* an essential new perspective on things as the lamp draws near. Were I writing about *Hamlet,* I should begin by stressing the underestimated significance of the subplot in Shakespearean tragedy: a locus of events exploring what the main action of the play censures, a locus of resolution of conflicts that the main action will only have shown as unfolding in the most disastrous way. And so in the forefront of my reading I should place Hamlet's view of Ophelia, in which, to my mind, the success or failure of his supposedly major undertaking is at stake—his becoming able, in his own eyes, to assume the responsibilities of kingship. It would be important to show, and I think it is possible to do so, that the faith in self that will allow him to assume the charismatic power of a sovereign such as the elder Hamlet had been, a figure of the theocentric order, may in these new times find its source of energy outside of filiations determined by God and in that simple human affection which is destined to become a center of reflection for those observing our society. This problem, however, is both absent and present in *Julius Caesar*, where, though there is no subplot, there are nonetheless many signs, beyond the exchange Caesar had wanted, that point to a space of missing action. In other words, in act 4, when Brutus's eyes cloud over, we almost expect the appearance not of Caesar's ghost but of Portia's, the murderer's wife.

Portia is dead, and "by strange manner," as is the case with those who come to haunt the living. That Brutus loved her, in his way, is clear—and Shakespeare wanted it to be clear—from the moment when, in the second act, and just as Lucius has fallen asleep, she comes in search of her husband, having wounded herself "here in the thigh" to show him she can endure pain and thus to convince him to share his concerns. "You are . . . / As dear to me," he so movingly says to her then, as the blood "that visit[s] my sad heart"; and he promises to confide in her completely. Brutus loves Portia, so much so that when he learns of her death, he cannot help hoping against hope that the news is false. This is the meaning of the scene that has greatly troubled critics—some have believed the text to have been modified—in which Brutus pretends to know nothing of the matter when a second messenger arrives. Brutus loves Portia, but has he loved her as he ought to have done? Doesn't this desperate hoping mean that he is experiencing far more regret than he admits? Regret, as with Caesar, that the opportunity to exchange words of trust is now forever lost?

That he kept his promise, however, and revealed to Portia everything she wanted to know in order to share his burden seems indisputable, even though the structure of *Julius Caesar* leaves no room for this conversation in its succession of scenes, as if Shakespeare had wished to problematize it as an event at the very moment he was announcing it. But then, did a significant meeting even occur? It is clear from Brutus's words, when he agrees to explain everything to Portia, that he will speak to her only because he has been persuaded that, as Cato's daughter and his wife, she is capable of behaving as she has assured him she will, that is, as a Roman, a man, "stronger than [her]self," to use her own words. But Portia is not all she has dreamed of being. When, in the hours that follow, she understands that Brutus is at the Capitol with the intention confided to her, a short scene shows her wild with anxiety, giving Lucius conflicting orders, and on the point of betraying her secret. "How weak a thing / The heart of woman is," she admits to herself; and when Brutus has departed from Rome, she loses her mind. Where inflexible determination seemed clearly indicated, there lay hidden the tumult of a human being divided between a desire to help, the dream of being recognized and loved, and all those aspirations and urges that are part of an understanding of the world that is denied, even scorned, by the group of men in power—aspirations and urges that thus remain in darkness. Something other than Brutus's values would have been needed for Portia to liberate her own strength and put to use her energy. Only if he had listened to her, and not simply informed her, might she have been able to offer him help—pointing to clear signs in his relationship to Caesar and to himself that, having never been heard, will lead to his death. In short, Brutus sees Portia only through his projection upon her of what he believes her to be; he loves her only as an image. Here again, his evil spirit renders him incapable of truly encountering the other.

But the fact that the same deep, dark fault line that runs between Brutus and Caesar also runs between Brutus and Portia, Shakespeare thus extending it more or less explicitly to relations between man and woman and to the very place—the intimacy of marriage—to which it ought not to have spread, shows full consciousness of the extent of the disaster and, at the same time, reveals the discovery, in a new society where the teaching of love is vanishing from traditional structures, of another locus in which the problem may be posed. Hamlet—the hero of the tragedy hinted at in *Julius Caesar*—may henceforth be observed in his conflicted attachment to Ophelia as well as in his equally ambivalent anxiety over the crown of Denmark. And Shakespeare himself will have to look over the shoulder of his own creation, in this and in other later plays, so as to better perceive and reflect on the women that a Hamlet or an Othello gaze upon and to free himself of his own prejudices. The fault line that separates self and other in *Julius Caesar* runs, in fact, through Shakespeare himself. It is visible in the ease with which he lets Cassius dread being merely "womanish," governed by "our mothers' spirits" rather than "our fathers' minds." And it perhaps explains, for lack of attention to Portia, why something that might have assumed the proportions of a subplot remains in the shadows.

But there was so much to mull over! Why didn't Shakespeare bring over from Plutarch the fact that Brutus had struck Caesar "in his privities," as Amyot's translator, Thomas North, says? Why, on the other hand, did he retain the other proto-Freudian detail concerning Portia's injury, "here in the thigh"? And why in *Julius Caesar* can he only vaguely evoke an adult's interest in a child, yet in *Hamlet* and *Lear* can give ever greater significance to the father figure? A space opens up in writing, a space that medieval thinking, which focused symbols on external reality, had kept closed. And this space is also and above all the author himself, with his particular way of dealing with the repercussions of the great crisis—and his need, too, to gain greater self-knowledge, though the means of attaining to it are in need of profound reform. The greatness of *Julius Caesar* lies in its growing awareness, through Brutus's delusions, of the more secret dimensions of human speech. After which, the "anointed," the divinely chosen king, and the still archaic England will be able to fade from Shakespeare's stage—on the threshold, as far as self-awareness is concerned, of places unknown that are still our own.

TRANSLATED BY MICHAEL BISHOP

CHAPTER SIX

The Nobility of Cleopatra

He words me, girls, he words me, that I should not
Be noble to myself.
Antony and Cleopatra, 5.2.190–91

Cleopatra: What shall we do, Enobarbus?
Enobarbus: Think, and die.
Antony and Cleopatra, 3.13.1–2

WE MIGHT wonder why, six or seven years after *Julius Caesar*, Shakespeare felt the need to write another "Roman" play, or what seems to be one. The question has particular interest because the aim of the earlier work, which was essentially political, seemed likely to lead to other kinds of reflection, especially in a mind that was used to thinking about situations of power—all the more so because power in Rome, after the death of Brutus, had taken on new forms, which later generations would always find exemplary. So there have been critics and historians—and there still are—who have advanced the hypothesis that Shakespeare had thought about writing another tragedy on those decisive years and, more precisely, on certain aspects of the collapse of the triumvirate. This hypothesis led, of course, to speculation about Shakespeare's relation to his own society, marked by new ways of thinking and acting, after the death of Elizabeth.

Such political subjects, likely as they were to capture the interest of the most diverse audiences, could not but arouse the attention of those who were in power and made decisions, and consequently the subject of Rome implied a certain danger for any author who might risk treating it. Certainly James I liked to think of himself as another Augustus, the initiator of a new universal peace, and he used propaganda to further this perception. It follows that a playwright referring to the first Roman emperor in a flattering way could have been warmly received. But the reminder that Rome was not long to mobilize against apprentice dictators, and that the top place was often bitterly disputed, was rather less welcome in an England where monarchy was absolute. In these same years, Ben Jonson had been worried about his *Sejanus*, and a less famous author, Fulke Greville, had thought it advisable to burn the manuscript of his own tragedy about Antony and Cleopatra.

Still, I don't believe that it was for such reasons that Shakespeare waited so long to return to Roman history, and I don't even think that he chose to write a tragedy about Antony and Cleopatra because he was primarily interested in the downfall of the republic and the opportunity it would give him to reflect upon political matters specifically. I think his aim was entirely different. And if he was still concerned with the problems of society and power, either in Rome or in his own country, his focus in *Antony and Cleopatra* was set at a far deeper level than, say, in *Julius Caesar,* as he observes human behavior and analyzes the rivalries and conflicts that disturb or paralyze society.

What is this other level of meaning, which is deeper than ambition, the love of freedom, or doctrinal passion? To recognize it we have first to remember several facts which, though well known, are sufficiently important in Shakespeare's awareness of himself to deserve explicit attention.

The first is that Shakespeare was always extremely attentive to the nature of theater, its place in society and its social value, perceiving them as essentially positive. This is the meaning, among other indications scattered here and there in his work, of the remarks he puts in the mouth of that character who is the most open to contemporary problems, and even the most clearly aware of recent events in London—namely, Hamlet. The theater holds up a mirror to society, he says. In this mirror it can recognize its vices and its prejudices and learn how to correct them, since guilty beings can on occasion— whence Hamlet's project in the play to dramatize in front of his uncle the murder he committed—feel stripped of their masks and forced to recognize their crimes. Theater, therefore, is not a meaningless diversion that flatters passions for no reason. Rather, as heir to the truth function of the medieval mystery plays, it transposes the search for truth from the realm of the divine to that of the human, and as such should never be subjected to blame.

But—and this is a second determining fact for Shakespeare—the beginning of the seventeenth century marked a moment when attacks against the theatre by Puritan groups began to proliferate. The theater was bitterly accused of destabilizing the social order by giving too great importance, for example, to women—thought by those harsh moralizers to be in league with the devil. Passions restrained or hidden in everyday existence reveal themselves freely on the stage, so that the deplorable example set by theater must be prohibited as soon as possible; and we know to what extremes these dangerous enemies of artistic creation were willing to go in London at that time, and how effective they were. Such rebukes, accompanied by such threats, were bound to disturb someone who was at the time both the theater's greatest dramatist and its most resolute partisan.

It is easy to imagine how Shakespeare would have been particularly concerned about the diatribes again women, since women are so constantly at the heart of his tragedies, his comedies, and even some of his history plays, where they do not appear to suffer excessively from the prejudices of the time. True, there is misogyny in the "nunnery" scene in *Hamlet,* when Hamlet, who has been wearying Ophelia with his strange demands, turns on her with violence, accusing her of faults and vices that according to him are the result of a woman's despicable nature. But it is clear that this ranting, which borders on delirium and scarcely manages to cloak his fascination and regret, is only one of the prince's character traits, studied by Shakespeare from the perspective of a prevailing melancholy. There is nothing in these vituperations that might be thought the expression of the author's own feeling; quite to the contrary, the scenes that follow show Shakespeare's sympathy, even compassion, for Ophelia, whose "Saint Valentine's Day" song reminds us in a poignant way both of the naive sincerity of certain girls and of the wrong they incur as a result of young men's egotism and irresponsibility. As for Lady Macbeth or Goneril, those creatures of greed and death are in no way proof of the evil nature of women: rather, they are merely examples, like Edmond in *Lear,* or the enigmatic Iago in *Othello,* of that capacity for evil being and for evil doing that troubles Shakespeare equally with respect to men. In truth, it is only in his sonnets that Shakespeare seems to be a denigrator of women, and there he is so in a perfectly traditional manner. But the only consequence I am tempted to draw from this evidence is to imagine that these poems, so literary in nature, are not the work of the actor who wrote the plays.

Despite the fog of commonplaces and stereotypical behavior that envelops some of his characters, particularly the more minor ones, Shakespeare seems to show no real prejudice or suspicion toward women. Ophelia's song, which I mentioned a moment ago, shows rather that he has reflected, fully and consciously, on the alienation suffered by women in his time, both in their relation to men, because of men's idea of women, and, indeed, in their own awareness of themselves. And so it is perfectly legitimate to assume that Shakespeare would become interested in a problem intimately related to this alienation: the way women appear, or, rather, do not appear, on that very stage where his dramas were worked out.

Women's roles were taken by men; Hamlet makes this very clear when the actors arrive at Elsinore. And however accurately young men may observe the way women walk, move, or speak, however capable of real sympathy they may show themselves to be, there can be no doubt that their imitations are always somewhat caricatural, somewhat excessive at any rate, since they will need to respond to the amused expectation of a not very discerning audience. This was surely a situation that someone as intuitive as Shakespeare and as open to the truth of others—all others—could not fail to notice. The interpretation of women by men is a metaphor for the subordinate character of women and the fact that their image is dependent on a consciousness other than their own. It follows that theatrical tradition contributes in its own way to perpetuating, reinforcing, even aggravating this dependency, together with the disdain it is apt to engender.

II

And so I think that Shakespeare had reason to be concerned, even alarmed, about this characteristic of the society of his time: the attack led by the Puritans against the theater, their incrimination of woman, and the linking together of the two. There was as much for him to reflect upon—what a society is, what its prejudices can be, how it distributes power and decides on its freedoms—as with the more explicitly political study of governmental structures and absolutist or republican ideologies. It is therefore from a perspective of concerns that are fundamentally sociological that we should look at *Antony and Cleopatra*, which we will see as no less political, in the deep sense of the word, than a tragedy that speaks only of freedom and dictatorship. To realize this, we need only turn our attention from one abuse of power and one attack on justice toward other sorts of abuse, other forms of injustice. It is in this deeper exploration of society that the real intention of the play is to be found, and also its way of being "relevant," as they say, at the beginning of a century so obviously destined to undergo changes in its consciousness of the world. Thus the action of the play is "Roman," like *Julius Caesar*, only because the society of republican or imperial Rome and the society of Elizabeth and James had enough in common that the study of the one easily became the mirror of the other.

This resemblance, at least insofar as the relation between the sexes is concerned, is what Shakespeare could readily observe when he read Plutarch, as he loved to do, being an equally keen observer of the habits of his own contemporaries, especially in circles where people had money or power.

Certainly Roman civilization is pagan, whereas Shakespeare's era is supposedly dominated by the values of a religion that has a completely different notion of the human person from the polytheistic system and the various forms of wisdom that developed under its influence. This religious outlook gives an absolute value to the human being, promising him salvation and not denying women this gift, even if it is a woman that the Bible accuses of having provoked original sin and the Fall. But this metaphysical difference between the anthropologies of two civilizations in no way affects the relations between men and women when social behavior continues to be determined not by an idea of being but by a concern for possessions and power—material preoccupations whose constraints weigh heavily on the encounter between the sexes and the meaning seen in marriage. In London, just as in Rome, marriage has as its end the procreation of children and the perpetuation of goods. A woman's place never exceeds motherhood. Anything else in her is viewed as suspicious, or is demonized, denied. Sexuality is thus excluded from marriage and confined to situations where a woman—estranged from important aspects of herself—becomes an object of scorn or is forced to be nothing more than her body, or the shadow of it. A man takes pride in sexual relations as a sign of his virility, but he does not listen to what they might teach him. Instead, he chooses prestige and power over other men, like Shakespeare's prince Hal, who gives up his life of dissipation when he takes on the responsibilities of king, or Antony—at least so it seemed in *Julius Caesar*—who is wakened from his own debauchery by Caesar's murder and thrust into the struggle for the top place in Rome. From the point of view of a "patriarchal" structure, the two societies are similar, and a play that seems "Roman" can speak of the relations between the sexes in England during the reign of James I.

And this is what *Antony and Cleopatra* does and, I would even say, means to do. It is as though the new play were rising from the bottomless depths from which at roughly the same time a play like *Macbeth* was seeking to unearth the very roots of evil—in order to explore whether this mysterious aspect of being could not somehow be lessened in ordinary society by an attitude toward the constraints imposed on men and women about how to live that would at last be direct and unbiased. It is as though Shakespeare were already explicitly raising a question that is so familiar to us today.

It is obvious that *Antony and Cleopatra* says a great deal about the relation between the sexes, but it is far more than this. It is a work that has this relation as its raison d'être, as a domain in which thought without concepts, the figural thought that is artistic creation, will be able to extend to situations, to symbols, that will reveal a new truth.

The first thing to observe is that to attain this goal, Shakespeare integrates into the play from the outset the accusation that the Puritans of his time make against women by associating them with the theater. In *Antony and Cleopatra* there is, of course, Cleopatra herself, who seems to be, as Osric would say in *Hamlet,* the "card and calendar" of all the defects, weaknesses, falsity, and deception with which the Puritans—while admitting women's skill in using their charm and intuitive guile—sought to condemn those women who do not put all their strength and purity into simply being wives. In certain scenes, this kind of dubious femininity is so concretely evoked that many critics have thought they could describe the queen's character by simply enumerating these grave defects and undistinguished talents, as if this were how Shakespeare wanted to depict her.

An example is Granville-Barker, who wrote (admittedly a long time ago), "This is the woman herself, quick, jealous, imperious, malicious, flagrant, subtle. . . . She is childishly extravagant, ingenuously shameless, nothing exists for her but her desire." And, indeed, opinions are voiced in the play itself that corroborate this reading, agreeing with and even intensifying this judgment, as if it were only too obvious. It is expressed in the very opening lines of the play. Two Roman officers, who exemplify the values of their society, are filled with indignation at the sight of their general in the hands of a lascivious woman, one moreover who is "tawny" and filled with "a gypsy's lust." Later, Cleopatra will be described in a gentler but still negative fashion by Enobarbus, the companion and confidant of Antony, who at times speaks in a way we would today call overtly sexist. When a great cause is at stake, he says to Antony, women cannot be taken into account. And later in the play he will view with absolute contempt the queen's desire to be the commander of her armies.

And it's not that he does not admire her, but his admiration only confirms his prejudice. This is apparent in the way he describes—somewhat ironically, as is his style, but nonetheless with wonder, even astonishment—Cleopatra's appearance in her great Egyptian vessel, the day she meets Antony on the banks of the river Cydnus. To try to describe her as she was then could only fall short, Enobarbus assures us. Surrounded by what seemed to be little cupids flying about and graceful Nereides, colored by the play of light and shade from the woven silk sails of her ship, whose strange perfume was wafted toward the shore by the breeze, Cleopatra surpassed Venus as much as Venus, the dream, surpasses nature. There is nothing here that recalls the "tawny front" or the scandalous "gypsy" behavior that Philon decried. We might think Enobarbus's judgment more favorable, the expression of a more open thinking. But we should note that his description of the beautiful sovereign closely resembles an *ekphrasis*—the kind of discourse whose object is not reality but a work of art. As he presents the scene, Enobarbus constantly shows us how it is composed like a painting, enhanced with carefully calculated hues and other elements that appeal to the senses; and Cleopatra is the artist of all this.

Now artists, as generally understood in Shakespeare's time, are those who use appearances to suggest in the ones they depict some form of excellence that would not necessarily be seen in reality. This is what Lucrece becomes painfully aware of in Shakespeare's famous poem when she sees a painting depicting the fall of Troy in which Sinon, the traitor, has been represented with a handsome face and bearing that ought to have been the expression of his moral quality. The artist is a master of illusion, fundamentally dangerous, even guilty, and it is obvious that Cleopatra often behaves and works the way an artist does, especially when she is trying to seduce Antony. She will invite him to her ship; she will be what "his eyes eat only," as Enobarbus says. And so, in spite of her beauty—or perhaps because of it—Cleopatra is suspected of being an agent of evil, a sorceress.

In short, Enobarbus's description is less about admiration than about refusal, a refusal that is an underhanded incrimination of artistic creation. And this is exactly the kind of condemnation the Puritans would have added to their reasons for disapproving of women if they had happened to see certain paintings of their own time or just before it, especially Italian paintings, such as the *Galatea* Raphael painted for the Villa Farnesina, which could so easily have been the model for the description of Cleopatra on the Cydnus. In his highly ambiguous lines, Enobarbus places himself on the side of those who condemn the arts, hate love poetry with its hyperbolic celebrations—and want to close the theaters. Listening to him, we are not led to believe that Shakespeare holds a different opinion.

Shakespeare even seems willing to give free rein to the disfavor attaching to Cleopatra and to be ready to suggest that she really is all that is said of her, since he puts these accusations in the mouth of Antony himself, his main male character, who becomes Cleopatra's judge despite the love he says he feels for her. Antony makes a long series of criticisms, of decisions to leave—"I must from this enchanting queen break off"—that seem to prove what a bad person the Egyptian queen is. He says that the "idleness" that holds him near her can only engender troubles without number. And when, in act 3, having returned to Egypt after his defeat at Actium, he sees her courted by Thidias, the envoy of Octavius, he rushes to the conclusion that she has encouraged those attentions, that she has always been false—"you have been a boggler ever!"—before scornfully evoking her lustfulness and reducing her past to the level of the vilest prostitution. "I found you as a morsel, cold upon / Dead Caesar's trencher," he cries—though with more anguish, it is true, than real hatred. Nonetheless, he will call her a "Triple-turn'd whore" and claim that "this foul Egyptian hath betrayed me."

The action of the play also seems to develop along these lines, since on one level at least it appears to be merely the all too familiar portrait of a supremely talented man of legitimate ambition gradually destroyed by the scheming of a depraved and malevolent being. Antony has conquered one-third of the known world through his merit alone, as everyone recognizes, and has had every opportunity of claiming still more. But now in the revels and debauchery he shares with Cleopatra, he has lost all sense of his responsibilities, the force of his former plans, and even the clarity of his judgment, for in the end he is almost delirious before committing suicide. And it is far from being a Roman suicide, although Antony tries desperately to believe it one. Antony wants to show himself greater than adversity; he imagines he will find freedom in death, but in his last moments he thinks only of Cleopatra, who, he is told, is dead. Killing himself in this way, he does not so much establish his equality with what is great and Roman in his enemy Octavius as acknowledge that enemy's superiority, to the extent that he still can be said to live on the level of the values and behavior that once bound him to Octavius even in their very manner of battling with one another. And it is easy enough to think that Antony's fall has been caused by Cleopatra, the one who appeared on the Cydnus painted and richly adorned—staging her own appearance and substituting illusion for reality the way the theater does. There is, therefore, a great deal in *Antony and Cleopatra* that would seem to support the champions of traditional order—the order determined and controlled by those for whom nothing has meaning or value other than power and possessions.

But that isn't all there is to it, and I would now like to suggest that when Shakespeare inserts the prejudices of actual society into his play, it is in no way to affirm their value but rather to question such social structures and to arrive at conclusions about them that will soon prove devastating.

This helps us to understand, for example, the role that Shakespeare assigns to Octavius's sister Octavia, whom Antony marries after his return to Rome in order to seal a paradoxical alliance, fraught with ulterior motives and suspicion, with the man who will remain his great rival.

Octavia has everything to make her appear as a foil for Cleopatra, especially since Shakespeare has emphasized that she incarnates the qualities and demeanor that the society of men in power like to see in women and that allow women to have a place and a role in that society. Octavia, who is a reflection of Octavius to her very name, is virtue itself, and her first principle is obedience to her husband; unconditional and uncritical devotion to him, even though he has been chosen for her without her consent. And if the play were merely an occasion for showing, uncritically, society as it is, Octavia would be held in high regard to the same degree that Cleopatra is vilified; or at the very least she would be regarded with sympathy and endowed with some substance. It would have been quite easy for Shakespeare to give her character some degree of self-assurance or to demonstrate some resoluteness on her part.

But this is not at all the way Shakespeare chooses to present the very worthy but colorless Octavia. When Maecenas and Octavius present her to the man she will be asked to marry, he does not find it necessary to wait for her response. Later, when she finds herself torn between the conflicting interests of her brother and her husband, Shakespeare—though he often lets Cleopatra express herself in truly remarkable ways—has Octavia, who always seems so remote, speak like a book. It is not her deepest being that Shakespeare wants us to hear, and for a very good reason: she is in the play only to demonstrate through the degree zero of her role the function a woman performs in the calculations of men, and the resulting lack of freedom and even of life. Observing the few scenes in which Octavia appears, we understand

The Nobility of Cleopatra 141

that she is merely a bargaining chip on the table around which men are conducting their affairs. And through this neutral or, rather, neutralized figure we can see that Shakespeare has sought to address the problem of the subordination of women.

From this point on—and it is a central moment in the play since the action changes orientation when the link that Octavia was to have been is broken—the whole space of *Antony and Cleopatra*, the whole field of representations and judgments that make up the play, will be extended and clarified, less as a confrontation between people pursuing their action on the stage itself than as a network of the significant aspects of a social order, seen in its structural reality. When we look around Octavia, everything immediately crystallizes. Octavius, the new Caesar? He is fundamentally a politician who thinks only of power, and whose action—thus determined, thus ruinous to every other aspect of a person, though it may demand the use of intelligence, at least when plotting strategy—obliterates all capacity for feeling. We have seen how, without the slightest hesitation, he disposes of Octavia, despite his protestations of affection for her—though later he will not disguise the fact that he has expressed them so publicly only to assure his own power. Even if he truly loved his sister, it would be with the kind of love that is a function of kinship and therefore only serves the cause of wealth and power.

Moreover, he will wish for Antony's death despite the great esteem he has for him, and this—as he will make clear when he learns of Antony's suicide—simply because there is no room for both of them at the top of the social hierarchy. As for Cleopatra, Octavius would not have felt the slightest remorse or compassion had he been able to lead her forth triumphantly in chains. He indicates as much to one of his intimates, and to assure himself this advantage, not to say pleasure, he will not hesitate to resort to the most horrifying threats—the murder of her children—and to the coldest of ruses. Octavius is not really vile. But bereft of all genuine emotion by the order he serves, he retains only the heart of a snake.

What *is* the world of which he is the center and that Shakespeare lays bare? It is a space where one has to exist in this abstract way or admit to being defeated, like the young Pompey, who is an impulsive and sentimental nobody because he hesitates to order the assassination of the rivals that fate has placed in his hands. It is a network of precise values, but for all that not a real order, a harmony, a music—like the one the Greeks dreamed of for society, in the Athens of Solon and Plato. Each successive state of a humanity thus devoted to competition among individuals or groups can only be an episode, a consequence, and soon a cause, of violent acts in an endless conflict.

So what appears most clearly through the perspective that Shakespeare creates around the figure of Octavia is that this society of possession and power is built solely on the rivalry between the pretenders to that power and on the violence with which they assert their claims. This is a world in which legitimacy is the result only of some previous exaction. Since one cannot imagine in others any intention but the kind of appropriation one wants for oneself, the only solution is to eliminate them, and war will thus be constant. In this joyless world, strength will be an asset and a value, and with it youth, since youth possesses strength—which explains why Antony, who has grown older, is obsessed about Octavius's youth. "The boy," "the young man," is how he refers to his rival, with a scorn that does not hide the anguish and the jealousy.

This, then, is the nature of the society that appears in the Rome of *Antony and Cleopatra*, and there is nothing about it that Shakespeare appears to like or to value. One can hardly imagine that in depicting human beings the way he does here, the author of *Hamlet* is seeking to deal with the totality of their nature—in the way that *Macbeth*, written in the same months, probes their depths. We have to see that this time he is not delving into an individual soul, at least not right away, but rather remaining for the moment on the edge of the action to raise a problem primarily in social terms. We have to imagine that he is asking himself how we can have gotten here. That perhaps he is asking himself whether the value placed on power on the one hand, and the vilification of women on the other—the alienation they suffer, as do men themselves—are not two aspects of the same lie, a lie that paralyzes life. He may even be hoping that the soul in bondage will all at once break free of its chains, dispel these unreal images.

Indeed, it is the fundamental alienation in the minds of his characters that concerns Shakespeare—a fact that is easier to see when we examine the protagonists in the play, Mark Antony first of all—a figure who has interested Shakespeare for some time since he has already appeared in *Julius Caesar*.

v

It is obvious that Antony, to a very large extent, partakes of the mental structure that seems to me to be at the heart of Shakespeare's thinking in this play, especially since Antony is a general and a statesman, and above all an ambitious, proud man—which was already apparent in *Julius Caesar*, where, as I have said, as soon as he hears that Caesar is dead, he leaves his life of dissipation and throws himself into the action that might lead him to supreme power. But it should also be noted that Antony's allegiance to a way of life that gives priority to political considerations is at the very least somewhat qualified and, indeed, highly ambiguous, for in the presence of a consummate politician like the young Octavius, Antony acts like a person who cannot quite find his place and who experiences this difference as a weakness, which gives him a slight feeling of inferiority. This is something that Shakespeare, taking his cue from Plutarch, doesn't just underscore but repeats, out of context on one occasion, as if he were haunted by it. The first instance occurs in *Julius Caesar*. After setting the future in motion, not without brutality and cynicism, Antony allies himself with Octavius—the first of such alliances—in order to bring down Brutus, Caesar's murderer. And on the eve of the decisive battle at Philippi, he decides on a plan of action that is doubtless the best one to follow, but Octavius coldly, calmly, says they will do the opposite, and Antony immediately acquiesces.

And then there is a moment in *Macbeth*, when Shakespeare had no particular reason to be thinking of Antony. Speaking of Banquo, Macbeth, who could hardly be imagined to have any idea about the Romans, says, "under him, / My genius is rebuked; as, it is said, / Mark Antony's was by Caesar." And finally there are passages in *Antony and Cleopatra*, starting with the magnificent opening scene when the queen of Egypt tells Antony that he blushed when she told him that Octavius, "the scarce-bearded Caesar," was giving him orders. Antony knows only too well that there is someone within him who bends instinctively when Octavius speaks. The most revealing of these scenes is, of course, the encounter between the two men when Antony returns from Egypt, vowing to reestablish himself and filled with ambition for supreme power. I have "neglected" my duties to you, I was not myself, "poison'd hours had bound me up," he tells Octavius, almost apologizing. And he marries Octavius's sister less out of self-interest than because he seeks to identify with the man he nonetheless knows is and will remain his implacable enemy. Octavius and the Roman idea he incarnates seem to function as a kind of superego in a space in Antony's psyche, a space in which the contradictions of desire appear and the workings of the unconscious emerge.

And it is here that we find a quality, a "humanity," which is obviously what most appealed to Shakespeare. Already in *Julius Caesar*, Shakespeare, always the intuitive artist, shows a special interest in Antony the man because of his richness and complexity, not just because of his relation to Octavius. And this attention had taken the most intense form possible, through the identification of the author with his character in a series of superb lines that rise straight from the depths of his writing, from his soul, as if Shakespeare were one with his hero, communicating his whole being to him. Beyond the scene of the discovery of the murder, in which Antony expresses himself with great nobility despite his caution and even his cunning, there is also the great moment when, in the general stupor and confusion that follows, Caesar's young friend presents himself to the people to defend his cause. And his discourse is primarily a masterpiece of rhetorical skill. With coolness and extraordinary deftness, Antony makes use of arguments that will completely reverse an opinion that was predisposed against him. There is also a great deal of cynicism in the choice of these arguments, but through his words, as though from Shakespeare himself, there rises an emotion that can only mean love and that shows in Antony—for a moment at least, as he speaks of the bloody cloak and evokes the first time Caesar wore it, then sweeps it back to show the body—both an intelligence of the heart and a poetic way of looking at things. Starting with the first Roman play, Antony is more for Shakespeare than a representative of the "Roman" way of being; he is a man from whom nothing human seems to have been excluded.

Six or seven years later, in the second of the works that refer to Rome and were inspired by Plutarch, this complexity and this humanity are shown in other of their dimensions, thus rendering Antony, in the organization of the play, the one person who is real and who, by his very existence, confirms that Shakespeare sees in Rome the presence of a social structure, a system of values, a network of moral and metaphysical principles, that this counterexample will allow us to question more carefully in order to better perceive its limitations and denounce its falsity. In Antony, as he now appears, we discover what is lacking in Octavius, that is, a teeming inner life, a facility for self-contradiction, a propensity to indulge in pathetic declarations—in short, a temperament, as we now say—whereas all Octavius wants is to be reason and lucidity. And so we should understand from the outset that there exists between the two men not only the rivalry that is shown in the visible action of the play but also a difference in their very natures, on which a more profound action will be based, the one that will give the tragedy its meaning. Octavius, the new Caesar, represents reason that in fact is violence and war without end. His is the calculation that reduces all thought to strategy, not love. And he is also the architect who keeps himself at a distance from any real involvement in his plans, especially battles, because his eagle eye needs some distance in order to command the field of the possible. Why take up a sword in the front lines? There are other ways to die, he maintains without any false shame.

Antony, on the other hand, as Shakespeare says more than once, is someone who loves to fight with sword in hand; he wants to be in the first ranks of his troops, in the heat and danger of battles. He is one who, though already gray-haired (which makes him uneasy and even obsesses him), nonetheless, and with even more ardor in his last battle at the doors of Alexandria, seeks bloody skirmishes, elbow to elbow with the rough Scarus, the soldier stitched up with wounds whom he loves to use as a mirror. When he feels on the verge of defeat, Antony even dreams of fighting Octavius to the death, in hand-to-hand combat that would settle their respective claims; and had Octavius accepted the challenge (but he is careful not to), this would have been a duel in which Antony would doubtless have recovered all his former decisiveness, all his capacity for victory. "Now by my sword," he loves to exclaim—the "sword Philippan," the one he used at Philippi and has kept ever since, as we see when he lets Cleopatra hold it during the games they play.

In short, Antony is a man not of modern warfare but of archaic combat, not of intellect but of body, which is mind in another mode. And it is obvious that this body, these clashes, are also part of the sexual impulse, which, far from being reduced, as in the puritanism of Octavius or anyone else, to marginal places or moments or simply to the background of thought, is the other great passion of his life, if not the primary one, in that immediacy of a person's relation to himself which makes Antony, in the ambient modernity, an archaic figure. So in this aspect as well—which is so important in the play because it is Cleopatra, a much-desired woman, who will be the protagonist—the question of "Roman" puritanical order, or disorder, can be heard. We begin to see how Shakespeare uses his subject and his characters to approach the truth he is looking for. We can already sense that at least the problems and the forgotten or censored categories of this truth are being laid out. For example, where there is only abstraction, blind competition, war without real ideals or chances for peace—Octavius speaks of universal peace, but this *pax romana* is nothing more than the elimination of rivals and the defense of borders—wouldn't it make sense to reintroduce into the counsels of the mind something of the immediacy of old? Wouldn't it make sense to listen more sensitively to the body and to all it feels? Wouldn't one then be on paths that are closer to the harmony of life, to music?

What, after all, was the meaning of all the gods and demigods of the warmer paganism of yesterday—the gods of the poets of classical Greece, not those of the Roman pantheon of jurists—if not humanity delivered from limits that are perhaps born simply of the hunger to possess, self-interest, the overvaluation of conceptual thought? Humanity restored to what is infinite in it. And if not an actual possibility, at least a model that could be enriched were it to be used as a measure and rule of life. When Cleopatra, finally speaking with the words of poetry that were earlier denied her, tries to express what she loved in Antony, she will speak of all the things that made him like a god, but will add that his "delights," his pleasures, were "dolphin-like," having in mind those dolphins whose frolicking backs burst through the sea foam. The life of the sea creature, cherished in antiquity, is a life delivered from the alienation of what is purely mental, a life that is surely closer to the divine and more familiar with its joy than is Octavius—Caesar, Augustus— however divine those in his service may wish to make him.

It is certainly not by chance that Shakespeare has noticed and repeatedly mentions that Antony is the direct descendant of a demigod, Hercules; neither is it by chance that he underscores the importance for this Roman of the land of Egypt, the hellenized kingdom of the Ptolemies, where the gods of the most carnal existence, Venus and Mars, seem so present in this tragedy against the background of rites and myths of more fabulous eras, a presence teeming with the unconscious. It was only natural that Antony, an archaic figure, should go to Egypt, and that his voyage and his stay there should be complete only in the way that Enobarbus will tell him in one of his moments of doubt: by meeting Cleopatra.

VI

Cleopatra is quite obviously the great presence that Shakespeare sees rising on the horizon of his investigation of Rome—that is, of his examination of Puritan objections. In the presence of the incrimination by his somber contemporaries of the nature of women, of the increasingly intense denunciation of the perils that women are said to represent, Shakespeare had to recognize the fact of love, to take stock of it in a system of values related to that of the Puritans, and then to assess its quality and meaning. Above all, he had to wonder if there were not in love the possibility of an experience of mind and spirit that would annul and even transcend Puritanical fear, and that would allow a society debilitated by the idolatry of material goods and power to be renewed: love that needed to be "reinvented" for "true life" to return, or to begin.[1]

And it is thinking of this kind that Shakespeare has pursued in *Antony and Cleopatra* through a series of scenes that show to what extent the empirical work of poetry, as it encounters and examines dramatic situations, as it recognizes their symbolic value, as it cuts into what is inessential to get to the presence of beings, can become a path to knowledge.

In other words, Shakespeare was trying to understand whether the attraction that brought together the queen of Egypt and the Roman commander was simply a carnal reality, of the kind that his enemies in London would have found in keeping with their thoughts about women and yet another proof of the danger of these Circes, or whether there was something more in their relationship, though difficult to situate. The first hypothesis is far from absurd, and it is clear that Shakespeare has not sought to wipe from the canvas of his thinking those signs that could give it some weight, never hesitating to record the various charges made against Cleopatra, including those of Antony himself. Antony vilifies and insults Cleopatra; he claims more than once that she has betrayed him. He evokes her "idleness"—that is, to some extent, her hysteria. The way Cleopatra herself often behaves, either with her entourage or with Antony himself—behavior that is as capricious, irrational, "childishly extravagant," and "ingenuously shameless" as her critics claim—is unlikely to counter the view that others have of her, so vibrant and "true" is Shakespeare's portrayal of this kind of stereotype. In the scenes that appear to be comic, the playwright may have been thinking of the actor who was to play the role rather than of the woman who would be oversimplified by it. And we could conclude from these aspects of the play that in the social structure he is beginning to understand, Shakespeare felt obliged—for historical reasons—to consider Cleopatra as just an example of female alienation in one of its classic forms: from which it would follow that he would not be able to find in her any reason for hopefulness as he undertook his critique of society.

But let us look more carefully at what takes place in the scenes in which Cleopatra does not appear in a very favorable light, such as the one when a messenger comes to announce to her that Antony has married Octavia, concerning whom she shows her jealousy in a clearly childish way. Childish, too,

---

1. Bonnefoy is making use of terms employed by Arthur Rimbaud in his *Une saison en enfer*. See "Délires I: Vierge folle / L'Époux infernal."—Trans.

is her attitude toward the bearer of the bad news—she falls upon him, striking him, and threatening him with torture as if he were responsible for what she considers her misfortune. Her behavior is so extravagant that one of her attendants, Charmian, urges her to control herself. "The man is innocent," she protests. At moments like these, Cleopatra undoubtedly gives some basis to the criticism and even to the judgment brought against her throughout the play. Yet the words spoken by Charmian—the young woman who will accompany Cleopatra in death, participating in her spiritual maturation, the one of whom the soothsayer in the first act was surely right to say that one day she would be "far fairer" than in her first frivolity—immediately begin to bear fruit. "Call the slave again," says Cleopatra, "though I am mad, I will not bite him: call." Then, thoughtfully, she adds:

> I will not hurt him.
> These hands do lack nobility, that they strike
> A meaner than myself, since I myself
> Have given myself the cause,

words that show the complexity as well as the range of a thoughtfulness she may simply be rediscovering in herself. Is it because she is a queen and he, the messenger, an inferior and a weakling that striking him would not be "noble"? But notice that in the context of the "nobility" that for a moment she lacked, the word "myself" appears three times in two lines—evidence that the nobility to which Cleopatra feels accountable is less a function of her rank than an aspect of something deep within her very self. And almost the same words reemerge later in the play, when the queen of Egypt feels herself threatened by Octavius on the most intimate level of her relation to herself: as the woman that she is and that he tries to dupe, to deprive of her awareness of herself, in order the more easily to lead her away in chains—as a woman, vanquished—so as to enhance his triumph among men. "He words me, girls, that I should not be noble to myself." It is this recollection of what she is—or should and could be—that appears in the brief exchange with Charmian, and so there is some shame, but also pride and hope. Despite her "idleness" in the presence of the messenger, we can sense that she has not forgotten an innate "nobility"; we get a hint of the anxiety that allows her to recover it.

We sense this all the more because of that earlier scene in act 1, in which Cleopatra's first reaction as she separates from Antony, who has abruptly announced that he is leaving her to return to Rome (where he will view her as women are viewed in Rome), is one of jealousy, accusation, insult, and tears. She demonstrates the "idleness" for which Antony will explicitly criticize her, while accusing her of feigning it as much as truly exemplifying it. Their voices rise sharply; they are on the verge of shouting. But in the end Cleopatra tries to have her lover understand something more serious, close to her heart, which suggests recesses within her in which something she knows to be true resides — the kind of truth we instinctively feel is superior:

> Courteous lord, one word:
> Sir, you and I must part, but that's not it;
> Sir, you and I have lov'd; but there's not it;
> That you know well. Something it is I would—

she begins to say, but at this point, alas, she lacks the words that would allow her to formulate the thought or feeling she wants to communicate to Antony, so that, breaking off, she can only conclude:

> O, my oblivion is a very Antony,
> And I am all forgotten,

which is certainly very moving. We understand a great deal here: the seriousness, the lucidity she feels building within her before Antony as he wrestles with the contradictions she fears might prove fatal, the quality of the love they feel for one another and that she wants him to understand, the gift of reality and the future she would like to offer him—all this is on the tip of her tongue, but the condition of women in a man's world is such that she has been robbed even of words; language is not for her; she is forgotten in it, forgotten first of all by herself, who can speak only as people want her to speak. Her forgetting is the forgetting of her own being; she has forgotten herself in the way Antony, rejoining the world that censors her, has forgotten her. She betrays herself, without wanting to, as he betrays her, giving in to his ambition. And the obvious pain in these lines—one can almost hear the sobbing they try to repress—is all the greater in that Cleopatra knows perfectly well that in "betraying" herself as she does, in not knowing how to give voice to the woman within her, to her "nobility," she is betraying Antony as well, for in weeping, in expressing herself through irony and insult, and now in just keeping silent, she is acting in accordance with masculine prejudices that impoverish Antony and abandon him to his own misery and to his likely very sad destiny. Love asks for more than what she can give at this moment. But this may be the moment when the project of recovering herself takes shape— a project I will try to follow in other of Cleopatra's actions.

For the moment, however, this great coming together of the two lovers has not taken place. Indeed, it is precisely Cleopatra's silence that Antony targets with his accusation of "idleness," of hysteria, which he bases on everything that has led up to it; and Cleopatra, understanding that nothing true will now be said, limits herself, with dignity and a new gravity, to assuring Antony that her natural womanly agitation does come from the heart and that he can break away from her, deaf to her "unpitied folly," since "honor" calls him far from Egypt. With the words "your honor," which seem to be lacking in the idea of "nobility," we sense that the problem that will dominate the action is now being raised. Will the "nobility, " the repressed dignity of the female condition, manage to triumph over the "forgetting" that weighs so heavily upon it? Will it manage to speak? Will it manage to convince men that "honor" is not the absolute value that rightly should obsess them, but rather a barrier set up against self-knowledge?

For however much Cleopatra may be lacking in the essential words that might have made her confrontation with Antony a true sharing, she has nonetheless already shown—and this is the moment to make note of it so as to better perceive the depths in her that are hidden by "hysteria"—an understanding of the other and of herself that Antony clearly does not possess. Space does not permit me to dwell on this, but we should be aware of the perfectly lucid way in which she has always observed him, and of the way in which, almost from the outset, she foresees the kind of relationship that would allow both of them to pursue the "betterment," the spiritual deepening, that their love should aim at. As for lucidity, let us simply remember what Cleopatra has said to Antony about his confusion when face to face with Octavius; or the way she notes his capacity for lying, which is great indeed, though poorly served by his meager acting skills, which she mocks; or her sadness when she sees how little he is affected by the death of Fulvia, his abandoned wife, in spite of her own jealousy of her. She has become attached to a real human being, with faults of which she wants to be aware and that she certainly notices, whereas he moves toward her through a world of fantasies.

And as for the project of deepening their love, let us simply think of the way Cleopatra evokes, when Antony is away, a happy moment from their past—fishing with him and the joke she made then in rather poor taste and the lovers' quarrel they had, then their reconciliation in the fever of desire and their jousting at dawn, when she put her "tires and mantles" on Antony while girding herself with his sword, the very one with which he had spilled blood at Philippi and vanquished Brutus. A famous sword, the symbol of his virility. Here is an exchange in which it would be easy to see nothing more than erotic play; indeed, some might suspect the cynical control of a frivolous "enchantress," destructive and petty, over a man of great action and honor, symbolically stripped of himself. But another intention is emerging here, which we will have to take into account if we want to understand what is about to happen. What Cleopatra lets us see when she takes the "Philippan sword" is that she wants to free Antony from his obsession with public grandeur, from his passion for "glory," "honor," ambition; and isn't this in order to keep him in a private existence where, in a deeper, more intense relationship with her, he might come to see what men and women truly are? It would mean that a better future, or in any case a truer and thus a "nobler" one, would be possible for this man she now sees driven by his sword toward endless wars, as he ages and then dies. The symbol of virility in this game does not exist simply on the level of its obvious sexual suggestions; it takes its place in the larger context of a society whose emphasis on possessions and power has driven it from its indispensable equilibrium. And so, when Cleopatra seeks to turn Antony from what ordinarily he affirms without question, her act implies a social and a moral revolution. And even if that night, as dawn is about to break, she does not really know what to expect from the games and pleasures she has dreamed up, Cleopatra may already be, in part, the more lucid and courageous woman we shall see her become.

VII

For it is a fact—one we now need to take fully into account—that Cleopatra's character does develop during the course of the play, and her evolution and maturation will become the driving force of the action, as well as a way for Shakespeare to verify that the kind of society valued by Romans or Puritans is not the end of human possibility. After doing so, he will be able to discover, and make manifest, one of the great functions of theatrical truth.

Cleopatra is encouraged to change, to look within herself for the "nobility" that is so easily forgotten, since from the outset of the action, if not from before, a call to order can clearly be heard, a call that will be echoed with increasing urgency as the play unfolds. It has to do with the passage of time, and time passes even in the palace of an Egyptian sovereign. Cleopatra has been beauty incarnate; she has reigned by her beauty even more than by her riches or her armies, but everyone knows that she is growing older, as several comments in the play make clear, and she herself is the first to say that her complexion is less alluring, that she now has wrinkles. Even her sensuality can only cause her exasperation: since the "salad days" of Caesar's love—the "broad-fronted Caesar" who kept her more admiring than truly in love—she has only known increasing anguish as her body stands on the threshold of its autumn. Antony too is growing older, and not only does he admit this to himself, but does so repeatedly, obsessed as he is with his gray hair, with his arm that one day will lose its strength—and with the youth of Octavius, of whom he is jealous, covering him with contempt that scarcely conceals the irrepressible fascination he feels.

Antony and Cleopatra are in the hands of time, and they know it. This is the cause both of the ardor they bring to their love and of the anguish that smolders beneath it. But it is important to understand that they do not live this anguish in the same way. For Antony—as is made clear by his obsession with Octavius—for this great warrior of times past, now won over to the Roman idea, it is power that matters, ambition that predominates; there is therefore no richness in the depths of the simple fact of existing; the moment, in particular, cannot be a place for being, for fullness—and so for Antony, in the war that must always be waged, the passage of time is nothing more than opportunities to seize or to miss, with an ever increasing risk of losing everything. This explains the agitation signaled on a number of occasions throughout the play. Antony goes through moments of depression followed by moments of unhealthy elation that disturb his companions, and he loses his head to the point of challenging Octavius to face-to-face combat. In the "Roman" milieu, the anguish of passing time serves only to break a person apart; it does not allow for spiritual development.

But it cannot be the same for Cleopatra, because, as we know, this woman has a very strong, almost painful sense of the reserves within her of innate quality, of nobility, to which the Roman world has barred access, which consigns her to being "forgotten"—so that her uneasiness at the rapid passing of days demands above all a way of thinking that has nothing to fear from age. On the contrary, the time that touches her body can help her toward a fuller awareness of herself by reminding her ever more insistently not so much of its passage as of its nature. In other words, time is reality, and at the heart of reality the only thing of value is that which can recognize time as its very substance, in other words, finite beings—like the aging Antony, who, by admitting he is mortal, accedes to what is absolute in him. The obsession with the passage of time is for Cleopatra the source of her search for her self; it is what makes her regret having struck the messenger and makes her suffer when she cannot find the way to tell Antony what is at stake, and what they have paid too little heed to, in their love. And it is what will make her look for another chance—beyond this moment of involuntary speechlessness, of missed communication—to exchange true words, words that might allow Antony to attain to the truth of life at the same time as she does, which would help her as well, since at last she would be truly loved, thanks to the luminous reciprocity of a common search.

This is the search for the "new heaven" and the "new earth" that Antony explicitly asks her for—and we should note it, as it is of great importance—in the very first words he speaks. A search that will not be easy to undertake, since Antony has his eyes still fixed on Rome, and his mind still clouded by sexist prejudices. To fully appreciate so profoundly intuitive a work as *Antony and Cleopatra,* we will need to examine this search and follow it along that path which the frustrated relationship of the two lovers keeps open if barely usable—that is, in the underpinnings of the spoken word, in the acts that Cleopatra and even Antony will carry out since they cannot communicate more directly, at a level of action in a drama soon to become tragic where it is surely the unconscious will that interprets and decides.

I am thinking, of course, of the battle of Actium, situated in the middle of the play like a great schema that allows us to feel the desires and strengths of all those who from the very beginning of the work and in every corner of the triple world—Rome, Greece, Egypt, each with its own thoughts about existence and being—have laid claim to the truth. Did Cleopatra, in deciding to take personal command of her ships at the moment when this decisive confrontation between Octavius and Mark Antony was being prepared off the coast of Greece, seek to regain her "nobility" by emulating Antony? Was she the kind of woman who seeks to gain recognition from a man by imitating him? This is exactly what she has given the Roman Enobarbus to understand: as the sovereign of my kingdom, she tells him, I intend to assume my part of the campaign in manly fashion, to "appear there for a man"; her intention could hardly be more clearly stated. But soon she will understand that this is not the direction to follow, that it is one more way of being overwhelmed by values she cannot really want either for herself or even for Antony, a losing way of letting herself "speak" through what she cannot want to be, and so she suddenly breaks with this level in herself on which the warrior's quest for glory and her own very real thirst for kingdoms and power are at work, and when the battle is at its height and victory for either side uncertain, she turns her great vessel the *Antoniad* around and brings all sixty of her ships back to Egypt.

It is, then, from the perspective of a radical lucidity that I understand this defection. And it is perhaps yet another moment when the unconscious has decided before consciousness has properly deliberated: "Forgive my fearful sails, I little thought / You would have follow'd," she says later to Antony, depicting herself as the fearful woman one might have expected, the one she can actually believe herself to have been, much as she had formerly wanted to be a man. But we can perceive nothing of the deep signifiers at Actium— the sea, the scattered ships, the flight of Egyptian sails like so many birds beneath the sky—without recognizing in this departure, which unsettles all the surface intentions, another quite essential fear of Cleopatra's, that of losing what gives life its value and love its reason for being: an aptitude for the lived moment, for its fullness, its light, when the ambitions of the powerful and the calculations of the strategists might veil, might blacken, everything around us, and, as a consequence of this fear, the wakening in her, though it may seem mad, of a supreme, desperate hope. She "reasons" in the following way: either Antony will win this battle or he will lose, but in either case he will be lost to the truth that matters, since he will be anchored even more deeply than before in the logic of plunder and war. Shouldn't he then be offered, before it is too late, the chance to become, as another Egyptian drama says, "better than a prince, a man"?[2] All of which would give Cleopatra herself, as the lover Antony could return to, access to her own truth—that truth that risks being lost forever if she remains entangled in the battles raging that day.

To this end, however, Antony must be confronted with a choice that involves their destiny: either to accept that Cleopatra should break with him, that she should return alone to an Egypt which henceforth will be nothing more than a pawn in his battle with Octavius, or to follow her in her departure and thus lose on the level of the naval battle, perhaps even on the level of his political ambitions as well, but in order to pass from a reality based on mere appearance to one that at last would be truthful, the reality founded on an existence lived in the depths of one's relation to oneself, in the awareness of time, this existence being the only one that truly matters, especially as death is drawing near. It should be noted, as Shakespeare himself surely did, that the name of Cleopatra's ship is the *Antoniad*. Antony is obviously what

2. The reference is to Mozart's *The Magic Flute*.—Trans.

the queen keeps foremost in her mind when at first sight she might seem only to be responding in fear to the noise and fire of a battle between men.

The flight of Cleopatra from the battle at Actium is thus a major proposition, formulated in the heart of a reflection about what life might be; and through the magnitude of a richly symbolic event, which affects two armies, two parts of the world, we can see that this reflection is made on the level of the representations, the values, the investments in reality that constitute human society from one end of the Roman world to the other and constantly paralyze it. This flight of birds disappearing beyond the earthly horizon and opening onto an Egypt of the spirit—the full relation of a person to himself—is a call to Antony, and to every man and woman with him, to move from blind action to the project of knowledge. And the astonishing thing is that Antony seems to accept this great invitation, since he in turn abandons the battlefield in solitary pursuit of the *Antoniad*. At this point we see a new development in the action, in which the two protagonists are bound to be far closer to one another tomorrow than before.

VIII

But let us not forget that Shakespeare has set himself, from the beginning of *Antony and Cleopatra*, as in all his plays, the task of observing society as it is, looking for the paths that truth might follow, but without surrendering to utopian dreams; throughout the rest of this play, therefore, he will follow to the very end of their effects the misunderstandings that separate men and women, depicting clearly the pitfalls that can ensnare and cripple them as well as their ability to overcome them.

For a while, at least as far as Antony is concerned, what happens after Actium will involve a consciousness more agitated than changed. It is clear that when he follows his first impulse, when he commits himself passionately and without thinking to following Cleopatra, Antony is lifted by a great wave of inner illumination. He sees what he has not suspected: that a loving relationship suffices, that it has the capacity to reveal the vanity of many other concerns and undertakings. But soon he is prey once more to his habitual contradictions; his concern for his "honor," for his "glory"—the values of male society—reasserts itself, and all the more violently in that he is not unaware of the degree to which his desertion from battle will be condemned, even despised, by the military and the politicians. The unbearable sting of lost honor clouds the intuition that was active for a moment and leads him to take the appeal Cleopatra has made at Actium not for what it truly was, an act of fidelity to what she still hopes from their love, but for an act of betrayal, motivated either by a cynical egotism seeking advantages in Octavius's camp by seducing the new Caesar, or simply by the supposedly irresponsible nature of women. "Your ribaudred nag of Egypt," the soldier Scarus says to him, with everyone around him approving. We see an Antony held back by an uncontrollable passion for Cleopatra but also stirred by malevolent feelings that inspire loathing if not fear in him—which explains why his ways of thinking and acting will become progressively more troubled and dark.

But there is nothing of this in Cleopatra, whose behavior shows that she is taking stock of the new situation and drawing consequences from it that are related to the yearning she still feels so intensely. As for Antony, she knows full well that in this war, which will usher in a new era, he is a man whose time has past, a man who will soon be vanquished. Octavius, master of the rest of the world, already has envoys in Egypt to propose to the queen, whose power he is about to break, that she turn against her lover or have him killed. It may be that something of the woman she once was still lives in Cleopatra, the woman shaped by masculine values, who still admires the god of war in an aging Antony, who loves to think of him triumphant in the final clashes, and who still plays with his armor as once she did with his sword—dreaming, against all evidence to the contrary, that he will protect her from her own vow of pure nobility, which is so difficult to adhere to and so destructive of any hope of simple earthly happiness, by defending forever a bit of Egyptian land against the Roman. Even so, she now understands that the time has come to prepare herself for one last supreme attempt, to demonstrate to Antony, so that his eyes may be opened to life, the truth that she carries within her, although on the day of a previous departure she had not known how to tell him of it. This demonstration will be deeply serious, intense; a revelation of what true reality is, beneath the delusions, so that Antony, discovering what true values are, for him as much as for her, may become conscious of what life is, "real life"; may cure his love of disastrous prejudices and other illusions and thus be able to live his love to the full, be it only for an hour. Then die, saved.

It is, in short, a second invitation, following the one made in Actium. But one which, since it will have to be based this time on the evidence of "nobility," can be clearly expressed only if Cleopatra knows how to devote herself to her own being, to her quality, in a deep and irreversible way: in other words, if she learns to dominate what in her is capriciousness, thoughtlessness, nervous agitation—all those ways of being that men have encouraged in the behavior of women, all those "frailties," as she herself will admit to Octavius, that "have often sham'd our sex." And so she must undo in herself what has always been so deeply and strongly rooted in the human psyche, which can mean nothing other than a confrontation with death, a willingness, if necessary, to seek in the absolute of death the breaking of all those heavy chains that have until now kept even a queen of Egypt from moving as fully as she would have wanted toward herself and toward another. She must know how to die without hesitation or doubt, to bring about in the depths of her being the possibility that when the day comes, if it must, she can prove her readiness, offering in that moment—doubtless a double suicide, given the last disasters—the keys to an intensity of exchange that had been missing. "What shall we do?" she had asked Enobarbus after Actium, terrified by what she had put in motion that day and worried about the consequences. "Think, and die," Enobarbus had answered her, without realizing—he who was preparing to betray Antony—the momentous event his words might incite.

An accepted death, a suicide, at least potentially, "in the Egyptian way," we might say. For there are many references in *Antony and Cleopatra* to another way of choosing death, again through fidelity to an intensity in moral conduct; in advocating this way of dying, the Romans claimed that it allowed one to escape an adversary, specifically a tyrant, without relinquishing one's freedom. This "Roman" form of suicide haunts Antony from the moment he feels he has lost his honor; he sees suicide as a way to recover it. And Cleopatra herself, as she says explicitly, considers it a model for the transcendence of ordinary motivations that she is seeking. But the intention of the Roman act is obviously quite different from what she has in mind. For it takes place in the context of a society whose principles and values are never called into question by this act—quite to the contrary. Influenced by this society's fatal tendency toward competition and war, Roman suicide is never based on the assumption that such a society is devoid of meaning: Brutus in *Julius Caesar* is ready and willing to die in this way in order to demonstrate the validity of the laws of the republic. By contrast, the "Egyptian" suicide Cleopatra is thinking about seeks to challenge, if not to dismantle, the structures of the social realm she has had to live in; it intends to accede to a higher reality, one ordinarily denied, overshadowed, and robbed of the most legitimate desires. In short, whereas "Roman" suicide is a triumph for death, since it merely confirms the social impoverishment of existence, "Egyptian" suicide bears witness to life. Whence the word that this death will allow Egypt's sovereign to utter when the time comes. Advancing in her death toward Antony, who, having learned and understood that she is capable of such action, has finally recognized her true quality and felt joy in the knowledge, she will be able to address this man, with whom she has lived through so many debilitating clashes patched up by so much feverish debauchery, as "husband." Beyond Roman marriage, which is devoid of being, and beyond their personal past, which was so full of misunderstandings, she has established as fact a relationship that at last is complete, eros together with nobility, which others, in future times, will have to adapt to moments less extreme.

IX

In short, after Actium, and aware of how insufficient, how uncertain, the sign of presence she had given that day had been, Cleopatra seeks once again her own inner "nobility," seeks to become one with it through the acceptance of death, which until then she has certainly feared—the acceptance of death, of total sacrifice, thus acceding to supreme freedom, to a recentering of being on the seriousness of freedom. It remains nonetheless true that such a vow of maturity, which could cure Antony's blindness if he knew how to recognize it in her, is not easily perceptible in a world of men, where so many prohibitions and prejudices cloud the true meaning of human behavior. In this second part of the play, Shakespeare remains as much the psychologist and sociologist as before, so as to observe the increasingly painful persistence of situations devastated by misunderstandings. This is immediately the case after Actium, since Antony can only see his own loss of honor and glory in Cleopatra's flight. And when Cleopatra, Octavius having dispatched an ambassador to her with the order to send Antony away or have him killed, pretends to listen to the officer with respect and even lets him kiss her hand, Antony immediately interprets the situation in the most offensive as well as in the most traditional way. "You have been a boggler ever," always inconstant and false, he tells her before sinking to even worse insults, since, as we have seen, he goes so far as to say that he has picked her up like a piece of meat from the late Caesar's table.

Soon afterward, love wins out again over distrust and fear, but when a second naval battle sees Cleopatra's ships join with those of Octavius, Antony, without hesitating, chooses yet another time to believe what is totally untrue: that "this foul Egyptian," this "triple-turn'd whore," has betrayed him for the "novice" who—this is always his obsession—is young while he is old. Still the same accusation except that this time they are no longer mere insults.

When she appears, Cleopatra cannot interject a single word in the torrent of reproof, and she leaves Antony with the well-grounded fear that he will kill her or have her killed. "She hath sold me," he has proclaimed, "she dies for it"—a death that would be just the opposite of the one for which she is preparing herself. This is the darkest moment of their long exchange.

But it is also the moment when Cleopatra conceives the stratagem that will allow her to break through to what she knows is most valuable in Antony, to that which is life and intelligence in the love he has always had for her. Since returning from Actium, the queen of Egypt may have had in her thoughts a tomb that North (the translator of Plutarch) and subsequently Shakespeare called "the monument," an unusual and unexpected word that has a special radiance and mystery. And when Charmian, given the danger her mistress is in of being killed, suggests that it would be a good idea to shut herself up in the "monument," which is fortified, and get word to her lover that she is dead, the queen takes up the idea at once, but not without adding an element that totally changes its meaning and will prove decisive. Charmian thinks only about deflecting an anger that could become fatal. But Cleopatra is counting on something entirely different from the message she will send to Antony. Death, the eunuch Mardian tells Antony, is something that Cleopatra has already brought about, and with a hand that will only have been one with yours: for you should know that, as she killed herself, the last word she uttered was the name of the noble, the "most noble Antony," a name she repeated, with a groan so broken, so incomplete, that it was as if she were carrying this name buried deep within her.

What is the meaning of this act, which we must remember is Shakespeare's invention, since Plutarch simply wrote that Cleopatra "had Antony notified that she was dead"? Essentially, it has to do with the fact that Cleopatra is afraid that the great exchange she has dreamed might be effected by her death will not be possible if she sees Antony again right away. And so she has to initiate in him a supreme state of consciousness through the representation from afar of the act that she knows she has already accomplished in the depths of her own being. A stratagem without any risk on the one level that matters: the life of the spirit. If Antony, on learning that the queen is dead, could feel so much sorrow that he in turn would want to die, it would mean that he was totally overcome by the repressed love he felt for her; by the knowledge, inherent in this love, of the other; by the awareness of the moment, of what is absolute in the moment, which is born from the recognition of the other; and thus he would die saved. And perhaps Cleopatra would have just enough time to come and share his last moments with him.

And this is certainly what takes place—henceforth necessity will separate from chance, as always happens at the end of tragedies.

"Dead, then?" Antony murmurs, and then immediately adds, "unarm, Eros." "No more a soldier," he says, knowing that with her death his own day has ended in a world where he has never known how to live. He begs Cleopatra's forgiveness for the relationship of illusion and lies he has imposed on her; he says he no longer wants to live in this "night," but it is also as if a dawn were rising in his words and another place opening and offering itself to a life this time truly shared with the woman he has until this moment loved only in ambivalence and fear. "I come, my queen," Antony cries, and adds, "Where souls do couch on flowers, we'll hand in hand, / And with our sprightly port make the ghosts gaze." He discovers what life can be at the very moment when his time on earth is ending, and this is exactly the revolution that Cleopatra has sought from him, since now he can be heard to render homage to her with the very words and the very categories of thought that she herself has so long been meditating upon.

Antony evokes her courage and praises "her noble mind," and when he imagines he hears her say to Octavius ("our Caesar," he calls him, for Octavius has been his model more than his rival), "I am the conqueror of myself," it is clear that he is thinking not that Cleopatra has sought to escape the power of others through a "Roman " suicide but that she has known how to free herself from the psychological bondage to which the world of Octavius reduces women. And, furthermore, Antony will confide to his servant Eros—a name that Shakespeare was sure to have been struck by—that since Cleopatra is dead, living for him can only mean "dishonor," and "baseness," words through which we understand that the values he once held, his idea of honor and grandeur—hacking the universe to pieces, filling the sea with ships—no longer have meaning when compared to this great example of true life. From now on, Antony is not the same; he is a new man, and to such a degree that he too, killing himself now with these new thoughts in mind, will be able to escape the power of Octavius as formerly he could not have done—not just with his body but also with his soul.

However, we should not expect to hear Antony say anything explicitly when, dying, he is borne up to the monument in which Cleopatra has taken refuge. He will not use the words that would clearly express the intimacy of their final hour together and the more open perspective on life that such intimacy encourages. Shakespeare is too much of a poet not to know that plenitude can only be expressed indirectly, allusively, and paradoxically, and it is far more moving to observe that in their final encounter Antony is directly concerned about what will happen to Cleopatra, pointing out the one person in whom it seems prudent for her to put her faith. The true exchange takes place on a much deeper level, in silence: either in the kiss these two beings exchange, a pathetic reminder of the kiss Antony had asked for, and gloriously affirmed, in the opening scene of act 1; or, just after Antony's death, in Cleopatra's fainting, from which she emerges changed. She was the queen of Egypt, and when Iras bends over her, this is still the word she uses: "Royal Egypt! Empress! " But coming back to herself, Cleopatra answers no—"no more but e'en a woman," one who no longer feels any difference between herself and "the maid that milks and does the meanest chares." It is as a woman and not as a queen that Cleopatra has claimed her nobility.

And it remains for her to keep the commitment made to Antony when the news of her suicide was first brought to him. This she succeeds in doing in act 5, through difficulties that make this last part of the play an occasion for Shakespeare to verify the extent of Cleopatra's determination, the steadfastness of her "nobility."

X

It will take, in fact, some obstinacy on Cleopatra's part to accomplish "what's brave, what's noble," as she says at the end of act 4, when she assigns herself "the briefest end" to do so.

For she must postpone her suicide so as to obtain Octavius's assurance about her son Cesarion, while at the same time preserving her own freedom to end her life. Now Octavius wants to display her in triumph when he returns to Rome, and he profits from this period of discussion to take her into custody and keep her from killing herself, as she immediately tries to do once the soldiers have surrounded her, after which they keep a careful watch over her.

Though deprived of power, she still has the resource of deceit, and she uses it to dupe Octavius into believing—a situation that is full of painful irony—that she is too much a woman, too much a woman of the sort that Octavius thinks women are, to think seriously about death. She does this by pretending to be attached to adornment—"lady trifles"—and by setting up a scene in which she lets herself be caught blatantly lying and then reacting childishly toward her accuser, Seleucus. With the result that Octavius can withdraw reassured. "Feed and sleep," he tells her when he leaves, with as much scorn as egotistical relief. In fact, Cleopatra now knows that she has time to receive the basket of figs that contains the mortal weapon of which her enemies are quite unaware.

The death of Cleopatra is one of the supreme moments in Shakespeare's work, one of the supreme moments in poetry, and there have been critics, like George Bernard Shaw, who have felt that this last scene, in a sense, is even too beautiful, since it uses a poet's art to give sublimity to a character such critics can see only in negative terms and to a situation that would seem to sanction a whole series of disturbing events, brought about by what Philon has denounced in the first words of the play: the taste for debauchery and foolishness.

This is obviously not what I think, and it seems to me, on the contrary, that the poetic quality of the end of the play, far from being the product of verbal art, adorning what is without value, ensues naturally from the intuitions that Shakespeare has detected in the richness of human potential and freed from what ordinarily stifles them, so that they can now speak as if by themselves and accordingly with that intensity, that purity, which makes for poetry. It is not Shakespeare who is the poet in this last scene, it is Cleopatra herself, whom Shakespeare could see as having existed under the burden of alienations and prejudices that have spoken in her stead, often through the very voice of a woman not yet equal to herself.

From now on, Cleopatra speaks out clearly, and her words are poetry in the direct way that great moments in one's relation to oneself can be, as thinking deepens, and hope becomes clear. For example, why are we so moved to hear her say—no doubt at the height of her own emotion as it becomes luminous—these few words that are yet so simple: "I am again for Cydnus / To meet Mark Antony"? There is no stylistic figure or flourish in these lines, nothing to dazzle or surprise us, but rather the immediate expression of a thought which, as cause for compassion, allows everything we consider to appear, for a moment at least, in its essential finitude, and for this reason as presence, and so speaks to us of unity and restores the world to poetry. What is this thought? When she was on the Cydnus the first time, Cleopatra wanted to present only the kind of fundamentally unreal image of herself that would serve her purpose at the time, using with great art all the marvels of appearance to seduce Antony. She thus agreed not to be the real person that she perhaps already was or would one day become in order to conquer a man whom she did not yet seek after for what he was in himself. And in this she played the role assigned to women by society. She played it so well that Enobarbus, in describing the famous encounter much later, combines a connoisseur's appreciation of things artistic with a condemnation that remains profound.

But time has passed, love has been declared between these two great figures, driven earlier only by ambition and self-interest, and when, in this new state of mind, Cleopatra remembers their first meeting, there can be no doubt that she recognizes in it the original sin of their relationship; the silks, the perfumes, the strange music—the whole beautiful painting, with cupids even, and nymphs—which had almost undone the great potential of the relationship and obscured the reality—a "rough" reality perhaps but the only true one—that their future held. And so there was a "return" to the Cydnus that Cleopatra, grown older, felt she owed as reparation for the original seduction and as foundation for the kind of exchange between Antony and herself such a return would establish. A return whereby she would still appear in all her beauty, and even with her queenly adornments—what she calls "trifles" when she mentions them to Octavius, because she has thought deeply about their meaning—but no longer to fashion illusion with these vain signs of distinction; no, rather to express what she has recognized as her nobility with signs that will indicate how, beautiful as she has remained, she now intends to show this nobility in the appropriate way, as the sovereign of her being and her fate. To Iras and Charmian, she says, "Show me, my women, like a queen. Go fetch / My best attires," and Iras brings her the crown that symbolizes this kind of royalty, the only kind that is not illusory, even though it is over the waters of the river Styx that her barque is now setting out.

And it is certainly not for Antony alone that Cleopatra puts on the robe that solemnizes this conquest of self and the gift that will make her the wife of the man she has called her husband: it is also to affirm before all of society, of which Octavius will be the representative when he arrives in the suicide room—the "monument," henceforth rich with all its meaning—that she has triumphed in death, and through death has won the freedom that she never had when she was only a queen in the world as it exists, devastated by the desire for power and the illusions of possession. Let us recall the fear that Cleopatra expresses, just before she prepares for her suicide, of being led away alive to Octavius's triumph in Rome, where boors would present her to the crowd and singers and actors of the crudest sort would caricature what she and Antony had been for each other. And let us understand that her abhorrence of such a fate was fully justified, for aside from the outrage she would have had to endure, her very condition as a woman would have been openly insulted. The triumphs that rejoice in victory, the crowds that admire the powerful and idolize a great leader, a Rome that has grown accustomed to such servile festivals as the very essence of its self-consciousness—what is all this if not a symbolic manifestation of the many tyrannies that society exerts, in particular its effort to appropriate and diminish women? By her absence from the triumph of Octavius, Cleopatra has some reason to feel herself victorious, even at the price of her own existence.

XI

This doesn't mean, alas, that the "scald rhymers" and the "quick comedians" of the triumphal day will be deprived of putting her on display, and that a young actor won't mimic her in a borrowed dress, assuming lewd poses and changing his voice so as to reproduce the ostensible image of a woman. At this point in the network of the action a concern seems to surface proper to Shakespeare, the one I hypothesized may have caused him to pick the subject of Antony and Cleopatra one day when leafing through his Plutarch and thinking of the attacks by many of his long-faced contemporaries against the theater and against women. Shakespeare was sure to have noticed the profound analogy between Roman triumph and the theater of the era of Elizabeth and King James. In a number of plays that he knew, the action is imagined and moved forward with the aid of masculine values; and the fact that women's roles were ordinarily taken by men was as much the symbolic manifestation of this situation as a factor that contributed powerfully to maintaining or even aggravating it. Shakespeare knew that when *Antony and Cleopatra* was staged, the role of the Egyptian sovereign would be entrusted to a young man, or to a boy who might not "squeak," as happens on more vulgar stages, and who might even try to be true to the play's intention, yet would still not be in any better position to feel in his own being Cleopatra's need to recover her "nobility," to coincide fully with what she knows she is and remains, despite the effort made to have her forget it. A male actor will be unable to express this kind of relation to the self in all its great potential, in its quality, in its eventual gift of new harmony to a society in disorder; and under these circumstances it is not surprising that the Puritans should have seen in the theater an irruption of the feminine that might seem to be that of the devil himself. A schematic representation animated by a life of a nature other than itself, as is the case when a woman's role is played by a man, can merely grimace, can merely seem spectral, can evoke only nothingness and all its destructive potential.

Such is the situation, more or less the same on the London stage as on the Roman stage in the final analysis, and there is certainly food for thought here, especially for the man who had Hamlet say that theater is the mirror of society. It was precisely the criticism of the Puritans that Shakespeare had to take seriously, but as Cleopatra's great refusal makes clear, he gave it a meaning opposite to the one those frightened minds wanted to assert. Does woman appear in the theater as the principle of evil? Yes, but only because she is presented most of the time in a grossly simplified form, in which the denial of the truth gives ample play to fantasies, and whose fundamental unreality adds still more to the fear she arouses: whence, as always, the need to censure, with a consequent increase in inhibitions, in disequilibrium in an unhappy society.

And might we hope that this situation will change? Yes, but this would at least require that the "boy actor" no longer be there to weigh down with chains a woman who committed suicide so as not to have to submit to these humiliating insults.

And as I end these remarks, let me advance a hypothesis that seems to me far from absurd and even to reflect rather well what takes place, if unperceived, in poetic creation. One cannot help noticing that the verse in *Antony and Cleopatra* often has the suppleness, the inner freedom, the capacity for abrupt change that characterize Shakespeare's last plays, the "romances" that he began to write only a short while after his second Roman play. There are remarkable breaks in this verse; it opens onto a number of images which, even more than in previous works, short-circuit ordinary acts of the intellect—as when Cleopatra describes Antony's pleasures as "dolphin-like," while considering them "god-like" as well. There is clear evidence here of what is called *écriture*, that is, an act of mind that transgresses the paths taken by the conceptual interpretation of events and things, with their classifications and their simplifications, in the interests of an apprehension of a unity beyond, where what has been held back, repressed, reappears, revealing the form of the world and offering the possibility of harmony to a reconciled existence. What might we find on the level of conceptual constructions, even ideologies, that is called into question and sometimes even undone by poetry, if not the distribution of roles between men and women in society as dictated by the emphasis on power and tangible goods—a society devoted to precise action, to thought that analyzes and rationalizes? Poetry, with its eyes fixed on what is beyond the concept, is thus beyond the structures that define and paralyze the relation between the sexes at any given moment of history. At its most advanced stage—for we should not use the word poetry for everything that rhymes or is embellished with images—poetry dissipates what Cleopatra called the "wording" of women by masculine values. And whoever follows her along this path transcends in his own self-presence his socialized body and becomes once more his natural body, perhaps with an innate understanding of the other sex, which is equally natural at this level and whose repression arouses bitterness or anger in the other that a "nobility" has been belittled.

But if this is so, the dramatist who wants to hold a mirror to society, showing not only its flaws but also its potential, its hope, may ask himself whether the actor, even if a boy, who plays the woman will be, as it were, freed from his difference, with all its reductive potential, by the poetic quality of the words he speaks. If, in Cleopatra's name, he says, "Now no more / The juice of Egypt's grape shall moist this lip," or "I am fire and air; my other elements / I give to baser life," will we not be forced to see that the dying queen is now alive in him, that in the "nobility" she has won back from society and herself she has passed through the curtain of ordinary speech and is expressing herself now in the name of everyone? "I have immortal longings in me," she adds, magnificently, as she prepares to give herself to the asp, and these are indeed words that have meaning for many others besides herself. Why? Because what was "mortal" in her aspirations, in her "longings," was what condemned her, through her acceptance of the ideology of her time, to being nothing but a shadow in a world of appearances. And what is "immortal" is quite simply the real, the "true life," which is certainly the wish of all those for whom poetry matters. In *Antony and Cleopatra*—a theatrical work but one created by a poet—poetry has slipped into the network of the action to dissipate mirages, to undo knots of prejudice and fantasy, to denounce injustice. It is not an ornament tossed onto something just to entertain an audience, as George Bernard Shaw seemed to think, but a fermenting agent that allows the categories of the spirit to develop—perhaps for a better world.

TRANSLATED BY MARY ANN CAWS

CHAPTER SEVEN

Desdemona Hangs Her Head

> I have much to do
> But to go hang my head all at one side
> And sing it like poor Barbary.
> *Othello*, 4.3.31–33

THE MEANING of *Othello* has often been sought in the clearly essential relationship between the Moor and Iago. Is Othello simply a victim or is he more or less the accomplice of his aggressor, Iago? This approach is inadequate, however, and one of its most regrettable aspects has been a simplified, profoundly reductive understanding of Desdemona. More recently, attention has finally been paid to a problem that is everywhere present in the play and revolves around the relation between Othello and Desdemona and around the status of women—or, more precisely, of married women. This viewpoint has allowed for considerable progress in interpreting the play and has rendered many readings obsolete. The only critics who have seen this perspective as "feminist" are those who have fallen back on defensive positions, even if at the risk of replacing discussion with a form of blunt refusal that is at times reminiscent of Othello's disturbed behavior on the second day. Murder by criticism does exist; or, at least, some have found it tempting.

We now no longer have to wonder if the play ought to have been called *Iago*, as W. H. Auden suggested in "The Joker in the Pack," [1] since the current temptation—still a simplification—is to join in one title the names of both unhappy lovers, thus situating the play, which is clearly a tragedy, between *Romeo and Juliet* on the one hand and *Antony and Cleopatra* on the other. The former records the disaster that ruins the relationship between two people, while the latter's equally dramatic outcome lets a bit of light

---

1. W. H. Auden, "The Joker in the Pack, in *The Dyer's Hand and Other Essays* (1948; Vintage Books, 1989), 246–72.—Trans.

shine through. Although such new ways of thinking about *Othello* are surely relevant, I don't think they rule out an approach I shall endeavor to present here, which might prove useful and plainly overlaps with some of the conclusions of recent criticism.

This approach, ontological in nature, is applied to situations or, rather, to levels in human situations that are inaccessible to the various tools of ordinary psychology. Shakespeare's thinking was certainly continually sustained by observations that may be called psychological, as well as by others that were sociological, moral, and political. As I have tried to show, *Antony and Cleopatra* derives from a consideration of social conditions at the end of the sixteenth and the beginning of the seventeenth century, in particular the ways of being or of wishing to be that agitated the Puritan faction and threatened the theater's existence, and it concludes with the question of women's place in society and their understanding of themselves and their worth. With great insistence, Shakespeare attributes the words "noble" and "nobility" to Cleopatra. He also shows the progressive maturation of this vilified queen's moral experience. In so doing, he reevaluates the categories of thought and the value judgments whose heavy clouds, gathered for centuries, have stifled both women's rights and their deepest sense of self. By showing the gradual development of this relation to oneself, Shakespeare was speaking of Cleopatra's *being,* of the being of those women that the societies of antiquity and of Shakespeare's own time regarded essentially as objects.

Shakespeare could speak and think in such a fashion because of his extraordinary ability to perceive—in a manner more spontaneous and profound than any other way of looking at life and at a person—the relation of a person both to himself or herself and to others. He perceived this relation at a deeper level than that of its milieu or historical determinations, and deeper still than the supposedly innate characteristics defining exchanges, especially those connected to gender relations and conflicts. This ability is at the root of Shakespeare's exceptional greatness. It allows him to encounter men and women precisely when they are preparing—consciously or not, and most often without being explicitly aware of it—to respond, not to some immediate cause that may be inherent in the context and even the urgency of their present situation, but rather, in a more inclusive and radical fashion, to their feelings about themselves as beings, as presences in the world, presences that cannot rightfully be masked by the imposition of simplified, self-interested, and manipulative representations. To have this renewed sense of themselves also means that the predetermined network of meanings to which they have fallen victim may and perhaps should be replaced by another order—one born from a true and mutual recognition of the fundamental unity of all life.

Shakespeare observes the way humans either do or do not remember their own being and their right to being. He observes the way they live their condition, either with despair lodged in their innermost depths or, on the contrary, with a hope that mysteriously remains alive despite all the evidence amassed against it. In this second instance, confidence is not simply the metaphysical good humor that accepts whatever happens and goes on to face the future. It is, rather, a disposition of the relation to oneself at an even more intimate level, one prior to all ideas, even if these are gradually affected by it. Given that being comes into being only if we want it to, this confidence establishes and founds the very object to whose existence it attests.

Anyone who considers this deeply rooted place in the human condition must also note the weaknesses and failings that occur in the need or the will-to-be, precisely when this will-to-be remembers what it is and strives to achieve its object. For what most often happens in this relation of the speaking subject to itself is the defeat of its project in the networks of language. It fails when persons who are in peril lose faith in themselves when confronted with all the traps inherent both in the way others represent them and in the way they imagine their own desires, alienated as they are by the very dream—which they cannot help dreaming—of what their freedom should be. Shakespeare's observatory dives very deep, like a bathyscaph in the swirls of what well may be called the soul since it is a medium more mobile and more conductive than reason. His surprising premonitions have to do with his observing, from this vantage point, strange behaviors emerging from the unconscious.

Shakespeare's vantage point offers the best view of what overdetermines such principal motivations as love and jealousy. Psychology knows how to recognize and to analyze these but is unwilling to sense the workings of something more essential, so it can sometimes be mistaken. The study of self-awareness, for which the fact of being or not being is more important than ways of being and more decisive than an appetite merely for objects, is what I have called Shakespeare's ontological concern. It would be easy to show how it is ubiquitous in the work of an author who had Hamlet say, "To be or not to be, that is the question." If only by way of the tragedies I have mentioned, consideration of Shakespeare's plays confirms that this underlying dimension must be taken into account in order to resolve the enigma of *Romeo and Juliet*. It also pinpoints the source of the lyricism in *Antony and Cleopatra*, expressing as it does the wish to see a new form of speech emerging on the human stage, one fully aware of its potential alienation, a speech I would call poetry. And if we look at *The Winter's Tale*, a pivotal play in this context, we can see that the goal of Shakespeare's reflection clearly is his concern for a bold way of thinking that quite deliberately draws out the truth hidden in the pastoral tradition.

II

Ontological concern is everywhere in Shakespeare's works, nowhere more so than in *Othello*. Here it is more present and perhaps even more self-conscious and ready to reveal itself in ways that are different from the situations, deeds, and other factors emblematic of ideas that cannot be reduced to the order of concepts, which are burdened with prejudices hidden in pseudo-facts. Right at the beginning of the play, in one of those expository scenes that Shakespeare so artfully maintains at multiple levels, someone is heard describing himself in terms meant to evoke the whole of his being. This description goes beyond a judgment that could, for instance, be easily differentiated into psychological observations. Rather, it becomes the radical, immediate expression of rejection, the expression of a strong aversion for what this person is, or thinks he is, for what he might have wished to take on in the midst of a world order for which he might then have found some meaning. "Abhor me," Iago says in his very first lines, and then quickly adds, "despise me." In both cases, these very strong words are unjustified by the reasons Roderigo might have for reproaching him, since at this point these reasons have to do with offenses that are rather venial. A feeling arises in Iago that continues to be felt throughout this entire scene, in which a young officer, who, we soon learn, is respected by everyone, displays his villainy in a way that his present circumstances can hardly explain. For surely it is dangerous to proclaim one's dishonesty, as Iago does, in front of the fool one wishes to deceive. Iago even flaunts this feeling with a bitter, vehement glee: I am a liar, a thief, a sensualist, he says. I hypocritically and cynically betray those I am low enough to accept to serve. These declarations are all the more surprising since we already have a premonition that gold, the apparent stakes of his projected treachery and plunder, hardly interests this person, who remains preoccupied with thinking about himself. What one can sense, what one has to sense, is that these affirmations—which appear as value judgments—are simply the disguised expressions of a more fundamental affirmation. Iago considers himself evil not only because of his deeds but also because he can see nothing but meaninglessness and darkness at the heart of the human condition he represents.

In this first scene we could be led to believe that what is central to Iago, what makes him insist with such bravado that a servant's true task is stealing and treachery, is his humiliation at being a servant. Just when he hoped to be promoted to the position of Othello's lieutenant and could therefore have participated in his decisions, he finds himself demoted to the rank of ensign, which will force him to proclaim someone else's eminence and power. The choice made against Iago has clearly upset him greatly, and it is after it is made that he speaks with such imprudence to his friend Roderigo, who is, in fact, his dupe. But why is Iago so ill at ease with the master-servant relationship? It is because he is incapable of the "ontological" confidence that might counterbalance what he lacks in the world of social relations. Iago senses himself not as being but as pure nothingness. Where another person might be completely one with himself, if only in an illusory way, through an energy that was still his life, Iago, when he turns toward what he is, sees not a unified person but rather an ego divisible into separate elements that together have no meaning, like flotsam and jetsam on a beach. Where this other person might live positively, Iago is nothing but negativity.

Echoing Hamlet's famous words, Iago concludes his first monologue by saying, "I am not what I am." What does this sentence mean? It does not mean "I am not what I *seem* to be"—a reflection that might appear natural coming from someone who has just suggested that his calling is dissimulation and treason. For in this case there would be an "I am" within him. In other words, there still would be a reality beneath the pretense that is the true level of the illusory. On the contrary, Iago takes note of the uniqueness of what he is, someone with a secret design or whose conduct is a sham. Quite simply, Iago simultaneously *is* and *is not*, since what he might consider his being, what he might hold and proclaim as his self-presence, is nothing more, in his eyes, than a heap of meaningless characteristics, as opaque and as devoid of self as a dead animal. Whereas Hamlet hesitates between "to be" and "not to be," between having faith in his right to be and knowing that he is only nothingness, Iago has made a choice; or, more precisely, he has no choice.

Iago experiences himself as nothingness, as a "vain form of matter."[2] All the goods accumulated at the master's expense cannot fill the emptiness felt within such anguish, which is quite different from what a humiliated servant feels. With the same ill design and apparent efficacy, the gaze that "nihilates" all that might fulfill a person's connection to himself also falls upon everything that exists around this person or thinks it does.[3] As does Arthur Rimbaud's "Infernal Spouse"—though Iago does not have his capacity for hope, proof of a nobility that is only momentarily disconcerted—Iago laughs "atrociously, lengthily" at everything in society that, to him, seems mere baseless pretense, mechanisms devoid of meaning, such as the hierarchies and promotions in the army: there is nothing anywhere but marionettes clattering in the wind.[4]

Iago's gaze extends over nothing but desert. Sexuality, for instance, which has a hold on cynics but not on those who are desperate, is for Iago merely something dirty, something he does not hesitate to designate by his usual "pish." People are all goats and monkeys, as he finally and victoriously gets Othello to believe. Not surprisingly, women in particular are the object of the negative judgments he lays out in the sarcastic distichs he utters on arriving in Cyprus—remarks he makes in the presence of Desdemona, who is worried by the delayed arrival of her husband's ship. Women are nothing but lechery; they are deceitful and vicious, and Iago repays them for it with his disgust. When Desdemona gives her hand to Cassio out of courteousness, Iago immediately imagines "lechery" and something "pestilent." Likewise, all the acts one normally takes pleasure in are discredited in advance and are consequently replaced by boredom. I don't know whether Iago's boredom has been sufficiently underscored, but it is real and makes up his entire inner world. Consider the unrelenting activity that allows him to experience the sole pleasure left to him, escaping for an instant the feeling of his

2. Yves Bonnefoy is paraphrasing Stéphane Mallarmé, whose letter to Henri Cazalis (April 1866), characterizes mortal beings as "vaines formes de la matière, mais bien sublimes pour avoir inventé Dieu et notre âme" (vain forms of matter, but quite sublime for having invented God and our soul). Mallarmé, *Correspondance 1862–1871*, vol. 1, ed. H. Mondor and L. J. Austin (Gallimard, 1959), 207.—Trans.

3. The verb "to nihilate" (*néantir*) was coined by Jean-Paul Sartre. It implies that consciousness arises only by surrounding an object or being with nothingness or nonbeing.—Trans.

4. "Infernal Spouse" is the translation of Arthur Rimbaud's poem "Époux infernal," in *Une saison en enfer, Oeuvres Complètes* (Gallimard, "Bibliothèque de la Pléiade," 1972), 102–6.—Trans.

own hollowness. As he says: "Pleasure, and action, make the hours seem short."

Such is Iago, and so could he live, or rather survive, without any particular pain, though unhappily. Yet what also appears at the beginning of the play is that in this vision of the meaninglessness and evil of everything, which theoretically should steel him against pain or lull him to sleep, there are certain aspects of life that keep their color even in the grayness of Iago's world. These aspects thus can surprise him and, more important, hurt him. By escaping his judgment, they judge him, turning his nothingness into something that is not only lived but also suffered. What are these troubling factors? Unquestionably, they are the noble feelings of friendship and love, contradicting the sadly misogynist remarks Iago has made in Desdemona's presence. Through his mockery, he can believe he has rid himself of these feelings, and that he will only have to take them into account if there are men and women capable of confirming their reality.

The problem is, such beings do appear to exist. In the sphere of lucre and debauchery in which he thinks he lives, Iago feels that these beings have faith in themselves and in others who are like them, ensuring their presence in the here and now. They are witnesses to being, and they hurt Iago, for despite his sharing in their existence, he cannot help wondering whether they might not benefit from some intuition he lacks, one that transcends him and reduces him to a feeling of relative inadequacy even in a despicable society where he might otherwise have been able to consider himself the same as any other depraved being. In other words, these beings do not allow Iago to forget himself, to give himself over to the diversions of gold and power of which he boasts in his opening speech, and that he presents as the goal of thieving servants. These other beings fascinate Iago; he is, in fact, jealous of them. His jealousy is also ontological since it revolves around the capacity to be, not around any form of having. This is the most fundamental kind of jealousy, even though it settles into jealousy's more particular forms, as when Iago senses in those who fascinate him some sort of happiness that is not his own. As Iago resentfully points out, this is the case with Cassio, who is so at ease with himself in his dealings with women. Iago is jealous of such self-assured beings. He hates them.

He also wants to destroy these beings or, more exactly, he wants to destroy their inner capacity both to be in the world and to find what he cannot: a meaning to life. "I'll set down the pegs that make this music," he says, thereby indicating his intention to upset the keyboard on which they create their harmony. I clearly have no need to furnish evidence for this desire, this need, the project Iago has in mind when he says that he is acting not "for love and duty" but "for my peculiar end." It is the overwhelming motivation for the entire plot. Yet this desire also extends to every level of society and is immediately wakened whenever and wherever the capacity for being appears. It is shown on several occasions in the play, each time with the same destructive passion that can even wish physical death upon the one whose spirit resists.

This is the case with Cassio, who escapes with his life, but only just. As for Roderigo, who totally succumbs to the evildoings of his so-called associate, things are certainly different. This rich man of leisure is too worthless to excite Iago's jealousy, and if Iago chooses to have Roderigo die, it is only because it serves his purposes. It is again Iago's jealousy, however, and its dangerous effects, that appear in the case of Bianca, and strikingly so. This young woman's role is minor, and she has previously aroused no other feeling in Iago than his disgust for her "lechery" and "lust," since she is a woman of easy virtue who sells herself, most notably to Cassio. But it turns out that Bianca loves Cassio, truly loves him. When she sees him lying in his own blood, after the brawl Iago has instigated to bring about Cassio's demise, her anguished scream immediately troubles Iago and makes him want to destroy her too. Nothing could be more sinister than his sweeping down on her with the words: "Look you pale, mistress? / Do you perceive the gastness of her eyes?" Iago thus pretends to interpret her signs of pain as the indication of a confusion that would prove the young woman's complicity in a crime of which he obviously knows he is the sole author. He declares to those who are close by—who represent the law—that he strongly suspects "this trash." Had his plot succeeded, no doubt an hour later he would have had Bianca condemned and tortured, with the additional wicked pleasure of having distorted the signs of love on her face—a love he cannot dislodge from the world.

III

But it is obviously Othello who is the most important and immediate object of Iago's ontological jealousy. So demandingly and overwhelmingly is Othello that object that he fully confirms the jealousy, which thus gains focus and intensity; it no longer simply dreams of destroying souls but becomes an actual project, the main action of the play, culminating in real deaths, including that of the assassin. Iago's obsession is apparent from the start, and we know from the very first words he speaks that Othello is on his mind. Othello is the "he" toward whom Iago says he harbors rancor, and his frustration is nowhere more evident than in the presence of someone who has being, who has certainty of his being and solidarity both with being and with society's purpose. Iago's is the frustration of a man who cannot attain such a capacity for confidence.

As the general entrusted with a critical mission by the Venetian Senate, Othello clearly is in perfect harmony with his duty, which is as well founded in his eyes as his role in it is legitimate. As I have said, Iago, who seems to be a valuable and extremely experienced officer, had hoped to be named Othello's lieutenant, his second in command—he even has had three "great ones of the city" solicit this position for him. This demonstrates the desire of an apologist for thieving servants—a blatant cynic—to reach a level of responsibility which would allow him to free himself from precisely the kind of degrading position it has been all too easy for him to see in the miserable terms that obsess him. But Othello has turned Iago down for the position, assigning him the role of ensign, which makes him almost a lackey. In other words, Othello has thrust Iago back into his own wicked plans. Worse yet, Othello has chosen Cassio in his place, one of those whom Iago envies because they make living look so easy, because they are at peace with what they are, and consequently at ease with others. Iago cannot find words harsh enough to demean Cassio, attempting to extract and distil from the man's outward demeanor that mysterious substance of self-confidence which he himself lacks. In the first scene he tries even more to belittle Othello, of whose prestige he is well aware. He speaks of Othello's "loving his own pride" and of his "bombast circumstance / Horribly stuffed with epithets of war," a judgment belied by Othello's moving address to the Venetian senators in the council chamber .

Iago resents Othello as an unbearable example of what he is not. Othello forces Iago to experience as enigma and misfortune the feeling of nonmeaning and nonbeing that he could otherwise have accepted as a dismal, though tolerable, part of his worthless existence. It is thus clear why Othello polarizes Iago's worries. On the one hand, this officer coincides with one of the noble commitments—the army and defense of one's country—through which a society can exist, knows it exists, and can be assured of its being. Furthermore, the Moor—who has come to Venice from who knows where in Africa—has just been granted the love of a young Venetian noblewoman, along with all the signs of her passionate feelings. Their union renders

Othello—more essentially still, since the stakes become those of everyday life and, soon, of procreation—someone who benefits from the being that permeates society. Worse yet for Iago's peace of mind, the union shows that Othello possesses or seems to possess within himself the desire and the will to be. Othello is thus clearly the man the ensign has to take down. Devoid of any subplot, *Othello* is all about one grand action: Iago's efforts to subdue the Moor's faith in himself and in others. And perhaps to reveal that this self-confidence is not truly what it thinks it is; that the Othello who has discredited Iago in his own mind might himself be as devoid of substance as is Iago, though perhaps less lucidly so.

A question necessarily arises—as it should on the threshold of any well-constructed tragedy—at the very moment the protagonists enter the scene. Of what value is the feeling Othello inspires that he is sheltered from every threat except those posed by mere accident? Will the same internal self-assurance that allowed the Moor to win over the Senate's confidence and Desdemona's heart be able to protect him from the blows dealt by someone who can only muster up weapons that seem as laughable as they are dangerous to handle: negative readings of his deeds and gestures—slander? Shakespeare, the master storyteller, does everything he can in act 1—which is important since it takes place in Venice, the site of Othello's successes—to indicate the Moor's firmness in the face of danger. He thus also gives us some insight into the strength and nobility of Othello's soul, which is precisely the object of the scene in which Othello appears before the senators. His calm and self-assurance already were plain to see when Desdemona's father came with his officers to arrest Othello, who literally succeeds in sheathing their swords. He finds himself accused by Brabantio, a senator himself, but this time he stands before his peers as his judges. In one of the greatest speeches in the play—the other being his utterance just before his death—Othello's words are of exceptional gravity and beauty.

What does Othello say that lets him be perceived in such a favorable light? He claims it is not through magic that he has won Desdemona's heart, as Brabantio claims. He captivated the young girl's attention solely through telling the story of his past life and its tumultuous episodes. And there was something more, compassion for so many trials and, of course, for so much solitude that made her love him, truly love him. Desdemona recognized this stranger as a being—in the absolute—and she wanted to comfort him by joining her being to his, for all at once she lives her being as an overabundance whose calling is to offer itself fully. In return, this gift of love gave rise to another perhaps similar gift. Othello evokes an exchange that cannot be reduced to sexual attraction, although the two are not mutually exclusive. The exchange does not deny the attraction—it even finds roots in it—but it seeks to go beyond. Othello suggests what Desdemona soon confirms with a conviction that is as radiant as it is simple, namely that love is its own cause, like the sense that one exists, which is the necessary condition of love. He demonstrates a force at work that maintains human reality above mere matter. And Othello's right to say all this seems confirmed by the very nature of his words, which are imbued with an inspiration that imparts to the situations he evokes—the stages of his "pilgrimage," a word that sums up his past life as a quest—the beauty of an object become life and presence. Othello is henceforth of this world or at least seems to be; a world that appears through his words.

This sense of internal certainty, this *virtue,* can surely be recognized in Othello during his next appearance on stage, when he lands in Cyprus, which he must defend, and where the perils of the sea have brought his young bride just ahead of him. Desdemona is waiting for Othello along with several officers. He is surprised to see her, and lets out a cry of joy and pride that beautifully expresses his sense of being fully himself when united with the person he loves. "O my fair warrior!" he exclaims, thereby indicating to what an extent husband and wife feel close to one another in a battle that is not so much against the Turks who are menacing the island as against the uncertainty of life: a battle, which will surely be victorious, of meaning against meaninglessness. In this happy moment, preceding by just a few hours the consummation of the marriage, Othello feels a "calmness," a state of inner peace that he unhesitatingly characterizes as absolute.

How, then, could we doubt that Othello, when faced with Iago's intrigues, will stand firm as a rock, like the island itself, which remains a locus of faith against the infidels, a metaphor for the quality of its defender? Cyprus is the scene of a battle with an as yet unsuspected but equally fearsome adversary, Iago, who has arrived on the island aboard the same ship as Desdemona. But why should this battle be lost? The sea has been crossed without incident, in spite of the great storm.

IV

But *Othello,* after all, is a work of Shakespeare, who, in his tragedies at least, never constructs a character without delving deeply into the substance of existence, molding life as it is, not as we might wish it to be. Since we know what happens in the play following this happy moment, it is not unreasonable to ask whether there is not some flaw in the warrior's armor that might allow us to understand why Iago can believe that the struggle he initiates is not lost from the outset.

Othello himself bids us stop at this point to reconsider the past. To his happy greeting, he adds the fear that the future might not be equal to his present joy. Desdemona does not share his view, exclaiming that heaven must not allow their love and thus their bliss to be diminished. But Othello is worried, which reveals, perhaps, that he feels some doubt about what he is and what he will remain. He kisses Desdemona, twice, confirming their initial commitment. Yet this is precisely when Iago—wickedly and eagerly observing them and noticing the "music" he is incapable of—persuades himself that he will be able to bring it all to ruin. Lost in thought, but soon ready for action, he whispers to himself: "Oh, you are well tuned now! / But I'll set down the pegs that make this music, / as honest as I am."

There certainly is much about Othello to worry about, as we can see if we return to Venice, where the Moor had come to live after his lengthy wanderings. Who was Othello in Venice, notably during the "nine moons" when he rested, all the while maintaining his relations with the senators and other "great ones"? He spoke before three of these in a way Iago judged to be pure "bombast"—like the padding used to line clothing. This judgment seems unfair, however, for we heard Othello's rigorous use of words and the authentic nobility and firmness with which he addressed the Senate. Yet even if it is only malevolence that sees padding in the shoulders of the uniform, the uniform does exist, and Othello wears it with obvious pride; he even refers to it in his last speech. Othello's pride is somewhat equivocal. Why this loyalty to the republic of the doges, and the devotion of at least a part of himself to a society that is as rigorously structured as it is prestigious and powerful?

This society is, in fact, extremely structured. It is an order, a construct of representations and signs, many of which are deeply rooted in reality. It is easy to settle into it, believing that in this reality one can do more than merely survive since the actions it authorizes or suggests allow its members to partake of this structure's profound unity, which seemingly transcends individual goals. Is this not a place and a legitimate backdrop for the sense of being, or of wishing to be, that I have mentioned? Unfortunately, this question is easily answered. Venice is no more the reflection or the authentic extension of the only structure that might claim to accommodate the desire and the project of being—that open structure, wholly founded on love, that brings together in an elementary endeavor, as close as possible to finitude, the major needs of the human condition—than is any other society in history. Unfounded beliefs, fantasies, and inescapably individual interests form knots in the articulation of concepts. They animate the unreal, circulate myths, undo or, more precisely, make a travesty of the universal, thereby producing baseless values, such as the notion that a Turk is a "circumcised dog" that can be killed simply because he has insulted his Serene Highness, the republic. The mind is thus more ensnared than truly sustained by excessive belief in such mental structures.

When someone is tempted to perceive this society as reality itself—which is all the easier to do since it is a Christian civilization, with a religion whose aims are thoroughly cosmic and whose keystone is divine being—something goes wrong at that precise moment when the person who embraces Venice takes excessive pride in its law. In other words, when there is this kind of adherence, being—true being—is only figurative and not truly present. Society has produced merely the image of being, one with lacunae and distortions, since any system that considers its forms as absolutes—even if they are partially true—will only be able to recognize things in general terms and so will never see individual beings grappling with chance in their own particular existence. And those who would expect that such a reduction of being might help them to become present to themselves and to the world will encounter only the disfiguring mirror that reflects, in a false light, an insufficient representation of what they might be. Such persons will know an emptiness and live in a false relation to their own unrealized potential. By agonizing over this vaguely felt alienation and trying to compensate for it by even greater adherence to common values, they run the risk, without even realizing it, of idolizing these values.

So it is not certain that Othello, in the deepest recesses of his will-to-be, has much to gain by becoming the defender of Venice in Cyprus. This is all the more evident—Shakespeare has gone out of his way to show it—since early in his life and well before his allegiance to Venice, Othello was disposed to dream of such image worlds. When, in act 1, Iago suggests the harm Desdemona's father could bring down upon him, Othello says that his merits will protect him and proudly maintains that because he is of royal descent he can speak to anybody in Venice as his equal: "I fetch my life and being / From men of royal siege." Not solely "life," but also "being." Now this being is obviously of the same fictitious nature as the one that can be received from

Venice. Even if kings claim divine right, it is only in the most illusory fashion that they participate in the absolute. Othello's delusion replaces "rugged reality" with the world of brilliant but deceitful appearances provided by the Image.[5] And one can only fear that Othello's search, throughout the battles and adventures that have absorbed his life since his "boyish days," has been to recover the kind of ontological security of which some accident has stripped him. In short, Othello's allegiance to Venice does not guarantee that when the time comes, his desire for being will stand like a rock, unmoved by the onslaught of the forces of evil.

It is true that when he evokes his adventurous years, when danger and misfortune had power to touch his heart as well as to strengthen his courage, he speaks of them, with Desdemona in mind, as a "pilgrimage"—a word whose reference to spiritual needs can in no way be attenuated. It is also true that so much intensity and so much chaos in his earlier life recalls an aspiration of an equally spiritual nature, the one Arthur Rimbaud emphasizes in *Une saison en enfer;* and this is not the only common point between Rimbaud and the Moor. Let me repeat, Othello indicates that he would not have wished to sacrifice his "unhoused free condition" for anything other than his commitment to Desdemona. This seems to demonstrate that his allegiance to Venice is only relative, whereas to Desdemona it is absolute. Put another way, in his relationship to Venice, Othello is both protective of his freedom and interested in championing this society as a leader of mercenaries or a *condottiere* in the previous century would have done. Through this relationship he can let his ego prosper as a construct of the self, made up of representations and values that are of the same nature and fragility as those of the civilization he has adopted. He can revel in the unreal, and leave his will-to-be exposed to countless snares. But with Desdemona, in a private relationship in which the real elements of finite existence signify both an obligation and a dwelling place, Othello would seem to have found a way to break away from his chimerical ego for the sake of a now fundamental "I" determined solely by the desire to go ever forward in recognition of the Other, in sharing the essential—in what can be called incarnation.

To appreciate both the authenticity of Othello's will-to-be and the robustness of his armor, we must consider his giving of himself to Desdemona. We must think about this love, which might be the rock on which the wave

---

5. The expression "rugged reality" is from Arthur Rimbaud's "Adieu," in *Une saison en enfer,* 116.—Trans.

breaks. It is a question less easily answered than that of Othello's allegiance to Venice. It addresses a deed that is decided within his own person, separately from his moral principles (often simply the reflection of the culture of the times). Irrespective of his value judgments, this deed can only be decided by subsequent ones and in terms of an existence that is yet to come. We should therefore hesitate before sounding out his soul. Is there not, in the deepest reaches of Othello's relation to himself, a free will that distinguishes between good and evil in a manner incomprehensible to the psychology of ordinary motivation?

V

It is difficult to make up one's mind about Othello, to know in advance whether he is capable or incapable of thwarting the traps inherent in his condition as a speaking being, alienated from himself by the illusions of the image world. But let us not forget that Iago, in one of the most important events of the play, chooses to follow an intuition which, though it may or may not be correct, he does not hesitate to act upon. He draws a conclusion and makes a decision, for when he sees Othello's double kiss in Cyprus that confirms to Desdemona Othello's happiness, his attachment to her, and his inability to imagine even the slightest possible discord between them, Iago whispers— with real determination—the words I have previously cited regarding the discord he plans to bring to their music. He sees before him two people whose confidence wakens the very music of the spheres, illuminates the great chain of being, and knows that heaven approves of their union through the sacrament of marriage. Iago is nevertheless unflinching in his decision to undo this harmony. A few minutes later he will already have begun to put in motion the plan that will bring him success.

Since Iago will in fact go far—very far—in his plan, it is useful to study how he goes about it, what his hypotheses are, what he concludes at various stages, and what unfortunately his successes are. As we shall see, Iago is not only someone who is amazed and frustrated by the experience of others, demonstrating as it does a will-to-be he cannot comprehend; he is also the perceptive psychologist who, while searching in others for the origin of this relation to oneself that so irritates his intellect, customarily taps the hidden behavioral mechanisms in which he has learned to recognize, to his great joy, the workings of bad faith and the beautiful soul's naïveté. He has thus become an intimate of all that is implicit if not unconscious, and he can behave like a psychotherapist, but not for the good. He acts, rather, to disturb everything that can be disturbed, to bring every tension to the breaking point, and to devastate what seeks to come into being. Like any true practitioner, Iago does not hesitate to question his hypotheses, to readjust them to their object by changing and refining his plan of action.

What is Iago's plan? Let us first note that if he hates—and he certainly does—the faith he sensed in Othello, but also in Desdemona, in the instant he described as "music," he clearly feels that she is not as vulnerable as Othello. This is apparent as of the first scene of act 2, when Iago speaks directly to Desdemona during a rather long exchange, which Shakespeare must have deliberately developed at such length. Cassio is present, and Iago, irritated by his chivalrous manners, has just lashed out against his own wife, Emilia, as well as against all women. In jest—to attenuate and hide the anguish Desdemona feels rising within her, since Othello is still in peril on the open sea—in jest, but also perhaps in troubled amazement at his hateful words, Desdemona asks Iago what, under such conditions, he could say in praise of her. The slanderer initially evades the issue, then throws all caution to the wind and lets himself speak.

At first Iago seeks to get around Desdemona's request by protesting that he is nothing if not critical, his caustic nature being the glue in which all of his other ideas are ensnared, like birds in a trap. Then he tries to put off answering, but cannot restrain himself—since his muse nonetheless "labours," and perhaps this particular word that came to Iago is worth considering more closely—from unleashing, from the depths of his wickedness, distichs exemplary of his ill will toward those who, whether beautiful or ugly, intelligent or foolish, he believes have only fornication in mind. After listening to him, Desdemona tells him sharply that he is wrong, but still insists that he answer her question. Despite his malice, what sort of praise should this obtuse satirist nonetheless bestow upon women who undoubtedly deserve praise?

Still ironic, Iago improvises a poem that brings together all the qualities of the perfect woman, but its last line abruptly falls back into derision and sarcasm: this perfectly virtuous woman will soon find herself ready "to suckle fools and chronicle small beer." In this straightforward dialogue with Desdemona, Iago has shown himself capable only of his most ordinary, stereotypical, and basest thoughts; nothing at the level of her resistant intelligence and calm confidence. Worse yet, Iago has shown his hand and unmasked himself, thereby perhaps compromising his plan, which requires him to remain for everybody the "most honest" and friendly officer, as he clearly has succeeded in appearing until now. Is Iago intimidated, hence troubled? Does he understand that he cannot break into Desdemona's inner world or unsettle her deepest convictions, her quiet strength, and does this throw him off course?

On this occasion, in any case, Iago has revealed himself as exactly the opposite of what he will soon be when speaking with Othello: all dissimulation and ruse. Doubtless his exchange with Desdemona would have left him with nothing more than an unpleasant memory, were it not for the fact that her words and deeds on another level have given him an idea that he immediately sets in motion. Desdemona was gracious with Cassio, who also has landed in Cyprus. She offered her hand, and he took it. She answered his gallantries with indulgent smiles full of goodwill. These are ways of the world that are meaningless to a young bride whose life has been fulfilled. But Iago wastes no time in classifying her deeds into the usual categories by which he judges women—hypocrisy, tantalizing invitations, lustful thoughts, adultery. This indicates to Iago that as impervious as Desdemona might be to his villainous attacks, her exterior behavior can still make his slander seem justifiable. So what is there to stop Iago, skillful observer that he is, from drawing Othello's attention to what is potentially equivocal in her outward appearance? Isn't this the way to ruin the Moor, to use the one person Iago cannot get to directly?

Iago is well aware, if only since Othello's speech to the senators before his hasty departure for Cyprus, that however much Othello is in love with Desdemona and however much he wants to love her with an intensity transcending more ordinary relationships, he is nonetheless bound to the system of representations that make up Venice. He is bound to its noblest values, but doubtless also to something that is occasionally caught up in their framework—its most dangerous prejudices. Iago figures that by presenting a woman reconstructed according to the "Venetian model," he can place her husband, Othello, in a position of being disturbed and even undone by those ways of seeing and judging which, though contemptible, are yet firmly rooted in the supposed good sense of a corrupt society. Othello might be able to survive such potential disenchantment, for Iago does not appear to wish him dead, at least not during this first part of the play. But the Moor will be deprived of his music, of what is best in his will-to-be, and of love as the means to this will-to-be, once he makes the devastating discovery that a woman's promise of love is only an illusion.

Such is Iago's plan, and we should note how truly diabolical it is, since the devil's only goal is to deconstruct a person's faith in what I call being, while he himself—the great outcast—can neither feel this attraction nor understand its resulting force. Just as the devil can only seduce, and needs the signature of those he deceives, so Iago has Othello freely choose, at each step of his progressive entrapment, to believe in Desdemona's unfaithfulness and guilt. Othello even adds other reasons to those offered him: "for I am black" and "for I am declined / Into the vale of years." The Moor works on himself to the point of signing the diabolical contract that he could have torn up, and so brings about his own ruin and damnation. Iago is also a very traditional devil, a direct descendent of medieval theater, when he places his victim behind a door to hear a conversation in the course of which Cassio refers explicitly to Bianca, which Othello—in his pain and anger—will take as yet another reason to incriminate Desdemona. Othello believes he sees what Iago wants him to see. The conversation between Cassio and Iago about Bianca is thus like one of those illusory representations the devil can dangle before those he seeks to destroy.

Such is Iago's plan, and as the play unfolds, we can see that it obviously works, gradually revealing to Iago and to us the conflict that can arise in a soul between the world it represents to itself—the world of its prejudices— and the nonetheless very real desire to be fully self-present as well as present to another being. The perverse psychotherapist makes great strides in his discovery of human truth, thus allowing Shakespeare, with Iago as his research tool, to rise to a consideration of good and evil that will become central in his subsequent plays, assuring their greatness.

VI

How does Iago proceed? He simply recalls for Othello the so-called keys to a woman's behavior that he had dangled, perhaps already menacingly, before an indignant Desdemona. Iago reminds Othello, whose anguish is beginning to build, that the beauty of "Venetian women" is only the outer appearance of their lechery, the way of the world. From this perspective, Desdemona is merely another Venetian woman, and Iago will immediately suggest that this typicality can be observed in her gestures, words, and attitudes. He does so with the authority earned from his supposed knowledge of life, which dictates that suspicion is the rule of thumb with regard to all women.

Let us not forget that the field was wide open for this maneuver, which seems crude in our eyes, in Shakespeare's century of ruses, plundering, unbridled trickery and jugglery, and endless play on appearances—whose ubiquity is revealed as much by Montaigne as by Elizabethan theater and Italian novels. Never so frequently as in that period, and never with such cunning, have masks been worn and roles been played on the social stage, which became the source of Ben Johnson's dramas even more than of Shakespeare's tragedies. Othello is nevertheless of a "constant, loving, noble nature," as Iago reminds himself, and it will take some work to dislodge him from his instinctive confidence. Is Othello jealous? No—as Desdemona knows perfectly well, and as she assures her confidant, Emilia—he is not inherently jealous. What needs to be cultivated, so that Othello will become jealous to the point of suffocating, is the weed of suspicion, with particular care given to the preconceptions that lie in waiting in his mind.

The subtlest part of Iago's strategy to raise suspicion is that he begins by reinforcing the preconceptions of the person he wishes to break—those allowing him to doubt and condemn. The greatest preconception is the unwavering conviction that purity and chastity, particularly in marriage, must constitute women's mode of being. It would be quite dangerous for Iago's plan if Othello, once goaded to think about the supposed relationship between Desdemona and Cassio, began to question the validity of traditional moral values. For this would make him too understanding of his wife, perhaps even willing to resume their relation at a new level of intimacy. Iago therefore must continually stress the importance of a woman's faithfulness and chastity. And he chooses Desdemona as his example since she imitates virtue so well, thus making her all the more guilty.

This is a difficult game, in which Desdemona must simultaneously be seen from the outside as the picture of virtue, and represented as truly shameless beneath the appearances she regulates with cool mastery. The game is worth it, however, since it will both discountenance Othello's love and draw him into the hazy areas of his own psyche, where this love will be bogged down more surely than by simple disappointment at being betrayed or his own harsh moral judgments.

Indeed, what happens when Desdemona becomes someone who knows what virtue is—as her artful imitation of it proves—but wants lechery? Through her ability to preserve the freedom of the most blatantly sexual desire beneath the network of values in which she has been brought up, she seems all the more resolutely a person whose only place, need, and truth is in naked pleasure. But can Othello see her in this way—no matter how disappointed he is in his love and in his esteem—and still resist the kind of attraction such licentiousness and depravity can arouse? Sexuality can adapt to society's representations of itself. Yet it always exceeds the pact it has made, and loves to transgress it in giving free reign to its wilder side. Much as Othello is taken with these values, and sincerely as he proclaimed his chastity before the senators, he still has dormant within him this background of desire. In consequence, when Iago evokes Desdemona under the harsh light of his insinuations, she suddenly becomes nothing more than a body, an occasion for forbidden thoughts—an object of condemnation who is thus all the more disturbing and seductive, leading the man who once loved her chastely to flights of imagination that trouble him deeply, even when he is not fully aware of it. In other words, when Desdemona is judged, she is eroticized—eroticized because judged. Where morality is scandalized, sexual attraction is intensified, and detached from a love devoted to soul as well as body for the sake of more primary satisfactions. This, in turn, sets out of tune the beautiful, pure "music."

This process is what Iago has in mind, as is clearly demonstrated by the work he is about to undertake. He starts by suggesting Desdemona's double game and then makes titillating comments on her secret habits, the goal being more to inflame Othello's desire than to confirm his suspicions. When Iago suggests to Othello that he should imagine Desdemona in bed—in *his* bed—"naked with her friend . . . / An hour or more, not meaning any harm," and when he recounts Cassio's purported dream and describes how Cassio takes pleasure in Desdemona's body, he intends to make Othello see this body, to drag him into the labyrinth of fantasies. This is also what Iago is hoping for: when the most basic urge seeks to be unleashed, it runs up against the representations and values that society accepts or reveres. It dreams of transgressing these values, but they nevertheless remain in place, conditioning the very dream that seeks to deny their existence. Contradictions thereby arise within this dream, allowing fantasies to proliferate that are as destabilizing to Othello as they are perverse. For instance, he immediately needs Cassio, needs him lying on Desdemona—which Iago suggests he might see by hiding, secretly watching the man possessing the woman— in order to maintain, in the image he has of his wife, the erotic intensity whose novelty is now a necessity for him. On the one hand, such images deeply trouble those who are not used to them. Othello is ashamed of what he feels, to the point of being willing to throw all of the blame onto Desdemona. On the other hand, and this is the most disastrous part, these images place him under the power of Iago, who has become their purveyor.

Othello eagerly listens to the one he ought to silence. He could have gone straight to Cassio to ask for an explanation. Even before that, he could have spoken with Desdemona rather than rebuffing and insulting her in a way that is actually quite enigmatic. No, Othello needs to preserve his doubt, to prolong the moment separating doubt from the impending punishment. In the meantime, he becomes Iago's accomplice—Iago who only wishes his demise. He accepts Iago's vile innuendoes and embraces his words as his own. Is Othello an accomplice? Perhaps he is more of a slave, as when, in a moment of complete degradation, he lets Iago hide him behind the pillar or the door and becomes a voyeur spying on Cassio's conversation, which serves both his outraged anger and the pleasure he cannot avow.

VII

Iago penetrates a mind and a heart with an aptitude for intimacy of which, with the possible exception of love, perhaps only "ontological" jealousy is capable. He has found a way to draw Othello, who is of such a "constant, loving, noble nature," to what remains most instinctive in his being. He draws him to what is most separated from the meaning and from the good he nevertheless dreamed of when he pledged his allegiance to Venice, and dreamed of even more when later he sought to be united, body and soul, to Desdemona. If Iago—the enemy observing Othello, and the servant who has successfully made a slave of his master—did not have more important things to attend to, he could now enjoy contemplating the initial results of his malicious alchemy.

On the second day, the situation is indeed catastrophic for Othello. Eros and love—brought together in weeks past through Othello's union with Desdemona—have now been set apart. Where eros makes its way, love is dissipated since its object is no longer perceptible. Worse yet, love lingers, but as a memory that cannot be situated under present circumstances. If Othello wanted to revive this love, he naturally would have to begin by destroying what has taken its place: both the body that he now desires too obscenely and—to free himself from the sin of loving so poorly—the demon he needs to believe now resides in that body and controls it. This dissociation of eros and love makes it tempting to kill Desdemona in order to free the previous image—that of an angel—from the body, the prison, in which it has perished. Thus, as Othello smothers Desdemona, he also movingly evokes the light he once saw in her. And he smothers rather than stabs her to avoid having blood sully the pure white beauty that death will restore to her. Desdemona dies not so much because Othello is convinced of her guilt as because he has desired her in the wrong way, thanks to the doubts Iago has spread and the perverse passions they have engendered in Othello.

It is not only Desdemona who dies in this degradation of what Othello was or thought he was. The fantasies that have taken over his thoughts arise from his perceiving only certain aspects of situations and beings—those that suit the desire that seeks satisfaction in them. Yet they are not everything. What is missing is the indivisible reality of beings as a whole. When this reality disappears, Othello's experience of the unity between one thing and another, between one person and another, also disappears, and it is this experience that assures the presence of being—a presence beyond those reductionist image-worlds. In recovering this presence, the mind also manages to hear a little of its music. The ability to apprehend beings in their immediate totality, rather than from a certain angle—to perceive their ties to others, moving from a seemingly distinct particularity to the underlying unity that is the true order of life and the place where such life becomes transparent—may be called knowledge through symbols. It means understanding existence through a few symbols, those that reflect finitude and retrace its real needs. The symbol and love are thus at the same level in the creation of a world suited to human society, the first producing "the sun and the other stars" (*il sole et l'altre stelle*), the other moving them. Should one of the two be missing, however, both can die. Thus, when fantasies stifle these symbols, Othello is deprived of the memory of being, and finds himself simply among things.

Othello's world in Cyprus is now made up of things: a reified and smothered reality. This is the world of his second day. Above all, Desdemona's body has become a thing; simply a thing. Until the dawn of this catastrophic day, her body had been an indivisible part of her confident presence, one of the music's registers. But in the Moor's distrustful eyes, objects all around this young woman that might have been experienced—through a life shared—as truly present have become merely the possible traces of what Othello has not seen and what obsesses him. Fantasies transform everything into signs, thus substituting the opaque and deserted materiality of enigma for the mystery of all that is.

This disastrous transmutation is most vividly revealed in the famous handkerchief that Shakespeare had the genius to carry over from Cinthio's novella, creating with it a spectrum of the successive ideas Othello reads into it. At the beginning, in Venice, before their marriage and departure for Cyprus, this handkerchief was one of the ways by which Othello had shown his love for Desdemona. It incorporated his active presence, found its place in the world the two were building, and had all the qualities of a *symbol*. When Desdemona lets it fall, however, she delivers it over to Iago, who will use it to prove to Othello the existence of an adulterous liaison. This handkerchief thus becomes a *sign* signifying solely by metonymy its accidental relationship to the situation it reveals. Its meaning is not intrinsic, to the point that its materiality freely turns it into something impenetrable, something beyond any human meaning, in a world of darkness where nothing can act as a guide except, as soon becomes apparent, magic.

Othello's degradation is surely the saddest part of the drama, for it also contaminates Desdemona. We might have hoped that in the face of adversity she would maintain if not the capacity for hope then at least her feeling for what ought to be, for what is worthwhile. But this is clearly not the case. Faced with Othello's completely unjustifiable behavior—behavior he does not even attempt to defend—and accused in a way she does not understand, though she knows she is innocent, Desdemona will nonetheless try to persuade herself that Othello is right while she is wrong. Such an attitude is surely bound up with the love she still feels, but it also reveals her tendency to accept unquestioningly the reductive precepts governing a wife's duties—which insist above all that she be submissive. Worse yet, her relation to herself and to her own speech has now been changed.

When confronted with Othello's incomprehensible anger, Desdemona—who was so firm before her judges in Venice—does not know how to assume responsibility for the loss of her handkerchief. She resorts to lying, which is perhaps her first fatal misstep, since it not only confirms Othello's belief that she is a liar but also deprives both herself and Othello of the possibility of an open, perhaps salutary explanation. And yet, from the outset, she had inscribed the necessity of and the right to such an explanation in her understanding of marriage. Such an open and direct exchange might have been the object of the "suit" of which she had said that Othello, by accepting it, would thereby prove his love, given the anguish he would have to vanquish in order to respond.

> Nay, when I have a suit
> Wherein I mean to touch your love indeed,
> It shall be full of poise and difficult weight,
> And fearful to be granted.

As Othello increasingly becomes the possessive husband, however, Desdemona forgets this great request—the very essence of her love. She becomes the wife who wishes to be nothing more than an object among her husband's other belongings. Her freedom is smothered, but with her consent, which thereby anticipates the murder whereby Othello brings about their mutual ruin. It is thus significant to see how the change in her words—ordinary words—goes hand in hand with the change in her being. As recently as the day before, she spoke frankly and boldly with Iago. She listened without flinching—severely but without flinching—to his many offensive words and vile ideas. But she has become incapable of uttering the word "whore," which Othello now uses and abuses. Freedom has abdicated before the most external of moral imperatives, one sadly conforming to the prejudices of the times.

VIII

As an indirect consequence that is clearly worth considering, Desdemona becomes the treacherous Iago's second victim, and this to his great joy, since it offers him revenge for the previous day's humiliation. To understand the fervor of Desdemona's attraction to the Moor before it was so surprisingly altered, closer consideration must be given to what Desdemona is or has been. Who was the Desdemona of act 1, and, above all, who was the girl who reached maturity around the time Othello appeared, and beneath the clearly conformist thumb of Brabantio, her father the senator? Whether she was loyal to Brabantio's values or not, it is clear that she felt their full impact and offered no noticeable resistance to them, as evidenced by her father's surprise when she flees his house. He thought she was perfectly calm and obedient. And it is true that she dutifully attended to household tasks, which Iago spitefully compares to chronicling "small beer," and that she only entered rooms where men were speaking when her duties allowed it. It should also be noted that while Desdemona's father represents only the most conventional and empty of social obligations, her mother is strangely absent from her life, despite her youth. In her final anguished moments, the only thing Desdemona says about her mother, who seems to have long been absent, is that she had had a servant named Barbary who had died of a broken heart and love betrayed. Through this allusion to the servant who presided over the first years of her life, it is almost as if Desdemona were indicating that her childhood attention had been focused on someone other than her mother; whereas, even at an age when one shares important thoughts with all kinds of people, one can hardly acquire all the teaching needed for life from a mere servant. In Desdemona's life, a weak father is matched by an absent mother. There was "no friendly hand," as Rimbaud would say; "Where is help to be found?"[6]

From this solitude, it follows that if the desire to be and to give meaning to life is somehow to exist in Desdemona as she reaches maturity, she will have to receive from someone totally new the support necessary to shore up her faith. She hopes for an arrival, an overwhelming encounter, but one to which she confers a special meaning. The person who arrives must be someone whose will-to-be is clearly free of conventions and prejudice; whose will, in other words, is for a future guided by the reevaluation of moral propositions, and by a need for simple, total truth. Desdemona is ready to respond to the one who will offer to share in the search for this truth, recognizing and loving him for this very reason. It goes without saying, however, that this recognition carries with it a major demand: that Desdemona also be recognized as willing to engage in this search. Not simply a wife in the old sense of the word, but a full partner in the dynamics of truth, where the necessity of trust is clearly the only true form of love.

At first, Desdemona behaves in a way that is both welcoming and demanding. Her words in the presence of the senators and her father are direct and frank, revealing a boundless commitment of mind and also of body, equally a locus of truth. When she asks to follow Othello to Cyprus—a courageous decision given the Turkish threat and the risk of defeat, followed by certain torture if not death—she makes it plain that she will not sacrifice what she desires, and that she owes her husband "the rites for which I love him." At this moment she clearly wants her destiny to be a life fully present to herself and to Othello.

A detail at the end of act 4 merits our attention since it confirms Desde-

6. Arthur Rimbaud, "Adieu," 116.—Trans.

mona's wish and reveals the whole of Shakespeare's genius. Othello has just subjected Desdemona to his contempt, which is all the more overwhelming because unexpected and inexplicable. She senses that her great desire for harmony and transparency is coming to an end. At the close of this second day, broken and apprehending disaster, she finds herself in her room, where the "rites" of love were only once performed, near those sheets in which she asks the dumbfounded Emilia to shroud her when the day comes. After one of Othello's outbursts, and to this same Emilia, Desdemona had already said, "Answers have I none." Yet now she does speak, pensively, like someone withdrawn into the depths of her being. She divulges what I mentioned previously, namely that her mother had a servant named Barbary who was in love with a boy who betrayed her. She adds that Barbary was fond of a song which, in its own way, pondered love—the "song of willow" that "she died singing." This song, Desdemona says,

> Will not go from my mind; I have much to do
> But to hang my head all at one side
> And sing it like poor Barbary.

What is the meaning of this clearly emotional memory? First of all, that Desdemona cannot repress the desire for the fullness and self-evidence of life, the willow, the "green willow" being the tree of life that grows green again, eternally, with every spring. It is the major symbol in the song, taking precedence over the other tree, the sycamore, in whose shadow the grieving soul takes refuge. It is not in the song as such, however, that we find the most moving avowal of the vanquished Desdemona. Rather, it is in the image of the bent head of the dying servant; for to bend one's head in this way—"all at one side"—is what newborn babies do before they have the strength to hold their heads up above their shoulders. This is also when they are still separated from language, when they exist prior to the world made up by words, prior to what language makes us live and suffer—which is to say, our desire for meaning, for happiness, but also, sadly, the realization of the vanity of such dreams. In remembering Barbary's posture, Desdemona understands at what depth in her being the poor servant bore her renunciation at the very moment when she nonetheless sang the "song of willow," the "green willow," an image of the good one might wish to share. Desdemona lets it be known that in her present situation she too could well use the affection and care provided to those little beings whose heads still hang.

Desdemona has therefore experienced the greatest of all desires, the desire to be, which is born and lives beneath all other desires, at a level even deeper than the unconscious. Othello's arrival into her previously deserted existence allowed her to shore up this desire. But was she justified in doing so? This is the question we now must answer, by reliving with Desdemona, more critically, the days when she still had hope. We shall come to understand that she might well have worried about what attracted her to the Moor, which was hardly unambiguous, as Shakespeare shows through the comments and speeches he carefully attributes to Othello when he is still in Venice. Consider, for instance, the Moor's eloquent speech to the senators and the doge. It is richly evocative of vast caves and "deserts idle," of "rocks and hills, whose heads touch heaven." Yet it also evokes strange beings, cannibals and monsters, along with the deeds of a young man and then of an older one, deeds that are as surprising as their twists and turns are endless: "moving accidents by flood and field." At first glance, we too might have the impression that the man so freed from ordinary ways of thinking and existing is present to himself in a way rarely seen in society as it exists everywhere and at all times, with its frozen representations and conventional, debatable values.

Yet can we forget that what we are hearing are words—words whose capacity for evocation is greater than any given situation in lived experience? So much so that these words can tempt the speaker with the pleasures of the imaginary, when it would be much better for him to experience life directly, in accordance with its own needs and laws—the most fundamental of which is finitude. A speech such as Othello's, impetuously imaginative and lyrical as it is, is nothing more than the kind of writing that poems are made of: sentences that transgress conceptual formulations only to find themselves captive of representations within the unconscious, which are themselves rigidly closed to presence. This speech is just the first level of poetry. Its second level is the only true one: the wish to free oneself of these dreams by systematically tearing up the specious writing of which the dreams are made. During his speech in Venice, Othello is a "poet" and, as such, is seductive. Yet, perhaps he is only superficially a poet, in a way that does not inquire into the real person, of whom we know almost nothing concerning the kind of life that might be shared with him.

Who is Othello, really? To answer this question—leaving aside his last words for the time being—let us consider the one other moment when

Othello talks about himself, openly, since his guard is down. In his monologue in act 1, when he is enjoying complete success, he is in total control. But
now, under the influence of Iago's insinuations, he is deeply disturbed and is
therefore likely to say things about himself that are more revealing, to be
caught unawares, especially since his ability to censor his thoughts has now
been weakened.

Othello tells a strange story that may very well be fictional but is nonetheless one of those tales that originate in the nocturnal regions where dreams
take form. And the handkerchief in question even seems to be an image of the
unconscious, with its many dreamlike folds and mysterious figures, whether
embroidered or painted, that fascinate Cassio when he sees them, although
his own worries ought to have diverted his attention from them. What is this
handkerchief? It is the gift Othello offered to Desdemona as a sign of love
and as a token of their union. But it is also the handkerchief that Desdemona
drops as she is using it to bind Othello's forehead when he claims to have a
headache—the disguised expression of his obsession with the horns attributed to cuckolded husbands. Desdemona loses the handkerchief, for which
Othello bitterly reproaches her since for him it is one more proof of her betrayal. He tells her—and this is the story that interests me here—that the
gift was a reenactment of the one his mother had made to him on her death-
bed. This woman—who, like Desdemona's mother and other mothers in
Shakespeare's works, is nowhere else mentioned in the play—had entrusted
the handkerchief to her son. He guarded it closely, undoubtedly out of affection for her, but also and perhaps mainly because of the power she had suggested inhered in this handkerchief, a power she had confirmed with her own
husband, Othello's father. When the time should come for the husband to
give the handkerchief to his young bride, it would allow her to preserve
the love of the man she married. "But if she lost it / Or made a gift of it,"
as Othello's dying mother told him, the husband's eyes "Should hold her
loathed and his spirits should hunt / After new fancies," which, as Othello
adds, would be "perdition / As nothing else could match."

What can be learned from this story? First of all that Othello's mother
seems to hold men in low esteem and has very little confidence in herself and
in women in general—since they need magic to keep the one they love. And
so we have to recognize that until the time—the "seven years"—when he
stopped seeing her, this mother was unable to instill in her son any great faith
in the reality of love, at least in its constancy in men. Othello did in fact
listen to this message, and believed it since he recounts it with such obvious

fervor. But there is something contradictory in his own gift. Desdemona clearly believes that this gift is a sign of his love. She holds the handkerchief most dear, and kisses it often, as Emilia tells us. It is hard to believe that Othello didn't regard it in the same way. But what a strange lover who can only express himself by offering his wife something that will allow her to be sheltered from his potential weakness, which could result in his despising her and hunting "after new fancies"! Why should Othello wish, out of love, to protect Desdemona from the deficiency of his own love? At the very least there are two levels to Othello, two ways of living his relationship with Desdemona that apparently are not mutually exclusive.

These two levels do, in fact, exist and are easy to distinguish from the first days of Othello and Desdemona's relationship in Venice. The obvious level is the love that Desdemona rightly perceives in Othello, since there is no doubt that one who knows how to envelop his stories in such an aura of presence truly does want to free himself from the rigid representations that veil the reality of others. He is ready to love: to love, for instance, the young woman who listens to him with such eagerness. Yet, this feeling may also be only the illusion of being and of the will-to-be that exists in the facile forms of writing. Indeed, in the same period Othello could say to Iago—who took careful note of it—that he fetched "life and being / From men of royal siege," a fact he some day will "promulgate." To think in such a fashion is to draw on a social structure which, with its values and images, encourages a person to build him- or herself up as an ego, with limited principles and ideas, and little desire to transgress these. And this ego does exist in Othello as a way of thinking and feeling borrowed from Venice and bound to Venetian ideology, as is clear from Othello's dying words, supreme expression of the contradictions he has never managed to resolve: "I have done the state some service, and they know't. / No more of that," he says as he sheds tears for the drama that has devastated his personal life. But he cannot help returning to this service of his, recalling how one day he "smote" a Turk simply because he had insulted Venice. And what has Othello just said of Desdemona, if not that she is innocent of all the crimes of which he has accused her? Yet he does so without incriminating the categories of thought he has received from Venice, the ones that have prompted him to think of her in just such a reproachful manner. The Othello who, for so many years, has lived his life as a "pilgrimage" may really be the "I" aspiring to be freed from the collective representations paralyzing love. But he is also the ego seeking an opportunity to be affirmed, to crystallize, and to take full advantage of the gift of self-confidence that pride constantly requires. Unfortunately, this gift is precisely what the beautiful young woman who admires and loves him can provide. It is hard not to see that if Othello's desire "to be" plays a role in his love for Desdemona, an even more powerful factor is the easily narcissistic self-concern that enjoys mirroring its understanding of itself in the eyes of another, and is moved by the sympathy and compassion it sees in the tears that well up in them. Othello loves Desdemona, but perhaps he loves her tenderness more.

Hence the handkerchief. Someone who loves in this fashion surely cherishes the object of his love for the confidence she brings him. This person wants what is his, even if only to preserve this confidence. He nevertheless obscurely senses that his own ego forbids a deeper attachment. This ego will always "hunt / After new fancies," feeling only disgust, as all dreams do, for existence in the here-and-now. In short, by giving Desdemona the handkerchief, Othello is thinking not only of protecting his future wife but also of freeing his highest aspiration from his wicked pride and from his dream. He is trying to hold in check what I call his ego by using what does indeed exist at this level (and only there): magic.

And this explains Othello's distress on noticing that Desdemona has lost what is above all a talisman. This gift demonstrates that Othello has put his hope in something whose efficacy is purely external. It also indicates, as Iago notes, Othello's refusal to confront the internal contradiction that weakens and threatens to destroy him. From the moment he first took an interest in Desdemona, some part of Othello steadfastly refused self-awareness. So there was no real possibility for the kind of exchange that would have gotten to the bottom of things, that might have undone the illusory for the sake of the truth, creating the dynamics of reciprocal presence and the musical cords that allow one to be. Hence the "suit" that Desdemona had hoped to make on some great occasion—the "suit" which, if granted, would have been proof of her husband's love—is destined for disappointment. And so we are sad when we see her give up her project, her dream, for it signals her unconscious acknowledgment that Othello is no longer capable of the effort required for a shared life.

X

In life, the worst is not always inevitable, since we still can believe in free will. Even with these somber thoughts in mind, we can ask ourselves whether things really had to turn to disaster. Was it fated that Iago should slip so promptly and perniciously between Othello and the object of his love?

This raises the question of Shakespeare's pessimism, at least during the period when he wrote two of his darkest tragedies, *King Lear* and *Macbeth*. Love could have been the basis for everything. Othello exclaims, "when I love thee not, / Chaos is come again." Yet, love, it would seem, is impossible. Evil exists at the very root of words. In *King Lear*, Cordelia nevertheless remains Cordelia. If she dies so unjustly, in a fashion more moving than anything else in Shakespeare's tragedies, it is because of blind chance. And the gods, if they exist, seem not to have granted success to Edmund—Iago's next of kin. Nor did they grant it to Regan or Goneril. Good wins out. And if dissension already begins to appear among the victors, Shakespeare makes sure to erase it. He places it in the background, as if to emphasize, by contrast, the mysterious power that ensures the ever-renewed struggle for justice, and for truth. In *Macbeth*, too, villainy and cynicism succumb. In *Othello*, whose conclusions seem so devastating, several factors suggest that the noble desire to be, despite being repeatedly bogged down in contradictions that cannot be resolved, yet remains a fact that cannot be neglected—which gives it its chance to be somehow effective.

One such factor—a not unimportant one—is provided by Iago himself. His jealousy of what he feels is Othello's authentic desire to be—beneath the contradictions and flaws that Iago is the first to notice—is evidence that the need to be is present even in those who are mired in hatred of the world and in fascination with meaninglessness. This feeling is so strong that Iago, an enemy of all that is good, will not hesitate to give up his life, to be cruelly tortured, in exchange for the benefit derived from feeling, if only for a moment, the palest reflection of being. What else can Iago expect from having brought down Othello? Will not the pride of success or the joy of vengeance immediately be swallowed up by his idea of the futility of everything and his indifference to pleasure? After the Moor's defeat, will he not have to visit upon others this same work of deadly destruction; the work of a Sisyphus who is plainly in hell? As the action unfolds, it becomes clear that Iago is taking more and more risks, as if at the very moment of his victory he wants to be unmasked. When he is finally found out, what a strange satisfaction he exudes! Before the distraught Venetians he envelops himself in silence and announces: "Demand me nothing: what you know, you know; / From this time forth I never will speak a word." The reason for this somber satisfaction, so obviously saturated with pride, surely must be that the apparent gratuity of the crime—monstrous as it is—makes its author an enigma to all around him. And enigma makes something visible. Iago thus will be seen and can imagine himself "being," if only for an instant, even if this being is opaque, lacking in depth, and consisting only in what rejects order in the world—rocky debris, refuse strewn along a path, noticed but largely ignored.

This turns Iago into something vile and unclean—something that in the Middle Ages would have marked him as the devil. Iago is on the outer edge of a human reality whose threshold he could not or would not cross. He has found a way to imitate, even if only externally, the presence he has denounced and decided to destroy. It follows that all of his actions during the past two days have been directed at reaching this goal, the only one to which he could aspire. We may wonder whether evil in the world, evil in general, does not always have this aim—to accede to being, even while denying, ridiculing, trying to destroy it, and even if only by grasping its exterior. It thereby sets the being of nonbeing, the presence of absence, against those humans who seem only able to think and live in terms of the need for being, even if in exile.

Iago, paradoxically, is proof of the desire to be. And if the proof he represents operates in an obscure zone, another, deeply moving proof is offered in the foreground: the tears Othello sheds during his final moments, comparing them to the "medicinable gum" of certain Arabian trees. In betraying Desdemona, Othello has betrayed being itself. He has not even understood his sin, and dies in astonishment, as much an enigma to himself as Iago is to those around him. Does Othello then have the right to this reference, a passing reflection of the Grace that only heaven can dispense? He does, for his tears prove that despite his errors and weaknesses there was within him goodwill toward existence, a desire for the desire to be. His former yearning was not the resolute beginning that was needed; it was unable to transform itself into love; yet it still testifies to Othello's sincere need to give meaning to human existence.

Othello the destroyer also attests to the fact that the desire to be, the desire for meaning and for good, maintains itself in the face of the greatest dangers. I would thus conclude that in this, one of his darkest tragedies, Shakespeare was less a pessimist who demonstrated what Jacques Vaché called the "theatrical uselessness of everything" than a dramatist who ventured into the abyss with all the necessary lucidity, yet without concluding that all hope is vain. Why would he write plays and persist in doing so if there were nothing other in his mind and his heart than the recognition of illusion and evil?

In writing *Othello,* perhaps Shakespeare had an objective in mind that we should try to understand.

XI

Is there an "objective" in *Othello,* an intention through which the play might find its place within the context of a broader investigation undertaken by Shakespeare? An investigation, a meditation, a proposition, and a hope that would be pursued in his later tragedies, perhaps above all in Shakespeare's "romances," *The Winter's Tale* and *The Tempest?*

I should note here that a figure like Iago can be perceived in two ways. The first resides simply in the way the play is put together, where meaning surfaces solely in the interaction of the characters—those highly complex figures that give such a strong impression of inner life that they seem real. From this illusion, spectator and reader alike are led to feel compassion for at least some of these beings, suffering with them and unable to forget their tragic destinies. They thus give full credence to what the author proposes regarding the nature of the characters' actions, the causes for which are to be found within the characters themselves, since they are presented as existing independently. Seen in this way, Iago appears as the evil that is sometimes absolute in a person, and, as such, he represents something terrifying in the human condition.

But there is another way of thinking about Iago, not at the moment when we are participating with compassion in the events of the tragedy, but later when we have closed the book or left the theater. It is then that we notice how this fictional character points toward a social reality existing outside of fiction, a reality that is articulated around beings not totally depraved as he is. And this gives rise to another complexity, in which absolutely negative conclusions are not necessarily the only way of thinking or the only rule of conduct. There are many people in real society—whether in the court or in the city—who are not unlike Iago. They are, for example, the "falsely jealous" who so preoccupied the popular narratives and songs in the Middle Ages. They were often husbands who hid behind the tree of life to spy on the happiness of young men and women giving themselves over to their bodily senses during the vernal season of their life. As the author of *A Midsummer Night's Dream* and as someone who often expressed his regret at the Puritans' persecution of the dances and games of the month of May, Shakespeare would have been the first to deplore the existence of those dangerous killjoys.

Shakespeare was also well aware that certain of these Puritans, already powerful during his day, might come dimly but unmistakably to the minds of spectators as they witnessed Iago's actions. Much in Iago's way of thinking and acting was in fact the Puritans' own. Like Iago, who arranges to have everybody call him the "honest one" or the "very honest one," these Puritans professed their virtue and, like Iago, attacked any woman who was not simply a submissive and self-effacing wife. Like him, they felt disgust for the flesh, no appetite for pleasure, even the same need to accumulate profits in order to compensate for their lack of being by satisfaction in having. The resemblance is striking, and it is quite possible that Shakespeare sought to draw our attention to it. Isn't Iago's reference to his "fellows" an allusion meant to prompt laughter or, perhaps more prudently, a smile on many faces in the audience?

The Puritans had no use for theater of this kind. Through their misogyny and their rejection of anything festive, they waged sustained and frequently effective attacks against the theater, suggesting it was a danger to society. In fact, what worried them most about theatrical representation, with its ability to unmask factitious values and deceitful behavior, was the threat it posed to their own image. Even if Iago was more wicked than they, he still could worry them. Here we see an aspect of Shakespeare's thinking that is founded on the capacity to point out and to denounce—which is not simply a satirical activity, not simply a distraction from his pessimism by means of relentless accusation.

Hamlet, written three or four years before *Othello,* explicitly presents a conception of theater that is the starting point for my understanding of *Othello.* While preparing several players to stage a play entitled "The Mousetrap," the prince of Denmark explains that theater holds up a mirror to society in which it can recognize its shortcomings, its sins, and its vices. The playwright's pursuit thus has truth as its task. Yet, as Hamlet says, or dreams, the playwright's role is not solely to analyze behaviors but to force those who are guilty to recognize and to admit their wrongdoing—truth thus controlling spirit, since truth is sustained by the authority of God and the threat of his wrath. In *Hamlet,* the guilty party is Claudius, who has become king by murder and usurpation, and the theater is represented by the "play within the play" that the poet-prince puts on for him.

Hamlet, of course, is not the mirror Shakespeare had theorized; nor is its effect the one he expected. From a theoretical standpoint, the play should catch sins and vices—virtues as well—in its mirror. But it should also let things emerge with enough clarity to allow the spectator to reflect upon them naturally and easily. During the Elizabethan and Jacobean periods, this was certainly accomplished by many playwrights. It is also true of many of Shakespeare's own works, in various aspects of his comedies and histories— and even in *Hamlet,* when, for instance, he presents Rosencrantz and Guildenstern, those pompous German university students. Yet, the mirror Shakespeare raises over the ramparts of Elsinore, bathed in nocturnal fog, or in the labyrinth of rooms in the great castle, which is such a striking glimpse into the psyche, is more often than not misted over.

What we do see in these waters, where truth and illusion intermingle their murky currents, is something quite different from mere ambition, or concern for the state, or sexual appetite, or even the oedipal complex. Like a vague glow or an indistinct background, it is a person's relation to the unfathomable depths of what he or she is, the place where awareness of one's self is rooted beyond the mind's reach. The mirror opens onto the infinite, the absolute; and its most striking figures, though unfinished and laden with enigma, will be those who, at the crucial moment when Shakespeare is writing, will most be disturbed by the collapse of the old world order—the structure that for so long has given hope to reason—and by the apprehension of nothingness, rising like a "sea of troubles" around the castle of illusion now in ruin. The mirror in *Hamlet* is not what ordinary psychology gives us to think about. By raising the question "to be or not to be," this mirror presents—but sheds insufficient light on—the problem of being-in-the world, of the will-to-be, or of the hatred of being.

Here we come quite close to *Othello,* where the desire to be, along with its failures, is Shakespeare's main concern. The difference between these two works is nonetheless remarkable. In *Hamlet* the question of being is posed in terms of a universe centered on the absolute reality of God. This medieval theology and cosmology still haunted the human spirit even as it stood on the threshold of its modern condition, thus impeding what was perhaps the necessary radicalization of its awareness of itself. For instance, Hamlet knows perfectly well, in one sense, that everything will depend on the success or failure of his relationship with Ophelia. Yet this intuition is obscured when he remembers his duties as heir to a royal power, his role as representing the divine solely through his being. It is also quite significant that the relationship between this young man and woman—the experience of a particular, private life—appears in the play merely as a subplot, and as the action unfolds, it loses its potential to become the center of that action. We can almost hear Rimbaud, in his poem "Royalty," proclaiming, "My friends, I want this woman to be Queen!" [7]

In *Othello*, on the other hand, the presence of the old order has fallen apart, or at least has been parenthesized. Goats, monkeys, wolves, and other animals are referred to occasionally, as the coded figures of human ways, but the starry sky has disappeared, and even God has all but vanished. There are no more kings and queens—reflections of God in the human mind. When Othello dies, society is not shaken to its foundations, as Claudius in *Hamlet* and certain Romans in *Julius Caesar* feared might happen when great men of this world mysteriously perish. Through Shakespeare's power of anticipation, the scene is suddenly narrowed onto an already modern and secular society.

What in *Hamlet* is secondary, a subplot, becomes in *Othello* the whole action, and it is precisely the same drama: a man who is suspicious of the woman he both loves and does not love, who insults her, threatens her, and brings about her death as well as his own. And as we follow the various scenes, the image that takes shape in the depths of the mirror has surely become clearer. What might have gone unnoticed in the earlier work is now readily apparent. In both plays, we are on the edge of the same abyss; from below we hear the same indistinct but insistent sound of a current flowing invisibly everywhere and in everything. But the problematic of "to be" and "not to be" is better formulated in *Othello* than in *Hamlet*. It is formulated almost explicitly, and with a conclusion we can think about. Even though the desire to be will always be ensnared in the dreams of particular persons or of the social group as a whole, *Othello* tells us that following that desire is the only path to take.

XII

Between *Hamlet* and *Othello*, Shakespeare thus reduces his predominantly ontological preoccupation to its essential categories. He even suggests a conclusion to be drawn. What I wish to underscore, however, is that once the mirror has been clarified, its very function can be redefined, revealing a possibility that justifies our accepting life in this world, no matter how somber it seems. It even explains our ability to find meaning in writing for the theater, as Shakespeare will continue to do.

7. Arthur Rimbaud, "Royauté," *Illuminations, Oeuvres Complètes*, 129–30.—Trans.

In this clarification we see first of all a redefinition of what is evil and who is guilty. In *Hamlet*, evil remains associated with cosmic structure. Evil imperils that structure, at least in its societal forms, which is why, by showing Claudius his sin beneath the weighty and irresistible gaze of God, theater might force him to admit his sin and repent. In *Othello*, on the contrary, Shakespeare anticipates a time when—as belief comes undone—the speaking being will recognize as transcendent only what is strictly human. He or she will feel responsible only to this reality, only to a fellow human being. What then will be criminal is the refusal to respect the being of the other or, worse yet, to subvert and to sap—while feigning to revere—the values upon which this respect is founded, which is what Iago does. But in a world of this sort, where God is no longer present, the theater too will change. No one can hope that an Iago in the audience will leap to his feet and proclaim his sin. Even in the play, the fictional Iago shrouds himself in silence. He may experience the vexation of forever remaining on the outside of being; the meaninglessness he sees everywhere and in everything nonetheless keeps him from feeling the slightest remorse.

Now if the society beginning to emerge no longer expects to receive its laws from heaven, and if it thus can take into its own hands the task of self-understanding, one might hope that theatrical representation—capable as it is of drawing the public's attention to the existence of Iagos, half-Iagos, and the shadows of Iago—would help people of goodwill, who do exist (as Othello proves even when his thinking is highly disturbed), to recognize those in their midst who spread evil, and to better understand the forms that evil can take, sometimes within themselves. This increased awareness might bring about adjustments in social relations or in private life. Even if only relative, these would allow people to escape disastrous situations, to attenuate misunderstandings, and to diminish suffering by deferring and circumscribing what cannot be made to disappear. Society's Iagos might be less dangerous if better perceived. This would also be true of the Puritans, in whose ranks a number of potential Iagos might lurk. They would be better explained and, through their very noxiousness, would even take on a certain value as examples of evil. In a word, theater would be concerned not so much with denouncing this or that faction or this or that sort of individual in order to wrench confessions from them, as with compelling them—by describing them—to collaborate with the theater, which is itself at the service of an ever imperiled community.

The role of theater—major theater—would then be to probe into the obscure dialectics of the self. Its project would be to work for the betterment of this self and to diminish the perils it faces. In following the same paths, Iago's design was, on the contrary, to create more mirages, to intensify fantasies, and to exacerbate the worst. The playwright, through the work he produces, might thus be thought of as an *anti-Iago*, a therapist seeking to attenuate the evil from which—given the pretenses of language—human beings can never fully recover. Something else becomes clearer through the invention of Iago in a work whose project thus transcends him, or at least relativizes him: the relationship between tragedy and what must be called poetry.

Why, indeed, has Iago been able to seduce Othello and mislead his desire if not because the Moor remained, as we so easily discovered, prisoner to a world of values and representations which, though sometimes generous, were always presented as absolute? Such is the force of verbal structures, capable of transforming society into a closed system and the human person into an "ego," equally closed in on what is only a dream. Iago's spade turns over the prejudices of his unfortunate interlocutor, thus burying with infertile soil the source of living water Othello sought to unearth. Yet Othello's intentions were good, as he himself insists in his final moments, and it is certain that in Venice, when he told his fiancée the story of his past life with such lyricism and poetry, he was ready to consider himself an open and free spirit.

But was this really poetry, this light that shone only in words? Was it not simply the self-satisfaction of a dream in search of its own form that thus remained the closure of egocentricity? As such, did it not mean forgetting and failing to know the listener—Desdemona—who is loved, thought to be loved, only or principally because she listened naively and, in so doing, gave credence to the mirages that were the only real object of the storyteller's affection? As I have already noted, true poetry constantly tears apart the dream that takes possession of words so as to keep open the path of the "I," which is always obsessed with the projections of the ego. Poetry is not the crystallization that occurs in a poem; it is a questioning which, by observing writing from within lived existence, deconstructs its images, disperses its dreams, and desires a new beginning—a more vigorous one—to the search for truth that the finest writings start but abandon. Poetry is critical of poetry, and it is only by making demands that it can fully be what it is. Othello has the misfortune of being only partly a poet. He is more of an artist, which is why Iago, the devil, can take hold of his thoughts.

If the playwright seeks to be an anti-Iago, penetrating the minds of the

spectators or readers of his work so as to show them what they really are—
spirits dawdling on the way to self-presence—and then to draw them farther
ahead, he must himself be a poet in this open and mobile way, always beginning anew, his gaze fixed on what lies beyond figures. This is the only worthwhile course, the only way of engaging oneself in speech and in the world
that can be called reality. It is what Shakespeare sought to do. After studying
his plays, especially after reading the tragedy of Othello and Desdemona—
but as much could be said of *King Lear, Macbeth,* and *The Winter's Tale*—
I conclude that Shakespeare, with respect to his characters' self-awareness,
always manages to place himself at the point where illusion assails truth.
From there he observes the action with the kind of lucidity—free of both
meanness and indulgence—that can only be explained by his affection for
the human situation, in its poverty and its beauty, which he seeks to restore
to its great potential.

XIII

One final remark: The specifically and profoundly poetic intention I sense at
work in certain plays in no way requires that social problems of the kind that
are debated in ordinary life be left outside of the author's and the spectators'
consideration. On the contrary, such problems can be better presented, open
to unexpected and truer solutions, because poetry is there to help dissipate
the illusions.

I am too far along in my study to consider at length what Shakespeare's
poetic spirit brought to the society he watched as it lived and suffered. I shall
note one aspect of it, however, since it leads to one of the most salutary observations that can be made about *Othello,* otherwise so harsh and somber a
play. In a society that alienates the desire to be, substituting the desire to
have, it has always been the rule that men make women both the instruments
and the stakes of their pursuit of possessions, which robs most women of the
possibility of mastering their own destiny. It is a situation that most eras and
milieus have rarely tried to understand. Such, at least, was the case in the age
of Elizabeth I and James I, when religion was quick to ascribe narrow limits
to women, even to upset their understanding of themselves by stifling their
voices to the innermost depths of their being.

With this question in mind, the tragic dialogue between Othello and Desdemona, with Iago in the wings, appears so rich in observations concerning
the relations between men and women that it is hard to imagine Shakespeare's

having failed to consider them carefully, along with certain proposals for "changing life."[8] Doesn't this dialogue, which exemplifies how disastrous human speech can be, forcefully demonstrate how the rule of men can work on a woman, and this from within her own self-awareness? Recall that this woman, who is as lucid and courageous as she is deeply in love, has demanded her right to a "noble exchange." But we have watched her give up this right, no longer understanding why she sought this exchange or hoped for transparency in her relation to Othello. In the end, she who at first was so bold comes to fear using the few simple words that give things a name. Shakespeare's remarks are applicable to many more women than to the one who hangs her head in discouragement in act 4. The critique that emerges on the stage can easily spread to the audience, and theater can thus begin to play its role as social reformer.

But *Othello* is also a play in which poetry works from within fixed structures of consciousness, and we should now focus on a passage that contributes to the kind of critique I have been discussing, though this time in a way that is not merely negative. Desdemona, having apparently renounced her rights and even her life, says to her servant Emilia, who has come to help her get ready for the night, that she would like to sing the "Willow Song"— which may surprise us. From the "poor soul" that Desdemona has become, we would expect her simply to want to sit under the sycamore, which is described at the beginning of the song as a tree of "weeping" and mourning. On the contrary, she wants to celebrate the willow, "the green willow," and for the audience nothing could be more profoundly moving than her recollection of this song, nothing could induce more compassion and also the feeling that some light is leading the human condition forward after all.

But why this emotion? Because in the first place it reveals to what degree Desdemona desired what she could not obtain; desired it with her whole soul, but also with her whole body, which had rightfully been wakened. She desired it with a capacity for simple joy that makes the maze of delusions, fears, and perverse lust into which Othello has dragged her seem all the more desolate and hopeless. And so it is the very voice of the truth of life that we hear in this spring song, and precisely when a demoralized witness to the play's ending might have thought this voice was lost.

Something else appears that helps to restore confidence, even in sorrow:

8. The expression "changing life" (*changer la vie*) is from Arthur Rimbaud's "Époux infernal," 104.—Trans.

this truth, which as such is irreducible, is not so much stifled by an unjust society as it is pushed toward the margins—margins that are nevertheless rich with the resonance of poetic expression. To tell life's truth where it is censored and repressed we have song, music, and words that are no longer a mirage but evidence. This is the clarity of consciousness that the unhappy Barbary sought to make her own—if only for a moment's dreaming—on the last day of her sad life. There is song, poetry in its simple unerring ways, and there are women to speak this poetry precisely because they have been driven away from what they might have been. Subjected to a world order whose values they do not share and whose pursuits they do not understand, women are deprived of the discourse that lays claim to truth. This deprivation, however, has its advantages. Any form of discourse, even if partially true, is an ideology that replaces the depth of being with an abstraction. It fails to recognize unity, which life needs to experience from within in order to attain what is best in itself—which is to become music, music as it is found in little songs and in great poems. All forms of discourse, by definition, forget the meaning of the willow and of the month of May. But in those who are not one with the dominant ideology, perhaps because they are its victims, the life that has been repressed in them is not falsified; it still has its share of light. It is not because women are women that they can sing the Willow Song, but because they are excluded from the common language of the dominant social group—that language in which evil can prosper and undertake its work of death.

What does the Willow Song mean at this point in the play when a pensive Desdemona is about to speak her mind regarding a new relationship between young men and women and the openness of this relationship? Through the poetic intuition so natural to him, which can dissolve the evil that seems to coagulate in and paralyze society, Shakespeare is surely suggesting that his audience pay particular attention to this speech emanating from within women and expressed in music, which is the essence of Barbary's message—Barbary, whom Desdemona, quite significantly, has never forgotten. Indeed, no sooner has Desdemona finished singing than her servant Emilia delivers a fiery defense of women's rights and a denunciation of the falsity and egocentricity of men.

From the point of view of the action, Emilia's remarks carry little weight, for Desdemona is now sunk so deep in sorrow that she has grown listless and barely listens to her servant, whose words have come too late. Emilia's eighteen lines, moreover, may have been borrowed from some totally different context, and they do not appear in the first Quarto, the earliest edition of the play. But the very fact that they seem to be appended to the developing drama makes them a kind of commentary on that drama, revealing its meaning just as it is about to conclude. As though inscribed on the drama from outside, in a way that seems abstract, these lines penetrate it, becoming, in turn, a part of the action. They enter deeply into Emilia herself, who, in the swiftest and most tragic fashion, claims their truth as her own, she who until then has seemed to be a perfect example of the social alienation of women. Wife to none other than Iago who is as cynical and disdainful with her as with everyone else, though more shamelessly so, Emilia has long obeyed her hideous companion with a naïveté that ultimately plays a disastrous role. For it is from Emilia that Iago received the handkerchief he uses to bring down Desdemona. During the last few hours of the second day, however, Emilia begins to become aware of what she has never wanted to see or understand. In the crucial final scene, she rises up in anger and indignation: spurred on by a sense of the truth, she unmasks Iago with a desperate courage that leads him to stab her, his malevolence thus made clear for all to see.

Emilia's speech—discourse that is grounded in society's own—comes after a song, like the passing of poetry to thought and action. Although the speech is crudely emphatic, it is supported by all the evidence in the play. It also indicates that Shakespeare has embarked on a way of thinking that he will pursue, for his most significant works, as has surely been noted, will henceforth focus on women, studied from the perspective of their awareness of themselves at the moment when their sense of their own truth asserts itself—unless it is overwhelmed by the alienation that oppresses them, but then specifically in a way that can be reflected upon. Cordelia, through her logic, her rejection of the lies of others, both men and women, is certainly the center of gravity in *King Lear,* just as Lady Macbeth is in *Macbeth* with her remorse and madness that are as striking and significant as the envious fear her husband experiences with regard to the realities of life. And *Antony and Cleopatra* is the preeminent tragedy of an alienated woman—an idol, painted and adorned, when the two lovers first meet on the dazzling royal barge— who nevertheless becomes aware of her true "nobility," thus aiding in man's spiritual recovery; even internalizing and expressing directly, with a voice that surpasses sexual difference, the speech of poetry, this theater's latent truth. With *Hamlet,* then with *Othello* and his subsequent plays, Shakespeare shifts from studying the civil war in English history to observing the war between men and women in the history of the West. And it is clearly as a consequence of his intuitive reflections that in *The Winter's Tale* he will suggest a "revelation," an "end to tribulations"—words I am borrowing from Rimbaud, so profoundly Shakespeare's kindred spirit, in whose poem "Royalty" we see a "magnificent man and woman" bound together in "essential health."[9]

TRANSLATED BY JAMES PETTERSON

9. Rimbaud, "Royauté," 129–30.—Trans.

PART TWO

CHAPTER EIGHT

Shakespeare & the French Poet

HOW MIGHT WE evaluate French translations of Shakespeare? Do we have a truthful image of him in French—or at least a compelling one? Have we, for instance, a French equivalent of the German translations by Schlegel and Tieck, which have enjoyed such favor and renown since the Romantic period? No, there is nothing comparable in French, and I believe it is useful and important to analyze this astonishing absence.

It is not that Shakespeare is unrecognized in France. We read him, as best we can; we evoke him; for quite some time we have had a general idea of his greatness, if only because an army of adapters, coming at Shakespeare from all sides, have managed to point out this or that aspect of a body of work whose essential feature is precisely its extraordinary diversity. In one sense, it is probably an advantage that we have no French translation comparable to that of Schlegel and Tieck—a "classic," beautiful and powerful enough to constrict us within the limited perfection of its own particular vision. The Romantic age, in any case, was incapable of truly understanding Shakespeare. The fact remains that to this day we still do not have in France a complete translation that is both faithful to the original and great literature in its own right—one in which the reader can get more than an abstract idea of the dramatic elements of the work and something of the substance of Shakespeare's incomparable poetry. Perfectly good translations of particular plays there are. I would mention, for example, those of Jules Supervielle, Pierre Leyris, and Henri Thomas—but they seem piecemeal and inconsistent when what is needed is an organic whole, a single profound vision combining anew all the aspects of the Shakespearean world—and this could only be attempted by a single poet working alone with authority and decision.

In other words, the French have only been *told about* Shakespeare, and if translating means catching the original tone of voice, that fusion of personal vision and word which makes the poetic dimension, then he has not yet been translated at all. Why is this so? I have no doubt that it is worth looking at the problem from a somewhat theoretical angle and trying to find out if there is not some basic, essential cause for this persistent failure. But in order to do this I shall first consider the earliest translations. What strikes me most about them, apart from any individual shortcomings, is one serious weakness they all have in common.

II

Although, historically speaking, the idea is absurd, it is a lasting pity that no one thought of extemporizing a translation in Shakespeare's own day. At the beginning of the seventeenth century, before Malherbe's influence turned the scale and while the impression of Garnier's breathless verse still lingered, something of the essence of Shakespeare could have seeped into our poetry and modified it, perhaps profoundly. But the taste for classicism soon barred any genuine understanding of Shakespeare. In an age dominated by Racine, one can hardly imagine anyone translating *Macbeth*. And when Voltaire takes it upon himself to initiate the French mind into what he calls "English Tragedy" (after Corneille and Racine even the word *tragedy* is charged with overtones very remote from anything English), the rendering he offers of Hamlet's "To be or not to be," for instance, is a complete travesty of Shakespeare, and precisely because of that facile and totally unpoetical alexandrine which was then the principal cause of the vapidity in the theater:

> Demeure, il faut choisir, et passer à l'instant
> De la vie à la mort et de l'être au néant ...

What is surprising is that Voltaire, with the intention of giving some idea of Shakespeare's "woodnotes wild," should have followed up this doggerel with a literal, line-for-line translation which has a kind of beauty of its own and, in its freedom and flexibility, is related to what we might welcome today. In rendering "Or to take arms against a sea of troubles" as "et de prendre les armes contre une mer de troubles," he shows a fine audacity, and in my own translation of *Hamlet* I have paid the unwitting forerunner of all modern translators the compliment of taking over this line. Voltaire, however, put it forward only to cut it out, as if he meant to show the kind of excesses from which the French genius had to be protected. And in the age of Louis XVI, when Ducis in turn composed "imitations" of *Hamlet* and *Othello* that were widely read and often reprinted (I remember they were still to be found in my grandfather's small library), it was from Voltaire that Ducis had learned to cut and rearrange and simplify Shakespeare's text so that the end product was a "five-act tragedy" of the utmost regularity and inanity. "I don't understand English"—this is how Ducis begins his preface, and he distorts the original plot to such an extent that Claudius, to take one example, is turned into Ophelia's father, and we can be fairly sure this is done so as to face Hamlet, like a character in Corneille, with a choice between revenge and love. From the neoclassical point of view of the Age of Reason, Hamlet's procrastination had to be justified on rational grounds that were *perfectly clear and distinct*.

Nevertheless, Ducis's clear-cut line is occasionally fuzzy; he has a touch of the *roman noir*, and I must confess that I do not find his renderings altogether intolerable, if only because they illustrate with such perfect clarity the difficulties of translating Shakespeare. Indeed, after Ducis, the problems were more often shelved than solved. Between the Revolution and the Second Empire, Shakespeare was continually being translated, but in the spirit of a vague Romanticism. Letourneur (between 1776 and 1782), Francisque Michel, Benjamin Laroche, Guizot, François Victor-Hugo, and Montégut all published *Complete Works*, with some progress in accuracy (though Letourneur had no compunction in cutting out complete scenes and bowdlerizing passages he thought coarse), and even in felicity—but with the same defect that is present in Ducis and is so subtle and elusive that it defies easy description.

Here is a famous passage from the first part of Henry IV, the one where Falstaff is in a black mood, repenting of his evil life: "Why," he says to Bardolph, "there is it":

> Come, sing me a bawdy song, make me merry. I was as virtuously given as a gentleman need to be; virtuous enough, swore little, diced not above seven times a week, went to a bawdy-house not above one in a quarter—of an hour, paid money that I borrowed—three or four times, lived well and in good compass; and now I live out of all order, out of all compass.

In these few lines, and in the background they suggest—a world of authentic bawdy houses and taverns—we are confronted with a real human being talking about himself, and any feeling of unreality arises only from the jocular way he himself contrasts his actual way of life to the impression he would like to create of it. Falstaff is fully there in the flesh, and for whatever universal meaning he attains, his starting point is the same as that of any other mortal: his individual reality, which persists in vivid unpredictability throughout the entire play. Falstaff is an archetype only because he is primarily a complex and mysterious being that we cannot fathom any more than we can really understand any other real human being. And the words seem to lend themselves to this total *thereness*. They seem to be one with the puffing voice, and even to be reabsorbed into the world of sense they evoke, so that we are left with nothing between us and its raw assertiveness, its undiminished complexity. But let us now look at a translation, a very meticulous one, by François Victor-Hugo.

> Oui, voilà la chose. Allons, chante-moi une chanson égrillarde. Egayemoi. J'étais aussi vertueusement doué qu'un gentilhomme a besoin de l'être; vertueux suffisamment; jurant peu; jouant aux dés, pas plus de sept fois ... par semaine; allant dans les mauvais lieux pas plus d'une fois par quart d'heure; ayant trois ou quatre fois rendu de l'argent emprunté; vivant bien et dans la juste mesure; et maintenant, je mène une vie désordonnée et hors de toute mesure.

Certainly it is the same passage: the ideas and the references are the same. But there is a world of difference between the original text and the translation. Whereas Shakespeare's Falstaff seems actually *in the room*, in the translation he appears distant, insubstantial, dimmed, *as if we were looking at him through a windowpane*. He is no longer a living being, he is a character in literature, but one striving, by his exuberant language, to resemble life too closely and hence all the less convincing. In all these translations, all Shakespeare's characters lose their roundness in the same way. Even where Shakespeare's "excesses"—the puns, the bawdiness—are scrupulously preserved, the characters seem insubstantial and their speech lacks life. "I have immortal longings" is what Shakespeare wrote at the end of *Antony and Cleopatra*. "Je sens en moi l'impatient désir de l'immortalité" is Letourneur's version, while "Je me sens pressée d'un violent désir de quitter la vie" is Francisque Michel's. Where are we? The words create neither reality nor myth. This is the ghost of Shakespeare.

And yet we can be confident that these translators chose a prose rendering so as not to be led into the unreality, the unnaturalness and lack of body, characteristic of the Voltaire and Ducis versions. They used prose because it served the Romantic aspiration to lay hold of the real in all its heterogeneity—local color and the picturesque, as well as the truth of beings as different as possible from ourselves—in short, to bring language and real life as close together as possible. Admittedly the earlier Romanticism (I mean that of Hugo and Musset) had no very profound grasp of this reality. But since Shakespeare could hardly have been less concerned with the picturesque, it is likely that one of the reasons why nineteenth-century translators missed the mark was just that they had lost touch with what is the real source of Shakespeare's truth—that vital force of human creation, that passionate depth of feeling, that his verse directly expresses. Even in the most recent efforts, that sense of looking through a windowpane is painfully persistent, so much so that in André Gide's translations (unfortunately very poor) we are left with the effect of a puppet theater—literary, artificial, and affected. Surely we cannot attribute this defect to a mere accident of literary history. It seems to be an inevitable misfortune of the French language when it tries to translate poetry without being able to escape from the hidden principles of its own very special and peculiar verse.

What I wish to do here—and this is all that I am attempting to do in these few pages—is to contrast Shakespeare's poetry with this unspoken assumption about the nature of poetry. For I am convinced that, quite apart from all the particular illustrations (I should like to have quoted more but nothing would really be adequate or decisive), the essence of this failure in translating Shakespeare lies in the opposing metaphysics that govern and, sometimes, tyrannize the French and English languages.

III

If I had to sum up in a sentence my impression of Shakespeare, I should say that I see no opposition in his work between the universal and the particular. In spite of scholastic tradition, he does not envisage these two poles of thought as contradictory because, in his plays at least, he doesn't focus his mind on them. Is Macbeth an archetype like Antigone, or even Harpagon, or is he rather an individual caught in a unique destiny, the product of pure chance? Is Othello the type of the jealous man, or the incoherent victim of blind and senseless forces that could not be further from anything "clear and distinct"? These questions cannot be answered because they are wrongly stated. For Shakespeare deals with people's actions, which are never "particulars" because they participate in the universal categories of the consciousness that conceives them, but which also never—not even in the case of Brutus and Julius Caesar—reach the fullness and clarity of the universal because they have to compromise with raw contingency. Human action cannot be fitted into the framework of logic because a person acts only in order to contradict his or her own nature, to be at once both individual and universal—and the essential ambiguity in Shakespeare means that his theater is the empirical observation, without literary or philosophical preconception, of people as they actually exist. The apparent subject of his tragedy is simply a means of capturing a possibility of human existence so as to examine it. The seemingly abstract setting of the action does not so much exclude the real world as concentrate it, like a framework within which all the variations of action that human passion might conceive could be instantaneously evoked.

And Shakespeare's language too is a means rather than an end; it is always subordinate to the external object, which is something English allows. Nouns fade before the real presence of things, which stand starkly before us in the actual process of becoming. The uninflected adjectives snap qualities photographically, without raising the metaphysical problem of the relation of quality and substance, as the agreement of adjectives and nouns must do in French. English concerns itself naturally with tangible aspects. It accepts the reality of what can be observed and does not admit the possibility of any other order of reality; it has a natural affinity with the Aristotelean critique of Platonic Ideas. And if its words with Latin roots to some extent unsettle this philosophical choice and grant a more abstract handling of experience to an intelligence shaped by this "devotion to the realm of things," they do not undermine the natural realism of the language so much as simply make it easier to express those moments in life when we are guided by a sense of the ideal. To quote once again that moment of the purest poetry, those sublime words of Cleopatra, "I have immortal longings": on the one hand, this phrase is capable of seizing hold of the living actuality at its most concrete, immediate, and instinctive, while on the other hand, by using a word like *immortal,* which is pure Idea, it retains the capacity to reveal in this same concrete action the timeless and the universal, which are our purest aspirations. At a deeper level, the English language tells us that immortality, this pure *Idea,* in some sense really exists and that it is a noble and veridical part of speech but also that its activity and life depend on our will to create them. English poetry, Shakespeare's at least, rejects archetypal realism but only in order to follow the inalienable liberty of man with greater flexibility.

And the greatness and richness of English poetry come from service to this liberty, as if offering it at every moment the entire range of its possibilities, so that any given word can open up a world, a "brave new world," to our perception. With French poetry it is a very different matter. Generally, with this more cautious, more self-contained kind of poetry, the words seem to state what they denote and immediately to exclude from the poem's field of reference whatever is not denoted. The poet's statements do not set out to describe external reality but shut the poet in with certain selected precepts in a simplified, more circumscribed world. For instance, Racine rejects all but a few situations and feelings in his plays. By stripping them of all the contingent or accidental details of real life, he seems to raise them to the dignity of the Platonic Idea, as if he wished to reduce his dramatic structure to the bare relations of congruence or opposition which hold between those ideas. A more coherent world of intelligible essences is substituted for the real world. Yet it is not an abstract world, for the Platonic Idea is profoundly double-natured, in the sense of taking on the life of sensible appearance in its most intense and specific form. But this world is nonetheless a *place apart*, where the bewildering diversity of the real can be forgotten, and also the very existence of time, everyday life and death. Poetic creation, in short, is hieratic; it makes an inviolable place, and while the rite of reading continues, it draws the mind into this illusory communion.

Not all French poetry, of course, can be identified with the art of Racine. Indeed, in Baudelaire's case it goes counter to Racine's design for poetry, but even then without moving out of this magic circle by which words circumscribe the mind. In rediscovering and reaffirming for himself the notion of poetry already implicit in the work of Villon, Durand, and Maynard, Baudelaire—in contrast to Racine—is asserting the very existence of sensible things, the particular reality as such, the stubborn entities that people our mortal horizon, as if surrendering totally to the phenomenal world and abandoning the hieratic use of language. Baudelaire is the most consistent and determined opponent of the Racinian theory. And yet this *principle of exclusion* I have referred to still governs his poetry. Even though he is dealing with *this* particular swan or *that* particular woman rather than with swan or woman as such—with the idea, that is, of swan or woman—what these particular entities are like are not what matters to him. What matters is simply this mystery—that the Idea should have strayed into the very marrow of the sensible world, that it should be willing to undergo limitation and death, and that, while retaining its absolute status, it should have entered into this world of shadows and chance. Baudelaire is not trying, at any level of penetration, to describe things as they are: he is trying to convey the act of being, and the passion and moral feeling that can be based upon it. An intense, narrow aim that restored to poetry the almost obsessional detachment from the phenomenal world that seems to be the fate of our main body of work. It is as if words, in French, excluding instead of describing, always encourage the mind to shake off the disintegrating diversity of things; it is as if they always make the work of art a world of its own, a closed sphere.[1]

I should like to conclude by saying that in English the word is an opening, it is all surface; and in French it is a closing, it is all depth. On the one hand, we have the kind of word that can call upon all the other words (more than 21,000 in Shakespeare, according to Jespersen) to aid precision and enrichment; on the other hand, we have a vocabulary as reduced as possible, so as to protect a single essential experience. On the one hand, unlimited dissociation, receptiveness to every dialectical or technical possibility, so that an alert awareness can penetrate always further into the phenomenal world. On the other hand, all these evocations of sense entering into poetry as one enters into an order, to be completely transformed, dying to the world, becoming one with the Idea that is constantly being realized in the poem. English poetry is a mirror, French poetry a crystal sphere. The French poet who, according to many, is least like Racine and most like Shakespeare is Paul Claudel. Yet in *L'Annonce faite à Marie*, not only Violaine but Mara, not only Pierre de Craon but Jacques Hury, speak with the same deliberate and highly stylized speech, a uniformity that symbolizes the unity of creation in the bosom of God, the nonexistence of evil at the heart of God's world. In spite of its richness, there is no poetry more organic, more closely knit than Paul Claudel's; it is still a sphere even though Claudel, with a medieval, pre-Copernican sense of the cosmos, thought he could succeed in making it into a correlative of the Sphere of Created Beings.

IV

English poetry, as I have said, can be represented by a mirror, French by a sphere. How can these contradictory forms of poetry be translated into each other?

1. And that is why English poetry "means" so much more than French poetry. The former, whose words have no pretension to be Idea—principle and origin of the world—can put the world

It may be easier now to see why so many French translations of Shakespeare are mediocre: they are nothing more than a compromise between two linguistic structures. The French poetic vocabulary irresistibly tones down and dims the particular reality, that stubborn compound of the essential and the contingent. How then could we expect it to preserve Falstaff, who is singularity incarnate, emancipated from all forms and laws, even moral law?[2] It is easier, too, to see how the majority of these translations came about historically. Romanticism thought it could be free of that inner law of the French language which I have tried to isolate. But the Romantics, who sought to revolutionize the old dictionary and multiply its references to the real world while still producing poetry, never achieved more than a shallow exploitation of this new territory. They were no more sensitive to the deeper stirrings of instinct and passion than they were to the dialectic of essence and existence, which had engaged both Racine and Baudelaire.

How, then, is Shakespeare to be translated? If I wanted to end on a pessimistic note, I could easily make a list of all the forms this fundamental opposition might assume, or, in other words, all the points of fidelity that a translation should realize and that French structure makes difficult, if not impossible. Thus the alternation of prose and verse in Shakespearean tragedy is true to reality; it witnesses to the opposing forces—the heroic and the commonplace—at work in the world: at the end of the cobbler's scene in *Julius Caesar*, the abrupt return to verse is a dramatic assertion of the will to nobility in a boorish world. But this plurality of perspectives is not possible in French poetry. Not only in Corneille and Racine but also in Hugo and Claudel, the minor characters speak in verse and, like the chorus in Greek tragedy, the less they share in the nobler dimensions of the action, the more strictly they are bound to formal poetic expression. Another difficulty is that wordplay has to be translated. Shakespeare's punning is genuinely ambiguous, reflecting the complex nature of the real world, but French does not take kindly to the pun, and it is unlikely to be anything better than a nihilistic (sometimes subversive) assault on rational mind. Indeed, the least significant

into words, interpret and formulate it. The latter can only reveal the Idea, manifest beyond words and concepts. From this contrast, the profound divergences of Anglo-Saxon and French literary criticism can also be deduced.

2. Of all Shakespeare's characters, Falstaff is the least understood and the least appreciated in France. In a country where the problem of good and evil is approached conceptually, dialectically, Zarathustra, who is *beyond* both good and evil (showing that he has at least considered them), is better understood than Falstaff, who remains, if you will, *beneath* good and evil.

word in a poem has latent within it the entire structure of its language. Mere literal translation of the word is not enough to break down the structure. Take that one word "Sortez!"—Roxane's cry in *Bajazet*. How much of its implication would we expect to survive, once translated into English? There is a great danger that this tremendous word by which Roxane severs herself from the world of sense, this word that implies a whole metaphysics, would wind up a mere theatrical effect.

But is there much point in making a long list of difficulties? It would be more useful to take note of the one remaining possibility that may, one day, give us the chance of solving the problem of Shakespearean translation—or at least of raising it to a new level.

If, as I have tried to show, every language has an individual structure, and the linguistic structure of French poetry is Platonic while that of Shakespeare's English is a sort of passionate Aristotelianism, then every true translation—and this quite apart from accuracy of detail—has a kind of moral obligation to be a metaphysical reflection, the contemplation of one way of thinking by another, the attempt to express from one's own angle the specific nature of that thought, and finally a kind of examination of one's own resources. From that point, translation goes far beyond the rendering of explicit discourse and the meanings that can be grasped directly, and penetrates into indirect ways of expression (prosodic usage or the handling of imagery, for instance). Translation becomes the struggle of a language with its own nature, at the very core of its being, the quickening point of its growth. Now I believe that French poetry today is much better prepared than it ever has been to wage this struggle with its own language. In general terms, we may have reached a point in Western history where the major languages have to emerge from their naïveté and break with their instinctive assumptions so as to establish themselves in a different kind of truth, with all its contradictions and difficulties. And without attempting to deny the existence of its ever-present structure, recent French poetry is undergoing a revolution which, by disturbing this metaphysical tendency, and curbing it, could at some time or other allow us to better convey Shakespeare's artistic intention.

What is the real point at issue? I have contended that a French word, in its "classic" usage, designates what it refers to only in order to exclude the real world of heterogeneous existences. I have contended, too, that Baudelaire affirmed this reality of existences but that it was not so much these real entities as our relations with them that he took as the focus of poetic contemplation; and so once again he made a closed world out of language—the world in which a soul struck by the mystery of presence is doomed to speak only obliquely of a reality he could never truly make part of his life. This kind of poetry is still a subjective account of the soul, it is a *psychology;* but there is another, more recent kind of poetry, which aims at *salvation.* It conceives of the real object, in its separation from ourselves, its infinite otherness, as something that can give us an instantaneous glimpse of essential being and thus be our salvation, if we are able to tear the veil of universals, of the conceptual, to attain to it. Whether this ambition is well founded or not is of little importance. The essential thing is the demand it makes on language—to be open to what is most different from us and most external to us, to what is most difficult to capture and express, the being of things, their metaphysical *thereness,* their pure presence before us, in all of its silence and night. While it continues to exclude conceptual descriptions, this poetry is an attempt to lose its identity, to go beyond its own nature, to the point where the universal *becomes* the particular (the ontologically unique), an ecstatic plunge into what is. This pursuit of otherness, of absolute exteriority, is surely not so far from Shakespeare. Is it not an attempt to contemplate what Shakespeare lays bare in particular beings as their secret source and background—when, for instance, he weaves through Macbeth's whole destiny the irreducible element of chance, which is the presence of the witches; or shows Hamlet's mind haunted by the voice coming from the shadows; or reveals, in *The Winter's Tale,* the hope—absurd but still triumphant—of a real resurrection in the flesh? After all, a mirror that truly reflects life must of necessity reflect an experience of being as well. Always a rational universe is given the lie; it melts away before the void, and human action projects itself into an obscure and incommunicable region. There is no great difference between the Hamlet who realizes that the rule of law has passed away (and that justification is to be found, if anywhere, in a subjective choice without ground or warrant) and our contemporary French poetry, which has abdicated its age-old kingdom and taken its chance, like the prince of Denmark, with anguish, impotence, and silence.

To put it another way, it is at the level of their deepest, most immediate intuitions that the realism of Shakespeare and the denial of idealism in recent French poetry may henceforth communicate. For the one presents, describes, what the other asks to live. And what can be *said* directly by Shakespeare may, perhaps, be indirectly suggested in a language of translation that, while honoring the explicit content of each work to be translated, can now contribute a profound feeling for the very being and presence of things, which will be an unremitting testing of all its poetic resources. Thus the necessary surpassing of classical forms, of closed types of prosody (which is not inconsistent with a concern for the real laws governing the verse), can become one, in translations of Shakespeare, with the need to preserve the poetic line and its tragic quality, but without giving the impression that the English poet believed in a hieratic and unreal world. In fact, Shakespeare and many other Elizabethan writers have become immensely instructive for French poetry in its process of finding itself. We ought to give them our most serious attention. And if we still fail to translate them properly, we shall certainly have less excuse than translators who have gone before.

The confrontation of two languages in a translation is a metaphysical and moral experiment, the "testing" of one way of thinking by another. Sometimes it is sheer impossibility, indeed vanity. From time to time, however, something may emerge that will add another level of interest to the mere fact of translation, raising a language to a new level of awareness through the circuitous ways of poetry.

TRANSLATED FOR *ENCOUNTER*, 1962;
REVISED BY JOHN NAUGHTON

CHAPTER NINE

Transpose or Translate?

IN A SPECIAL ISSUE of *Etudes Anglaises*,[1] Christian Pons proposes a new method of translation for *Hamlet*. He suggests that there be intentional transpositions, done in the broader rhythms and the unimpeded abundance of the *verset*—the long verse line favored by Claudel. He writes: "In the particular case of *Hamlet*—I would not say the same for all of Shakespeare—it would be better to transpose, that is, transfer into another movement that would be the equivalent in our language. . . . We should not hesitate to be more ample than the original wherever the French language requires a logical breaking up or the development of what in Shakespearean imagery is either implicitly stated or else concentrated in a few words." And, having legitimately criticized me for an inadequate translation of "to watch the minutes of this night"[2] from the opening scene in *Hamlet*, Pons unhesitatingly "develops" the meaning he sees contained in these words. His translation becomes: "Afin qu'il surveille avec nous les ténèbres, et ce lent écoulement des heures, tous les moments de la nuit l'un après l'autre" ("To watch over the darkness with us, and the slow passing of the hours, all the moments of the night one after

---

1. "Shakespeare en France," *Etudes anglaises* 13, no. 2 (1960).—Trans.
2. The full passage in Shakespeare reads as follows.—Trans.

Horatio says 'tis but our fantasy,
And will not let our belief take hold of him
Touching this dreaded sight, twice seen of us:
Therefore I have entreated him along
With us to watch the minutes of this night;
That, if again this apparition come
He may approve our eyes and speak to it.

another").[3] More oratorical than the original text, as Pons himself admits, this adaptation is nonetheless the way to true fidelity, through a movement "analogous to the Claudelian *verset*."

Let me begin with a comment that is not crucial and that has more to do with the psychology of translation than with its geometry. It is true that when an English word is rich in ambiguity, it is a thankless task to have to choose between meanings. To side with the principle of "developing," however, would mean having constant recourse to solutions through abundance, at the cost of breaking with the poetic tension of the line. The translator may have forgotten that the Claudelian *verset*, especially in his plays, can be quite short. I am convinced that constraints are necessary in the prosody itself in order to translate well, if not with ease.

More important still, what really is "meaning"? And doesn't the sort of "explicating" recommended by Pons lead to a kind of betrayal of meaning, since it might fail to recognize the duality, at the heart of speech, between what is formulated and what is held back, or, to put it another way, between the conscious and the unconscious? These oppositions, moreover, are themselves significant; they are a part of everything that has to be considered when translating. When Marcellus asks Horatio to stay with him and "to watch the minutes of this night," it is possible that these words mean all that Pons's translation has them say and would immediately be apprehended by the audience as such. Yet it is also possible that Marcellus is unaware of all that, or is unwilling to express it quite so fully. In fact, he is probably saying much more. But to "develop" almost to the point of exhaustion what is only one aspect of the meaning is to turn the mind away from its deeper reaches. One can no more deliver a word from its meaning than one can transport the density of a symbol into a concept, or cast the tragic dimension of immediacy into discourse, or put into a flat formula those indistinct stages through which the assertions or implications of the manifest meaning join the mysteries of what remains unconscious.

---

3. Bonnefoy's translation of the passage reads as follows.—Trans.

Horatio dit que ce n'est qu'un rêve,
Il ne veut pas accepter de croire
A l'horrible vision que deux fois nous avons eue.
Et c'est pourquoi je l'ai pressé de venir
Avec nous, pour épier ces heures de nuit.
Si ce spectre revient,
Il pourra rendre justice à nos yeux — et lui parler.

I would say that such ambitions sin through intellectuality; they presuppose the primacy of the idea in the act of writing, and even of a precise program of significance to be communicated, over every other function of the word—for instance, to *invent* a meaning rather than to say it; to *constitute* a world rather than simply to mirror it; to approach, while at the same time holding them at a distance, obscure and dangerous realities in a moment of conjuration. The rationalist view is not the best philosophy with which to approach the Elizabethan age. And I'm afraid it has little claim on Claudel, whose *verset* never had anything analytic about it, even in his translation of the *Oresteia*. A line of verse is always more than what it says. And a "developed" analysis of its meaning will always tend toward prose.

II

But I still have to formulate what strikes me as the most important reason for not translating *Hamlet* in *versets*. Pons presupposes that Claudel would have been a good translator of Shakespeare, but I disagree. It is a fact, after all, that this great dramatist, who did translate from the English, never tackled the Elizabethan theater. It is true that there is both a tragic and a comic breadth to Claudel that makes his plays perhaps the only body of work in French drama capable of competing with Shakespeare's variety. But on so vast a horizon a similar vision is not necessarily cast, and in order to translate *Hamlet* or *Macbeth* (this would have been less true of the history plays), Claudel would have had to abandon a good part of his own being and, in any case, his *verset*. For the *verset* signifies immediately, organically, an astonishing optimism, at once dogmatic and congenital, shot through with darkness and light, which is very far indeed from Shakespearean thought.

Listen to this line: "The time is out of joint: O cursed spite!" Nothing could be more pessimistic than *Hamlet;* nothing wanders quite so far from the security of faith. An intuition of nothingness darkens and fragments all of Elizabethan consciousness. Hamlet seeks but does not find the foundations for a viable order. And it is remarkable how well the Shakespearean line is able to express this torment. It identifies with the voice, breaks with its anguish, picks up with its newfound hopes, hardens when it might have come undone in the distress of the moment. The pentameter in *Hamlet* is by no means a secondary or negligible fact. And this is because it bears—like the decasyllable or the alexandrine in French—a power of metaphysical receptivity that is a good deal more specific and precise than is often thought.

Can we honestly believe that this length—five feet, six feet—has been imposed on Western languages by chance? It is the length in which the long and short syllables that make up each word can, in the midst of a visible ensemble, either come together or clash—creating this or that rhythm—with the greatest intensity, thus allowing the poet's relation to himself and the world to be expressed with a maximum of richness.

When the line is shorter, this activity at the heart of its sonorous reality is diminished; it tends to disappear, invariably at the expense of a whole dimension of feeling and thought. It is all too easy for the very short line to play, or to affirm; it risks losing much of its capacity for intuition. When it is longer, much longer—well, I will come back to this. In its average length—in English, five feet; in French, ten or twelve syllables—it helps to create between the various sounds of words, and also between their meanings, a system of reciprocal relations that is the very life of speech, and this fact has certainly contributed to its development, as evidenced by the history of poetry in recent centuries. And it has done more: it registers and expresses the structure of the world that the poet, at various moments of his relation to society, has had the power to create or the destiny to endure. An example? Doesn't the classical alexandrine, with its rhymes and its caesuras, require that clear and distinct ideas, a perfectly transparent form of Intelligibility, replace the dark night of empirical reality? And isn't the one who uses such verse not aware of this metaphysical demand, and in a better position to think deeply about it and to refute it than he would be were he to use any other form of language? It is in the hollows of Racine's verse that the horizon of the truer intuitions and the new illusions that will preoccupy Chénier, Nerval, and Mallarmé can already been seen taking shape.

In short, the line of five or six feet, or ten or twelve syllables, is the boundary between the mind's inner workings and the world outside on which that mind must work. It makes note of the order of things thought true by an era; it perpetuates that order, keeping thought fixed on it. But it also brings thought into contact with the unknown and with the unconscious. It is thus a form of speech that not only helps to constitute a society but enables it to visit the most distant regions of perception or the most hidden recesses of the psyche. This is why, historically, poetry has known a whole development from orthodoxy to revolt, to discovery, along paths that are sometimes direct, sometimes roundabout, and among which are the metaphors prosody itself can create. If the pentameter begins to "limp," it is not just because an actor in *Hamlet* does not know his role; it is also because the human being, the speaking being, no longer wants to play the role that tradition has assigned to him or her—that is, can no longer have faith in a myth, an ideology, a dogma, preferring doubt and confusion to the endless repetition of forms now devoid of being.

And this is also why the *verset*, be it Claudel's or Pons's, cannot be faithful to the truth of works written in the kind of verse practiced in Elizabethan England. For a line that is too long does not have the same constraints as do more tightly constricted meters; it therefore cannot create the same experience. In the longer line, form weighs much less heavily on the substance of the word, and the word is perceived less strongly as a resonant presence. It tends to be reduced to the notion it carries, and this encourages an entirely different relation to the world. I would say that, in contrast to the line of "average" length, the *verset* seeks from the outset to pass over that boundary in consciousness which is the idea of order, concern for the intelligible, so as to reach that happy state of plenitude and variety in which naming things and listing places takes precedence over the need for mastery and coherence, over the understanding of rules. And this can seem to be freedom itself, a perfectly appropriate welcoming of the future, and much superior to the "limping" I mentioned a moment ago, which is as much a prisoner of the past as a sign of changing times. But let us beware! Can this kind of fervor be called an authentic transgression when it has not known constraint? Is it not more likely to be the utopia that conceals a habit of thought we are unwilling to submit, in the line itself, to the test of the depths of the relation to oneself? The *verset* defers the examination of traditional forms rather than actually attempting it. After his series of words, in the aftermath of his wave, the poet appears to have settled on a shore decreed new and propitious, with the energetic, if debatable, self-assurance of a conqueror or a missionary. This seems to be the case with Claudel, whose verse for conquistadors hardly seems suited to the melancholy prince who gives up even his Denmark. To translate *Hamlet* with Claudel's methods would be to abandon the space of the question—which has value to the extent that it exceeds the resources of the intellect and must even, at times, be recognized as insolvable—for the arrogant genius of the answer.

TRANSLATED BY JOHN NAUGHTON AND STEPHEN ROMER

CHAPTER TEN

How Should Shakespeare Be Translated?

I AM SURE that none of my readers has not felt some irritation, some sense of disapproval, not only of the mind but also of the soul, when confronted with this or that translation of Shakespeare. It is not always the translator's ability that we are calling into question. Our impatience takes issue with a predisposition in the translator, which is contrary to our own personal sensibility and which influences, however subtly, the understanding of the text and the arrangement of the phrases translated. In short, since all translators have their instincts, their "genius" as we still might say, options were exercised at the very outset, whether consciously or unconsciously, that we would have decided quite differently. It is my intention here to explore those origins where sensibilities part; to isolate two or three of those fundamental choices that one makes with one's entire being; to understand them, as best I can, with the help of my notion of the poetic function—in short, to outline, within the limits of a thought that lays no claim to coherence, what, when systematized, elaborated, and extended to other problems, could become a typology or a general system of classification for translation and translators. This enterprise may well have its uses. Quite apart from the fact that, if done well, it would provide critics with ammunition to more easily dismiss inadequate translations, it might even allow budding translators to know themselves better and consequently to make better choices—a crucial first option!—of the works they want to translate. I certainly believe that many ways of translating are justified and can be shown to be fruitful, on condition that they are applied to works that bear some relation to those methods. Translate poets who are close to you! We can appreciate only certain minds and certain works. I am putting aside, of course, all value judgments.

But let us return to translations of Shakespeare, because it is the only experience, whether direct or indirect, on which I can base my argument. How in these illustrious translations, which we may or may not like, and in my own work, are we to trace those divergences that I wish to define? The best way, I believe, which is the method I will pursue, is to consider first and foremost the dilemmas and decisions that can be called *technical*, since we perceive these—from the outset of our undertaking, which they will help us to structure—as well-defined and very clearly formulated problems. For example: *Shall I translate in verse or in prose? Shall I choose regular verse?* The answers given to such questions cannot but be revealing. They are the reflection in the work-in-progress of those options I mentioned earlier, which are more deeply hidden within us and consequently more diffuse and less easily discernible.

I shall take this first question, then, as my point of departure: Should the translation be in verse or in prose? This is a choice one must make before venturing to translate the very first word.

II

On this choice, opinions differ widely. Obviously there is a tendency to prefer verse translation from the point of view of fidelity, but ambitious translators like Marcel Schwob or André Gide have certainly felt that their own particular undertakings made sense and were close enough to the truth, despite their use of prose. These translators justify their choice—or could well do so, for I see no other conceivable argument—by assuring us that an important part of the poetic substance—for example, the images, the symbols, the metaphors—is preserved in their translation. But what does this kind of thinking assume? Apparently, that verse itself is only a part of poetry. That the "content" of poetry is, to a degree, separable from its form. And thus that the elaboration of form is only one means among many of expressing, in a more striking and majestic way, in a manner easier to remember, what remains essentially the *description* of a state of our consciousness, or an aspect of the human condition. Poetry, in this view, is nothing more than a *better way of saying* what would otherwise simply remain something understood or expressed. We have no trouble remembering some of the endlessly thought-provoking situations that occur in *Othello, Macbeth,* or *Lear* that prose is certainly capable of evoking. The consequences of ambition, jealousy, or pride are revealed by the lucidity of the poet and are still authentic objects of reflection in the everyday speech that accommodates them.

However, is this really the essence of what Shakespeare has tried to do? Isn't there in the very heart of the truth that he expresses something other than the consciousness that perceived, analyzed, and formulated it? And if Shakespeare is distinct from philosophers and analysts of passion, isn't it because there exists, between his experience of others and his own existence, a more intimate sympathy, a more immediate connection between the particular and the universal, which, in its coherence and in its quite specific manner of being, is the very essence of Shakespearean intuition and, hence, of what it is important to keep vividly in mind? Take Hamlet, for example, that irrational presence that no objective description could ever reduce to a set formula. Hamlet really has meaning only if we recognize in him a great metaphor unfolding, which is only partly conscious of itself, by which the poet himself, and not some character that he imagines, projects himself into what is expressed; he has meaning only if we are able to understand that the true drama and the true tensions are just as much in the continuity between Hamlet and Leonte and Prospero—where Shakespeare deepens his thinking and strives to better understand himself—as in the apparently self-contained conflict that sets the young prince against his mother or the new king. At the heart of poetry, at least in its modern period, lies a subjectivity that is formed, felt, and constituted as destiny; and there is therefore a questioning and an uneasiness, which, because they are guided by a concern for true harmony with being, exceed all knowledge of a particular aspect of our being and every formulation of this knowing. If this is so, doesn't it follow that verse has a function as specific as it is irreplaceable, and that the translator cannot fail to recognize such a function without betraying the work?

I myself have no doubt about it. There may be a level of self-awareness where prose is a worthwhile instrument of expression. This is the level on which intelligence labors without any feeling for transcendence, determined to carefully distinguish between existence and the sacred, and seeking to know human reality only insofar as it remains an object, reducible to entirely natural laws, which are, in one way or another, immanent in our material needs or in the values of society. Instinct, then, and even passion and our highest aspirations are defined only by the proximate and tangible end toward which they tend. The irrational, even freedom itself, can be accepted as a fact, but the abstract universality of law, which prose seeks to apprehend, takes precedence over everything. Yet as soon as self-awareness develops in a serious way, I believe, it needs to realize that its tendency to generalize the description of the human object merely breaks up into varying aspects, finally obscuring the particular reality that we essentially are. And self-awareness needs to encounter what, on the contrary, immediately unites all the elements of our existence: the apprehension of ourselves as a presence that is at once evidence and mystery, and no longer object, which it is our task to enrich and deepen as we develop our destiny. Merely to attain to the idea of unity, or presence, we have to move to a new level and to recognize that what can claim to be called real on that level is no longer an *object*, indefinitely and vainly conceptualizable, but a *cipher* whereby we discover our meaning by constituting it. The responsibility that we have to ourselves can be exercised only by remorselessly exceeding what the West calls psychological knowledge. This is a development that fiction manifests when it tries to describe the "laws of the heart" but then, seized by a more religious concern, shows that it can rediscover the symbolic function of what we call things—as in Proust, in whose work, however, this act of transcendence is called to mind only by reflection that takes the past, and not the present, for its material. For the return to true being to be lived and not just talked about, for there to be a future as well as memory, we must disentangle ourselves from conceptual utterances and either tend toward the silence of elemental experiences or extend poetic elaboration beyond everyday language, where the word, become name and divine, no longer designates the "nature" specific to each thing, but points to its possible presence, its imminent presence, in our lives.

And this is where we rediscover verse and its function, which the translator must never forget. Poetry is by no means a denser or more pathetic *expression* of the nature of human beings, or even of the experience of someone in particular. It is one of the acts by which a consciousness tries to unfetter itself from the motivations that fragment it in order to place itself within a network of meanings and codes that assure our unity. Poetry is the constitution of a sacred order—and it is verse that allows it to be. For rhymes, assonances, and rhythms oppose the logic of analysis with their exigency, which seems to keep open a mysterious expectation in speech; they call attention to the material quality of the word, which is closed to the linking up of concepts, and which, by this very fact, comes to designate the thing in its being, which cannot be fragmented, in its presence in the world and for us. It follows that to put one's trust in verse will mean seeking, among these varied presences, those that will be mediatory. Writing in verse, we will no longer analyze our quest for unity, as Proust did; we will accomplish the quest here and now, in the free (at least in theory) unfolding of the poem. And as for feelings, which poetry lays bare as no other words can, let us just say that they are more *present* than apprehended in the poem, as if acting of their own accord, although each feeling is experienced there to its limit and must fade away in the transparency the heart at last acquires—which means that a certain kind of theater will be the natural setting for their fulfillment, as the author of *Hamlet* shows us. If there is speech, indeed, where feeling acts freely, in its essential immediacy—where what is lived prevails over what consciousness would describe—it is certainly the speech of the prince of Denmark, which I would call original and native. And if there is speech that is perfectly transparent without alienating its immediacy, its warmth in the act of knowing—transparent, dare I say, simply through loving—it is surely Perdita's speech in *The Winter's Tale*. Shakespeare was an exemplary poet in the sense that he imagined his main characters not by observation but by self-projection and risk; he lived each one of them as an autonomous and vivid metaphor of a part of what he himself potentially was, and by ridding himself of Othello, Lear, and Macbeth—all of them figures of doubt or obsession, and hence of nothingness—he cured himself of his bad tendencies. His whole theater is the conflict between an *I* and all its *others*. It is the diversification to almost universal dimensions of a lyric consciousness; which is not surprising, since consciousness may be vast, but the *I* alone is infinite.

The time has come, however, to give a precise answer to the question I have raised. I can now say that we must retain verse when translating Shakespeare or any other poet; otherwise, we lose the essence of what they have tried to accomplish. And translation that I would call literary—that subtle, ornate prose that maintains the illusion that it has preserved poetic specificity—is obviously dangerous. The poetic act is a space, the very space of existence, and the translator should at least know how to understand and evoke this space, if not restore it, in order to preserve its crucial value for us. But this is precisely the great task that literary translation is incapable of assuming, and its grandest stylistic refinements will only lead us astray. It is here that the first option is revealed, not only a technical option but also an existential one, whose influence I could sense in those unconvincing translations. In literary translation there is a denial of transcendence, of life conceived religiously. And it is certainly not surprising that this denial is illustrated by André Gide, who was enamored of a sensation that has no other end but itself and who could conceive of our freedom only by the trompe-l'oeil of the gratuitous act.

Nonetheless—and this is a point that bears emphasis—my criticism in no way implies that all prose translation should be proscribed, for there is still a case where, provided it is aware of its limits, the nonpoetic approach to a poem can contribute to the truth. Indeed, I am not forgetting that poetry cannot be the only impulse of a modern consciousness. Even if we have decided that poetry is the overriding goal, it is still useful to clear this experience of the deceptive approximations of half-knowledge, to rediscover the paths that historical changes have obscured, to confront the great moments of freedom of thought with the spiritual givens of their era so as better to distinguish, say, authentic utterance from mere vocabulary. In short, in a society like ours, where systems of reference are multiple and vocabulary not obvious, we need to be critical in order ultimately to be immediate. And, if poetry is an *act*, as I am convinced it is, then it will be so all the more intensely when critical awareness, taking it deliberately for *object*, and seeking to release its essence, will secure its radiance. It is in this spirit that the history of religions, for example, and religious sociology or phenomenology, striving to circumscribe the meaning of the necessarily impure elaboration of self-awareness in some confraternity from a bygone era, can maintain a true dialogue with one who is himself striving to make the impulse of faith exist among the snares of another time. I recognize, therefore, the value of scholarly translations, in prose of course, that seek to determine, from the point of view of that particular consciousness that keeps watch in the French language, everything that Shakespeare experienced—metaphysical or social features of his era, influences, etc.—and everything that relates or contrasts it to other projects of the mind. Yes, such translations, freed from all ambiguity, are desirable, and it goes without saying that when they exist, they can help the less learned endeavor of the poetic translator. But translations of this kind, it seems to me, have remained too timid. Out of respect for the continuity of the original phrase, they make the mistake of choosing between the hypotheses of meaning, the connotations, the buried implications, whereas each of these should be pursued, even if it means presenting a totality of signification, though in fragments, within the three dimensions of the page, like a new *Coup de dés*.[1] This would only be appropriate for a truly critical translation of *Hamlet*. The *prince amer de l'écueil* is precisely a mind that anguishes over its infinite

1. Mallarmé's *Un coup de dés jamais n'abolira le hazard* was revolutionary in its use of typography, making the material aspects of the book—the three dimensions of the page—part of the reading of the poem.—Trans.

potentialities.[2] Mallarmé may have wanted to gather them all together in order to escape his condition, which should have recognized the reality of chance. But critical awareness owes it to itself to examine, for its part, all those potentialities that *Hamlet* suggests so that the most elusive components of the Danish prince's hesitation may appear along with data that is more purely historical. Be that as it may, I end up either with the impassioned choice of poetry, for which the space of verse is needed, or with the enumerative absolute of science. Between these two poles of consciousness, between reason and faith, there is only inopportune literature.

III

But this first principle, or, if you prefer, this axiom, is surely insufficient for my purpose, which is to critique, in connection with problems of prosody, a number of important existential positions. There are, for example, some verse translations that I feel are unfaithful despite what may be called their artistic merit. Is choosing to translate in verse not sufficient obligation to be faithful to the spirit of the poetry? Let us continue, if you will, this analysis of modes of being and get to the most pressing of the decisions a translator must be prepared to make. I have decided to translate in verse. My decision is made. But what kind of verse? Free verse or regular verse?

Once again, as we know, opinions differ widely. But the most common thesis, at least until today, favors regular verse, which is still, as far as I know, the alexandrine, and this thesis seems to hold sway. It is obviously with good reason that the partisans of this thesis can argue that regular prosody, since it is the form of expression that Shakespeare himself used, is alone capable of bringing all aspects of his experience back to life. It is not without importance that a poet should dedicate himself to a form that predates him and that manifests in its very particularity something simple, inalienable, and impersonal. Such a form offers itself as a link between the particular existence and a common order of mind; at the very least, it evokes the possibility of a belief that all people can share. And if the poet is going to inscribe his own impulses of anguish, discord, or denial into this form, these deviations will still be expressed, and even imagined, from the perspective of a spiritual reality that is higher and more secure than that of any given individual. Regular verse is the

---

2. *Prince amer de l'écueil* (bitter prince of the reef) is a line from Mallarmé's *Un coup de dés*. The line refers to the risk of failure inherent in the poetic act.—Trans.

implicit acceptance—though sometimes stirred by rebellion or consumed with doubt—of the idea of an orthodoxy, and nothing in the translation to come should make us forget this initial commitment. Furthermore, the very length of the line of verse employed by the poet has meaning, as I have tried to show elsewhere: it marks a certain connection between inner life and world, and if Shakespeare chose pentameter, or if, more accurately, he could express himself profoundly in the theater of his era in which pentameter prevailed, then this is clearly a feature of his work that should not be forgotten. To these arguments, and to others that could easily be made, there is apparently no answer. I personally, however, have never for one moment envisioned translating Shakespeare in regular verse, for I believe that such a course of action is impossible to realize.

In other words, I believe there is a fundamental contradiction in the principle of this course of action that ruins it and irremediably misrepresents the truth it proposes. What happens if I choose to translate Shakespeare in alexandrines or, more reasonably perhaps, in decasyllables? On the one hand, I have a framework that is, in some ways, inviolable, and, on the other hand, a given meaning that is no less so. And it will therefore be necessary to adjust the content to the framework by procedures that at certain moments can only be exercises in pure form. I must confess that the best of the translations in regular verse strike me as artificial, and the ingenuity of the translator only aggravates this feeling; or, if I take the point of view of the characters that speak, the translations seem excessively conventional, and the brilliance of the translator only makes them more dangerous. At best, such brilliance is acceptable in Shakespeare's comedies, or in his tragicomedies, such as *Troilus and Cressida*, because in these works convention lies in the very essence of the utterance, manifesting the irony by which ambiguous and half-real figures become detached from the immediacy of life. But what an unnatural corset regular verse is for the brute force of Othello, what strange civility for Macbeth, what bizarre affectation, what unreal and excessive intellectuality, for the prince of Denmark! Isn't it true that we are now strictly in the field of rhetoric? In poetry, form is not a framework but an instrument of research. In its never entirely achieved potential, it represents, as if metaphorically, the sacred order that we want to establish; it carries on a dialogue with us, compelling us to abandon what is inessential, to give up much of what has been proposed about reality, and to devote ourselves to something it suggests is more intense—in a word, to change our lives. Indeed, poetry might be said to erase us. All poetic formulation is a crossroads at which we must assume, for our existence to come, what the absolute that lies waiting in form has sealed in the word. And if we no longer have this freedom of choice—where the paradox of free will comes to life in exemplary fashion—then the allegedly invented form will deteriorate into pure formalism. There is no meaning that preexists the poem; there is only a destiny that has *taken form* and knows how to state directly its adherence to itself.

Were you to accept this idea, it would allow us to analyze one of those entirely instinctive reservations that I mentioned at the outset, one of those disagreements suggesting that the mind itself is divided. If, indeed, true form is this choice, which translation cannot be, why have some translators who are very sensitive to the suggestions of poetry run the risk of fixed forms? What energy has sustained them? It must be another conception of the work, in which ingenuity and convention do not appear radically foreign to the creative practice. I remember meeting, not long ago, a translator of *Hamlet* who told me he had carried this sort of enthusiasm, which no doubt is sincere, to the point of imitating Shakespeare's rhythms, alliterations, and rhymes. He was striving to render the sound of the words in the translation of their meaning and what he saw as a carefully prepared harmony in the arrangement of Shakespeare's lines. Such an effort is surely futile. If the sonority of a word has a poetic value, this value differs according to the language and, at the very least, must be transposed. Harmony itself betrays a quite different intention in French, where it so easily conveys the platonic dreams of Mallarmé and Racine, than it does in the immediacy of Shakespeare's English. But the very extravagance of this ambition renders explicit the idea that determines it. What matters to this translator is less the act sketched out by Shakespeare but never completed than the remains of that act subsisting in the word. As an artist, this kind of translator worries about an ultimate form, the outer crust of poetry, indeed about an *object*, because he assumes—as Poe or as Valéry pretended to believe—that this object would be an end in itself for the poet. Here, then, is an idea of poetry whereby form no longer appears as a test of existence but rather as one of the elements in the construction of an object, so that everything will be subordinate to a fabrication that must be self-contained—everything, including the sensibility, the knowledge, or the passions of the poet, used in this autonomous space in the manner of trompe-l'oeil. Is this a valid conception, or rather, is it valid for Shakespeare? I fear that someone so disposed to understand his work would also be forced to realize, along with T. S. Eliot and, for that matter, Voltaire, that the object called *Hamlet* is poorly constructed. And, moreover, that it is unintelligible.

And so, if he wants to make himself creator of a new little universe, it might be best to forget the English poet who is so bristly and rough. In truth, there are two modes of being that go by the name of literature; though often parallel, their intentions and paths are profoundly dissimilar and may be contrasted as art and poetic ambition. Artists always seek to escape from themselves in order to produce an object that is sufficient in itself and that replaces them, a structure in which the wounds of the artists' condition, evoked beyond their personal interest, will change signs, so to speak, and become aspects of a new richness. Satisfaction is found in substituting aesthetic accomplishment for the great necessities of life. But go talk to Rimbaud about this kind of diversion! In his eyes, poets are those who want to restore the ancient balance of existence; who *use* beauty — rather than pursuing it as an end — to attain that goal whose essence remains an ethical one. They speak in order to know themselves, and at the expense of coherence. They are obscure, but they express themselves, rather than merely being made conspicuous, betrayed, like the author of a poem-object.

I will defend, for my part, the use of free verse in translation against this overly aesthetic notion of *Hamlet,* or *Othello,* or *Lear,* which are all meditative works moving toward truth. From the point of view of the "adjustment" I have been denouncing, free verse offers some very real advantages, for it can be a form in which poetic intensity asserts itself, without at the same time being a rigid framework. And in view of Shakespeare's prosody, whose regularity does have meaning, free verse also allows us to preserve some echo of it, as long as we know how to regroup its various measures around a mean, which, by returning frequently, will assume a controlling force. This number, which can reappear without becoming fixed, will be the regularity in Shakespeare in a form that is always close and yet always rejected, in the form of an emerging potentiality — and this too has some virtue. For in the era we live in, fixed forms are in any case beyond our reach for lack of a common ritual. Our desire for what they are can be expressed only in an indirect manner in our works themselves. Therefore, let this same distance, which aims at closeness, be established between us and Shakespearean verse, in which the spirit of orthodoxy is still asserted, sometimes fully so! And in translations in varying meters, let the controlling verse not be the alexandrine, which responds so ill to the specific properties of pentameter! As much as pentameter is compact, swift, capable of action, of deductive reasoning, of precise praise, as much as it can limp without ceasing to move forward, having at its disposal all the energy of what is real, so the alexandrine, that majestic structure onto which the powerful symmetry of equal hemistiches tends to impose itself, remains poised—perpendicular to the variety of all that is real—between the sacred and the profane, true only at the loftiest moments of lyrical experience. Of all forms, the alexandrine is the one that is both closed and unstable, which only escapes the excesses of harmony over meaning by the exceptional fullness of the latter or the depersonalization of some neoclassical beauty. It is a kind of all-or-nothing of the mind, and that is why it can welcome action only by agreeing to belie it.

The verse that seems to me the closest to Elizabethan pentameter has no name and scarcely any history—it is the eleven-syllable line. Breaking after the sixth syllable, it starts off like an indication of the ideal, but finishes, with the remaining five syllables that gather and secularize, like a fact open to the future of other facts. Thus the real and the sacred are, by its offices, in dialectical relation, as they are in the great decisions of life that the theater seeks to evoke, especially Shakespeare's theater. And when these decisions attain a genuine spiritual intensity, then the eleven-syllable line can move into the alexandrine. The absolute is given to us moderns only occasionally. And to us translators in particular. Eleven-syllable verse (and thirteen-syllable verse as well, no doubt) will be the shadow that an impossible regularity casts over the work of translation.

IV

But all this, I fear, is far too simple. All this covers only what is more or less possible in the practice of translating without really justifying its basis. When I spoke a moment ago of adjustment and illegitimacy in translating in regular prosody, I was underscoring a difficulty that free verse may attenuate but does not eliminate. As a matter of fact, it brings us back to what is fundamental. The work to be translated *has already been* invented. And however free I am to maneuver in the undefined space of free verse, this space, like any other possible form, has true poetic value only if it is the test of an existence and, consequently, the imprint of an invention that I will not be able to engage or produce if I must keep to the paths already cleared by Shakespeare. If poetry is to be translated, the translation must be located within the realm of poetry, and either this is my experience or it is not. How can I be faithful to an experience, my own, while living another? You see, then, the magnitude of the problem when put in this way; it is the very problem of our right to translate. Are there only false translations—false through fidelity to the poetic impulse—or, on the other hand, half-translations disguised as false poems? The fundamental question that must now be considered is: Should Shakespeare be translated at all? Isn't there an unraised contradiction, that is to say, an intellectual laziness, in the word-for-word confrontation with a work of poetry?

At this point, I think that the simplest thing to do is to admit my uneasiness, as well as my inability, at least provisionally, to attain the slightest degree of certainty on this truly essential point. On the one hand, I cannot rid myself of the dilemma just formulated, which seems unresolvable. I see Shakespeare's work as an entire world that he discovered little by little, and poetry as the tension of being and soul that allowed this discovery. And I also see my own effort at translation, however aware of poetry it may be, as merely an attempt to abide beneath its sign, without its having had to recreate this discovery, and without my having had to live, in my very ordinary life—as I imagine I should have done—the totality of those great moments. But, on the other hand, I cannot fail to recognize that translation sometimes associates poetry with fidelity. Is this simply a random fact, produced by the exceptionally close relationship of two poets? Or can a consciousness sometimes relive, as if *in memory*, the discoveries, the risks—in a word, the *change*—that someone else has undergone? In truth, I am at a loss as to how to answer these last questions.

Fortunately, I don't need to answer them in order to exercise my last option, surely the most radical one, which can only be decided by an act of faith. Even if poetic translation has no firm basis—and this is obviously an appalling situation—the poetry of Shakespeare still has a particular feature that attenuates the dilemma: namely, his poetry has taken the form of theater and so has mediated its always profoundly personal intention in figures that can be recognized by the common consciousness. For instance, Florizel's declaration of the love that will restore Perdita's royal essence is one of the codes in which Shakespeare has pledged to accomplish the discovery and the transfiguration, the "restitution," of his own being; but it is also an autonomous figure, incarnating one of the great moments in everyone's experience—and therefore an utterance that I too can understand and recreate poetically. In the order instituted by the poetry of theater, the given features of a specific existence constitute a smaller proportion than those essential aspects of the common consciousness. And these are the aspects that we can translate, recomposing with their help the space of the utterance that first drew them out, rejoining its primordial movement, and making authentic allusion, despite the contradictions I have been discussing, to the true, hidden Shakespeare.

TRANSLATED BY MARYANN DE JULIO

CHAPTER ELEVEN

Translating into Verse or Prose

I WOULD LIKE to make a few observations about the way in which the practice of translating sometimes interferes with the translator's idea of poetry. One of the problems posed by poems is the role of meters, rhymes, rhythms in their genesis; and how to decide whether or not it is necessary to preserve the prosody—or rather, to reenact the experience of it—when attempting to translate poems.

This was something I thought I was quite certain about. If poetry exists, it is because poets have wanted the sonorous dimension of words to be heard, to be an active element in the elaboration of form, so that meaning alone no longer determines the phrase, and the power and authority of the conceptual may be weakened and blurred, its veil torn, however slightly—for concepts deprive us of immediacy. Therefore the only way to read a poem, to translate it, is to relive the work done on the form that gave birth to it in the first place. This work is called its prosody. And so there is a certain inevitability about translating into verse what was written in verse, even though it means living the verse in the obviously new way imposed on the translator by his own experience of the world.

I have thought about this inevitability for a very long time, and it seems unassailable. I can even add one or two further elements to this basic principle, which seem to me well founded. If form is indeed what opens up our utterance to something immediate, something unbroken by words, something indivisible, beyond the concepts that fragment our experience of the world, it is form that restores to this experience the full dimension of the moment, since the concept, thought itself, is—reciprocally—an endless chain of separate events. But this moment must not divert us from true temporality; on the contrary, such openings onto the unbroken, onto plenitude, can give a real direction to our life, and therefore enrich—with desire, searching, straying, and returning—the time consecrated to the living of it. Poetry is the regeneration of time when we have lost heart, consenting to abstraction, exile. Poetry allows time, life's web—origin first, soon to be destiny—to be on the lookout in those situations where the absolute clearly makes its presence felt, for what might bring us closer to this absolute; and this explains the most striking, specific aspect of form in the poem: the line of verse, which can be written or heard only in the light of another line already encountered or to come.

Strictly as structure—long and short syllables, assonance, breaks, symmetries—form in verse is self-enclosed, which produces its separation from ordinary speech, its opening onto what lies beyond language. And this submission of writing to form is obviously a danger as well, the danger of reducing the utterance, which results to a handful of terms and a few figures, making it all the easier for the one expressing him- or herself in this fashion—desiring in this fashion—to construct yet another network of meanings, which once again veil immediacy. But words that have survived, however briefly, in this new light, provide possible guidelines for the work that always remains to be done; it is as if the form in which the indivisible is revealed, but disappears, were already summoning someone to the work that will allow the experience of unity to begin again, and thus what was closed off calls for what is yet to come—the line as such prepares the way for another line. Because the moment is never more than a fleeting glimpse, which passes quickly beneath the clouds of returning thought, its flash of light is always only a memory, but one that asks the storm to come back. The most beautiful lines of verse are those that make us sense an ardent desire for other lines in which the promise might flower again, the promise the first line avows it cannot keep.

Poetic form, in other words, is far from a structure proudly closed in on its handful of words like an oracle—that intervention of transcendence, when poetry is only the endless pursuit of it—or an inscription on a monument or a tomb. And the nature of lines of verse, at once moment and becoming, is yet another reason to see them as a very intimate part of the life of those who write them, coming from the most obscure region of their relation to themselves, and thus the very road that must be taken when, as translator, one has to keep clearly in mind what poetry is. And here, surely, the question becomes even more clear-cut. The text written in verse, that is to say lived in that form, must be translated—relived—in the same way.

But this doesn't mean that one must adopt the conventions determining the prosody of the text to be translated. For such rules do not reflect the specific and irreplaceable requirements of the full experience of the phenomenon of form, expressing rather the way in which a society, an era, can delimit if not vitiate this experience, thanks to philosophical or religious convictions, to say nothing of the demands of whatever power is in place, which attempts to redirect the always uncertain and unstable line-after-line of poetic intuition into the channels of rhetoric, whose flow is certainly easier, though not altogether devoid of charm. Prosodic conventions bear the stamp of the governing aspects of the culture of a particular time far more than anything essential to the transgression that may be brought about within their framework. In the complex reality that is the poem, they are on the side of its meaning and not on the side of what alone is essentially poetic, the break with this meaning. They should therefore be considered as just one element of the meaning, which one must indeed seek to translate but on the level on which this is merely the material that the writing, the new form of the translator, must work on with the freedom it needs in order to remain fully alive.

To submit oneself to a structure already precisely determined, even though one has also to remain faithful—sometimes for much better reasons—to what is actually said in the text, is clearly an impossible task: for the author invented the meaning at the same moment as he elaborated the form, whereas his unfortunate translator would have to adjust one to the other by means of a kind of acrobatics that would prevent him from reliving, in all its depth, the struggle between speech and presence. What the translator's text must recreate is the effect that the recourse to form, precisely when it is free, can have on the use of words, on their very meaning—which is disturbed even if not changed—and on the relationship of this sudden disorder to our encounter with what I have called the unbroken. To this end, "free" verse, which our era has made its own, will certainly suffice. From the outset, of course, free verse lacks what regular verse shows so clearly—namely the values and truths in play against a backdrop of consensus and common belief. But given that a line of free verse lacks fixed measures and clear signs of reprise beyond the word it ends up with, so that it is far less likely than a line of regular verse to elicit a kind of returning onto itself, through that fusion of temporality and form which is the very essence of the poetic, it has to make up for this lack, and can only do so—which is a major advantage—by paying deeper attention to what is played out in the relations between words where the form must do its work, not so much scorning rhyme, for example, as making it integral to the whole phrase.

In short, translating verse by means of verse seems incontestable, and I used to think myself fully justified in saying so. For example, after discussing the work of the philological translator—in my eyes perfectly legitimate—which deals with aspects of the text's meaning at the expense of the poetry, exploring to this end lexicons of a particular era or historical events, I once wrote: "either . . . the impassioned choice of poetry, for which the space of verse is needed, or . . . the enumerative absolute of science. Between these two poles of consciousness . . . there is only inopportune literature." And I glossed this, referring to yet another kind of translation: "We must retain verse when translating Shakespeare or any other poet; otherwise, we lose the essence of what they have tried to accomplish. And translation that I would call literary—that subtle, ornate prose which maintains the illusion that it has preserved poetic specificity—is obviously dangerous."

II

Yes, it is dangerous, and yet possibly not to be avoided altogether, for I have myself adopted it, and thus betrayed my own fine principles, in my translation of Shakespeare's *Venus and Adonis* and *The Rape of Lucrece*, which, having decided that this was the only possible solution, I did in a prose that may not have been all that subtle but was certainly ornate and obviously literary. Did I have grounds for this decision? And, hence, for being the first to contradict my own axiom, the validity of which, or at the least the limits of its application, I would then have to call into question?

Now why should one translate into prose something that is certainly poetry, despite the obvious fact that rhetoric, the delight one takes in language, plays such a large part in these two verse narratives? To answer this question, let me first observe that the line of verse is not the primary feature of the way we receive these texts for, to the eye as well as to the ear, the basic element of the poems under discussion is the stanza. And, on the level of the stanza, something happens that I should have taken into account, not only in my translation (where I did), but also when I was thinking, before or after translating, about the "principle."

Consider the first stanza of *Venus and Adonis* or, rather, the first two stanzas, for the repetition is needed in order to reveal what remains constant:

Even as the sun with purple-colour'd face
Had ta'en his last leave of the weeping morn,
Rose-cheek'd Adonis hied him to the chase;
Hunting he lov'd, but love he laugh'd to scorn.
Sick-thoughted Venus makes amain unto him,
And like a bold-fac'd suitor 'gins to woo him.

"Thrice fairer than myself," thus she began,
"The field's chief flower, sweet above compare;
Stain to all nymphs, more lovely than a man,
More white and red than doves or roses are;
Nature that made thee with herself at strife,
Saith that the world hath ending with thy life.

Here and throughout, the line of verse gives its fullness to the form, at least momentarily, since it immediately gives up this role while vowing to begin again, true to that oath we call rhyme. At first the rhyme is alternate, and this plays with the possibility of forgetting its exigency, but by the third line the memory of it is restored in a manner that is all the more acute—before the idea of the essential poetic renewal is affirmed, gloriously, by a rhyming couplet, the same sound struck twice. We thus move into a temporal continuity that we might think gives the line every opportunity to be simultaneously a pause and a development—that is, to live in us, to urge us on to this more-than-time within time itself, which I believe poetry is. And the stanza too moves on, for as soon as the second one is in place, a formal choice is confirmed, setting in motion the wheels that will draw all the other stanzas along.

But the rhyming of the last two lines, sounding the stronger since less expected, makes us pay all the more attention to the stanza, perceived now as a self-contained structure. For it has slightly increased the pause at the end, after which the form, separating from itself, decides to make a fresh start, forging ahead. And at this frozen moment—which allows us to see the stanza a little more clearly in its own form as an ensemble, that is, at the points where tensions appear as well as the verbal harmonies that the progression of the verse passed over too quickly—we discover that Shakespeare has corroborated this as yet discrete tendency by the richness of the rhymes, by shamelessly deploying the old rhetorical lexicon, loaded with stereotyped representations; and that this procedure is not at all without substance: for this sort of rich and easy rhyme supplies at one end of the line (just as the capital letter does at the other) what the garland of flowers and leaves and fruits on gilded frames brought to paintings of the same era. Rhyme in *Venus and Adonis* has that kind of decorative solemnity which allows us to more easily perceive the relations at work in the three dimensions created by all six lines together—the picture we are shown is what matters.

Now, these relations—and at this point they are no longer being summoned by the movement of the line to the meaning beyond it—peacefully proliferate in that immobility which is the stanza, and we see the crimson sun, the silvery tears, the rosy cheeks of Adonis, the beautiful body of Venus sick with love, flowering side by side, the one bringing the other into being. We are in a particular space, the space of dream. And because of this framing effect, which controls the borders of a line of verse already saturated with artistic metaphors and allegories that appeal to the eye, time—real existential time, which never ceases—is no longer anything but a thought repressed; from which it follows that our premonition of Adonis's tragic destiny, the fate that sweeps him away, seems to be drowned in the beauty one associates with Venetian painting: sumptuous foliage, purple skies, nudes like huge fruits.

It may be noted that Veronese's *Venus and Adonis* and his *Mars and Venus Bound by Love* date from 1580, twelve years before Shakespeare's poem, just the time needed for news of the works to reach England. And if temporal meshing plays its part in Shakespeare's poem, making it a succession of paintings rather than a single large one, we are surely reminded of the work of Annibal Carrache at the Farnese gallery, around 1600–1610. In order to recount the *Loves of the Gods*, Carrache juxtaposed and almost superimposed scenes with beautiful make-believe frames, so that his narrative project is equally a collection of paintings, each one leaving the development in suspense, each one therefore closer to dream than to tragedy.

In short, the earliest of Shakespeare's poems has several of the characteristics of a painting and is definitely akin to the art of the painters of his age, some of whose works may have been familiar to him, enriching his text with an abundance of essentially visual allusions.

III

And that is why I thought it proper to translate this text into prose. Is the "painting" aspect of the text essential? And to emphasize this aspect, is it essential to remain faithful to that which so strongly curbs the "forward movement" I have identified with poetry? In other words, how essential is the "frame" effect? It should be noted that free verse would not have the resources to render this essential element, since it in no way inhibits the temporal aspect of the verbal form, while regular and rhymed verse is even less feasible. How, then, can we find in modern speech those stereotyped yet well-received conventions which might play the part of rhyme frame without fear of ridicule? We have no "weeping morn" now; we no longer associate "love" with "forever"—not because of the idea the words convey but because our century tends to reject the commonplace and the cliché, to the extent, of course, that it is aware of them. And if the French language of today is to instill new life into "white colour'd faces" or "more white or red than doves or roses are," the translator will have to labor over the substance of his own words—an effort in which these conventional images will be of no value unless they are the result of his labor and not just a ready-made device for saving himself the trouble of sounding the depths.

Translating into prose, by contrast, will produce on the printed page a perfectly regular block for each stanza, perfectly separated each time, which will encourage readers to pause, to pore over this little universe of words for as long as they like, to try to perceive, as in a pond whose surface is partly obscured, the outcropping of images and the furtive cast of the colors, in the unforeseen reveling of the conventional metaphors. When a translation has to make do with these facile figures that move with an eel-like rapidity in a flux of alliteration and rhythm, prose serves it better, allowing associations and suggestions to join together and move apart without constraint. And the block formed by the stanza then has the function, and the effectiveness as well, of the elegant frame supplied by rhymes. So it is highly tempting and, it seems to me, justifiable to translate *Venus and Adonis* into prose, a prose as "ornate" and "subtle" as possible. Too much of the richness of this poem can survive in translation only on the level of prose, and we have to conclude that the balance tips in this direction.

But since this is the case, my "principle"—that verse must be translated by verse—has lost its universal value. One might be tempted to preserve the principle by suggesting that the verse, in *Venus and Adonis* or other texts of the same sort, is not verse in the deepest sense of the word, not the kind of verse that is fully present in truly poetic creations. It is "painter's verse" as it were, movements of the brush supplying rhythm to the canvas, hanging festoons around ideas as on walls in village halls—something almost as different from the real work of poetry as the meter of a mnemonic "poem." We might speak of "rhetoric" as opposed to poetry: a festive use of language intended to bring out its latent beauties, its undeniable capacity to create worlds and endow them with marvels, as opposed to that forcing of the truth of language, that beating of a path into the resistance of representations, of concepts, toward a bursting of pure presence, which is poetry as such, and as it already was in earliest antiquity, certainly in Shakespeare himself in his plays and sonnets.

We would not, however, be doing justice to this great poet, or indeed to lesser ones. For abdicating poetic potentiality in the interest of painterly effects is something that occurs in all written works, even those most devoted to the specificity of poetry, and it must therefore be retained as an aspect of the problems associated with it—for we would immediately misunderstand poetry's nature if we claimed that "pictorial" verses had no relevance to it. Every line of verse, every recourse to form in speech, to some degree goes through the same process in its ascent from conceptualization—from representation—to presence; and we must understand, and call to mind in this context, that if there is presence in a poem, it is there only in the most fleeting way. The moment poetic intuition has disturbed the conceptual network, Eros, who has been looking for ways to stage his desires, to satisfy them symbolically, will profit from this disorder for his own purposes, reconnecting, with the help of the relations he wants to establish between certain beings or things, words that have come apart: an attempt that recreates, at the very heart of perceived unity, the plane of the objects of this desire. And the world constituted by these objects—in fact these fantasies—is only an image, since it is constructed for play, which excludes our finitude from it; but this image is rich in the sensual aspects that Eros retains from life, and it therefore invades writing with seductions that are legitimate and that contribute, in no small way, to what we may call the beauty of literary works.

There is therefore an "image moment," a moment that easily becomes "painting" in any poetic production, even when the concern that engendered the work survives pure and intact. This concern seeks to recover itself and, in fact, does, and this is the essence of the development, the hope, that propels both line and stanza, opening up, as I think I have shown, the verbal form to a new, temporal dimension; but it will stall once again, and it will only survive by means of a compromise with the work of desire that is the secret weakness of poetry, the temptation that it can only resist in an ambiguous manner. The space that is dream shines forth, spreads itself out, breaks up, reconstitutes itself, despite the quest that desires presence within us. Two projects clash within the verse itself. In the final analysis, verse can be fully itself only if it does not pretend to ignore the fatality within it, namely the image; only if it is willing to venture wholeheartedly into the image. For such a venture puts poetry, what I understand by poetry, in danger, but it also makes it possible to better perceive and live out its drama. And if the image triumphs, the text born from this vanquished lucidity will perhaps nonetheless have been able to speak of poetry, at that point when for a moment it is being renounced.

In this case, translating the verse into prose in order to be faithful to the grand visual image that appears to predominate in the original, though it may seem more or less obligatory, is nonetheless a loss on the strictly poetic level, and the translator therefore cannot claim to have taken absolutely the right course. In *Venus and Adonis* for example, it may be less the case that Shakespeare yielded to the attractions of beautiful paintings than that he sought to appreciate their place in the spirit, their danger for poetry, thus embarking on that reflection that would lead him explicitly to condemn the seductiveness of the painted image in his next work, *The Rape of Lucrece*, and even more so in the sonnets, where he begs an all too handsome young man to remember that he is in reality old age in waiting, death, and to understand that he still has one chance: to give birth to another life. We can read Shakespeare's sonnets as embodying a problematics of the poetic, perceived in all its fundamental ambiguity, between illusion and lucidity, and thus using verse in a way that is more conscious of finitude—which is what Shakespeare's writing for the theater will become; the theater as he reinvented it. But this perception requires us to recognize that it is very dangerous for the overall translation of Shakespeare, for the transcription into French of the gradual development of this quest, to fail at the very point of departure by presenting the first poem without appearing to know that it was written in verse: all the more so in that it was already aiming—as the sonnets would do—at more than the image, for the portrayal of the death of Adonis indeed ends by tarnishing some of the brilliance of the colors. Recall the last line of the poem, where the goddess, "weary of the world," gathers together her silver doves, flies off in the chariot to which they are yoked, removes from our sight their conventional image as well as her own powers, and heads with her doves for Paphos,

> where their queen
> Means to immure herself and not be seen

A physical presence disappears, but in return there is an epiphany at the very moment of the transgression of the figures, a fleeting vision of what is purely divine in Venus, which further destroys any justification for my decision, since I will have translated "into prose" what nonetheless was clearly (albeit in a muted way) a threshold of poetry. Let us say I resigned myself to prose. But at the very moment when I felt that verse as such could not be saved, I was nonetheless convinced that it must be saved. I no longer have a principle handy that might promise solutions; all I have is awareness of our unavoidable incompetence: and it's probably better this way, since we are dealing with poetry.

IV

One last word. You may have noticed that I have discussed only *Venus and Adonis*—apart from a single mention of *The Rape of Lucrece* when I recalled that it contains a critique of the painter's spell and the power of images. Would the second poem lend itself less than the first to the justification—by faithfulness to the image—of translation into prose?

I think not. *The Rape of Lucrece* would have a different rationale for prose translation because it has recourse to another kind of painting. After practicing an art akin to that of Veronese, Shakespeare now approaches chiaroscuro, using rapid, violent actions that suggest Caravaggio, whose *Judith* dates from the same year as the poet's *Lucrece*. And this difference between two moments of the *ut pictura poesis* ideal is certainly important and has many facets, but for that very reason it would involve me in considerations irrelevant to the issue under discussion. A comparison between *Venus* and *Lucrece*, or between Veronese and Caravaggio, would provide rich instruction—not for the theory of translation but for a reflection on the nature of poetry itself.

TRANSLATED BY ANTHONY RUDOLF

CHAPTER TWELVE

Translating Shakespeare's Sonnets

I OWE SOME explanation to the reader, who is likely to be surprised that my translations of Shakespeare's sonnets have up to seventeen or eighteen lines, whereas a sonnet by definition has only fourteen, a number that Shakespeare's translators seem bent on preserving, unless they have resigned themselves to using prose.

But keeping strictly to fourteen lines, when one is already under an obligation not to make any changes to the ideas, feelings, and images that are the very substance of a poem, means having to produce a text in which a meaning decided in advance will be subject to considerable constraint on the level of form, even though, in all writing that is authentically and specifically poetic, form and meaning emerge simultaneously, the one stimulating the other, form helping meaning to explore its various possibilities and allowing it to discover, little by little or all at once, what the author, without yet knowing it, truly is. Poetry means searching; its rhythms find what is most immediate and spontaneous in us and help us to tear apart the representations of ourselves or of the world suggested to us by our concepts, and always too quickly. But poetry is also, dialectically speaking, the modification of these rhythms, of the prosody, by meaning, and poets who decide to employ a fixed form — as Shakespeare does with his sonnets — which would seem to hinder the dialectic, will have to make careful use of what remains open and free in the form by closely questioning what they thought they meant.

Now, it is precisely this calling into question that I find difficult when my role is that of translator. If I decide to preserve the sonnet form, I will no longer be able to see form and speech in a dialectical relationship in my writing; I will be faced with the sad duty of adjusting the meaning, which should be inviolable, to a form that will have ceased, at least in part, to be active and will instead prompt me to seek ways to adapt the substance of the text—by shifts in meaning, additions or subtractions supposedly venial, even padding—to the yoke of fourteen lines, eight rhymes, a fixed number of feet. All of which means forgetting about the kinds of operations and discoveries that take place in real poetry.

In translating the most regular meters, I feel justified, through fidelity to the spirit of real poetry, in claiming without question a form without any rules, which does not imply lawlessness, variable as to the number of syllables in each line and the number of lines in each stanza—in short, what we call free verse. With respect to the sonnet, I consider it permissible to retain only what is easiest to preserve of this structure and, moreover, what is sufficient to evoke it: its division always into four parts, one of them—the last—shorter in the case of Shakespeare. Four parts, but I shall not worry at all about the number of lines in each, or about their length, and as a poet I shall exempt myself—seeking as I am to make someone else's words live again in my own, both in meaning and in freedom of birth—from adhering to the conventions of a prosody which in this case would be like a Procrustean bed. I am not doing this to enable some idea found in the English text to develop in French simply according to its concepts and the logical articulations of those concepts, for, by definition, this would merely be prose. I am seeking rather to proceed freely with the rhythm, which, engendered within me in an unexpected way, will help me to relive what I have seen in the poem and, above all, to listen to it more intensely—even, perhaps, to draw out of the original text certain potentialities that were stifled by the fixed form.

Let us make no mistake, for this is at the heart of the matter: the material of the translator is less the "meaning" possessed by the text—a meaning that is extremely complex and is found or lost on various levels—than the translator's own experience of this meaning: an experience that can only take the form of a question the translator asks him- or herself about the value and the merit of the original, not necessarily with total approval but at least with a sufficiently open-minded and sympathetic understanding to give voice to them for a moment, in the play of hypotheses that constitutes our development. If this sort of agreement were not possible, it would be better to give up translating, for one can only translate well what one feels close to.

But when an opportunity for sympathetic listening is offered, so essential for a translator, translation becomes an activity that involves self-study as much as it involves a reading of the other, whence the need for free form, that great disrupter of stereotypes. My translation must also be a poem, rhythm and meaning each produced by the other. But note: this rhythm shall be my own. It can never fully relive the rhythm of the original because of the gap between the person one is and the person one admires. I have not tried to render the singular rhythms of Yeats into French: nor would I dream of trying to copy the verbal music of the Elizabethan poet; the result would be a mere shell. A translator must make such a sacrifice in order to enter, or at least try to enter, that place of invention called poetry.

But I certainly don't mean to imply that by ridding myself of a few shackles I shall have saved everything the English-speaking reader loves in Shakespeare's sonnets and rightly considers a major part of their quality. How can one preserve, for example, some of the wordplay—sounds tossed up and caught in flight in the space of meanings—created by a prosody so compact, so taut, so ready to send the ball back to the player on the other side for unexpected returns, that it becomes perfectly natural for that player to acquire a taste for these feats of prowess, for the almost poetic joy mental agility so often is? It is clear that the exercise of "wit" will suffer in my translation.

But I indulge myself in the belief that verbal prowess is, after all, only a brilliant envelope that must be opened to reveal the letter inside, which is the only thing that matters. I tell myself—am I wrong?—that it's all right to lose a lot of the rhetoric as long as some of the poetry remains.

TRANSLATED BY ANTHONY RUDOLF

Interview with Yves Bonnefoy

J.N. Can you remember when you first encountered Shakespeare and what your impressions were? Were you immediately drawn to his work? Was there a feeling of affinity?

Y.B. I can remember my first encounter since it was one of those moments that are not experienced in an especially powerful way at the time but that later come to dominate your thinking and to influence your choices. I was in school, and in the book of readings we were using to study English there was the most famous scene in *Julius Caesar:* "Friends, Romans, countrymen, lend me your ears," and that whole speech in which Mark Antony captivates his listeners, winning them over with cynical skill but at the same time speaking with such nobility and emotion about Caesar's remains. It's a great moment, not just of rhetoric but also of the lyrical essence of poetry. "'Twas on a summer's evening in his tent"—that whole passage that causes the "gracious drops" to flow.

Why did I find this scene so striking, more striking at the time than any other passage of English poetry, with the exception of *The Rime of the Ancient Mariner?* It was certainly because of the beauty and intensity I've mentioned, but today I think it was also because that superb English harbored a great deal of our own approach to poetry: the grand words of Latin origin, but also, and even more important, something of that resonant space that French poetry often maintains between words to allow their range of meaning a wider scope. In this case, the connection was somewhat closer than usual, and it allowed me to measure all the more fully the distance between these two paths of poetry, English and French.

I think I was also struck, though of course somewhat subconsciously, or, at least, in a not yet fully informed way, by the manner in which Shakespeare seems to consciously and deliberately bring together in this scene the aims and methods of rhetoric on the one hand, and poetry on the other. In a word, Antony's speech shows poetry in various kinds of relation to something other than itself. And this can help us to understand that poetry doesn't spring forth in a single bound from the depths of one's mind and spirit, but must free itself from various obstacles that are a function of the particular nature of language or cultural tradition. For someone like me, who wanted very much to devote himself to poetry, it was obviously important to understand this. I could almost convince myself that poetry is born in a more ordinary way in our lives and in our poems than I would have thought from reading Latin poets like Virgil, whose words seemed suggestive of an absolute; these poets were mysterious and seemed almost from another world because I understood Latin rather poorly, and there's no better way to find its words and phrases unsettling!

Need I add that these thoughts I had about Shakespeare were in an embryonic form? I had no particular capacity or knowledge or points of reference to develop them more fully. Let's just say that I thought a great deal about those speeches of Brutus and of Mark Antony; I wanted to translate them and, in fact, did many years later. *Julius Caesar* was the first play I translated, along with *Hamlet*, which I undertook at the same time—with the feeling of a very important rendez-vous with myself.

J.N. When exactly did you begin to translate Shakespeare? What were the circumstances?

Y.B. It was much later. I was in my thirties. And I hadn't been pursuing the idea. It was one of those chance occurrences that we marvel at later, since they seem to bring about what we've always wanted. In 1953 I published my first book of poems, which I sent to Pierre Jean Jouve, whom I had been admiring from afar. He asked me to come see him, which I did, and we found we had a great many common interests and tastes, especially in poetry. We talked about Shakespeare; Jouve had translated *Romeo and Juliet* before the war.

As it happened, Pierre Leyris, who had been friends with Jouve for many years, was planning to publish an edition of Shakespeare's complete works with the original English and translations by various French writers, his whole idea being to involve writers and poets rather than English language specialists. Leyris was the great translator whose work helped introduce French readers to Melville and Hopkins, as well as Djuna Barnes. Later on he also published a French edition of the complete works of William Blake. Leyris had contacted Jouve, since he knew of his translation of *Romeo and Juliet*, and had asked him to do the sonnets, an invitation that Jouve accepted enthusiastically. Then, without even consulting me, Jouve suggested to Leyris that he should offer me something to translate, which Leyris did. I didn't hesitate for a second; I felt I was ready, though my knowledge of Elizabethan English was still rather minimal.

Pierre Leyris asked me to do *Julius Caesar*, on condition that I first submit a sample, which was to be the first scene of the play. And so I did a translation of "Hence! home, you idle creatures, get you home!" and did it with such fervor and passion that Leyris immediately gave me *Hamlet* to translate as well. After these, I translated other plays, as well as Shakespeare's poems, for the volumes that appeared over the following years. The project made those happy years for me. I liked and respected Pierre Leyris, and he became and remained one of my dearest friends until his death, just recently, at the age of ninety-three, when he was at work on a new translation of Shakespeare's sonnets. Pierre read my work and gave me advice about specific details. But most of all, he gave me confidence. It was hard work, in fact. I was not in the least interested in producing, as many others did, a variation on previously existing translations without taking into account the difficulties of the text, and so I surrounded myself with critical editions and armed myself with dictionaries. I discovered Alexander Schmidt's superb lexicon and began to read various critical studies of Shakespeare that I happened to find.

J.N. What were the first difficulties you ran into?

Y.B. First of all, there were, of course, difficulties with the language, for I had a lot to learn, in particular about Elizabethan culture, and I spent much more time then than I do now with words and expressions that were unfamiliar to me. And then there was the fact that each new play brought its own problems: obscure patches in a sometimes unreliable text; passages, often famous ones, that the various editors interpret in quite different ways, all too often without coming to a decision. But those scholars and historians of the language certainly enable a non-native speaker like me to better understand Shakespeare, and without the editors of the New Arden Shakespeare, or the New Oxford and the New Cambridge editions, or, later, the Riverside edition, I couldn't have done a thing.

But what is especially interesting is a difficulty of a more fundamental nature, presented not by the vocabulary but by the prosody. This difficulty is a consequence of the difference between the two forms of poetry: Shakespeare's on the one hand, and our French traditions and experimentations on the other. Needless to say, I would never have imagined that translating works as essentially and profoundly poetic as *Julius Caesar* or *Hamlet* or *The Winter's Tale* could be anything other than a personal act of poetry, not merely restoring the meaning as fully as possible, but simultaneously reinventing a meaning and a form in the French version, a rhythm—form and rhythm being a part of the meaning in their own way, an irreplaceable part. Verse, real verse, emerging as such, is the only medium that can suggest Shakespeare's verse in my translation.

Yet the job is far from simple, for in the original act of writing poetry, form and meaning come into being at the same time, whereas for the translator the meaning has already been decided in the work to be translated. So you can't give yourself fully to the simultaneity of the two sides of poetic creation and receive its benefits. And there is also the fact—more important than you might think—that English verse, at its very inception, is an extension of the tonic stress that is the soul of each English word; it begins with the very first word in a line. It can move forward without thinking too much about the form it will assume. To become a form, it doesn't have to separate itself from existence as it is ordinarily experienced, and particularly from the experience of time, whereas form in French, where there is no stress of that kind, has for centuries been established in verse mainly by the number of syllables, which means that you have to make your way through twelve syllables to see that you're dealing with an alexandrine, for example. That's why the creation of form remains at a distance from the life situations of people who want to express themselves in a poem. Form is something spatial, something unaware of the temporal nature of hope or suffering or finitude. In short, a quite different way of approaching the world through speech, a quite different way of arriving at an experience of unity, which is the universal aim and intuition of poetry. It's another prosodic tradition, other customs and usages, all of which makes it problematic, or at least difficult, to articulate in French what is so immediate and spontaneous in the bursts of meaning in Shakespeare's pentameter, which often has no rhyme.

But this is hardly the place to dwell on such problems, and so I shall simply say, in answer to your question, that these difficulties are also golden opportunities for a translator because they force you to become more conscious of the specific nature of your own poetic traditions and prejudices, while the daily practice of translation helps you to see in your own work—in which the lack of tonic stresses is counterbalanced, when you wish, by the silent *e*—possibilities of shaking off the yoke of a prosody that is too abstract. From the moment I first read Rimbaud, who went very far in this direction, I became fascinated by the poetic potential of lines of verse with an uneven number of syllables, our *vers impairs*, especially eleven-syllable lines, which break up the symmetrical form of the old alexandrine and so open to a more immediate awareness of time. For me, the uneven line was one way of transgressing the burdensome rigidity of our classic prosody. And with this goal in mind, when I encountered Shakespeare I obviously received a great deal. I've mentioned the first scene of *Julius Caesar* and recalled my enthusiasm translating it. Think of these lines:

> Wherefore rejoice? What conquests brings he home?
> What tributaries follow him to Rome
> To grace in captive bonds his chariot wheels.
> You blocks, you stones, you worse than senseless things.

Or of the beginning of *Henry IV,* part one:

> So shaken as we are, so wan with care,
> Find we a time for fighted peace to pant.

Then think of the verse of Racine, or even Victor Hugo working the alexandrine like a caged squirrel on a wheel! English pentameter is perfect for making one forget the inner symmetries, the secret motionlessness, of the alexandrine. One of the reasons for my enthusiasm, for my wanting to stay close to *Julius Caesar* and *Hamlet,* was Shakespeare's verse, this surging of life in an utterance, his striking way of revealing what I would call the genius of the iamb.

J.N. So it wasn't totally by chance that you began to translate Shakespeare. There was also an element of personal vocation?

Y.B. Chance obviously played a role. When I began to translate, I was already in my thirties, as I've said. I wasn't prepared and had done nothing to prepare myself. But this is where chance can be invaluable, since it forces us to look into ourselves and to discover what may be lying dormant there. Chance offered me a translation; I could have refused. Or I might have done one out of curiosity or because I felt the need to at the time, but then stopped. On the contrary, I accepted the invitation and later did all that I could to prolong the experience, to explore what was occurring in the depths of the work I had taken on. Translating a writer means reading that writer. It means having the opportunity to truly read him or her, in a way that you would normally *not* read an author, since you have to pause at every word and even slide beneath a lot of them, which an ordinary reader wouldn't—and shouldn't—usually do. So translating Shakespeare meant getting as close to him as possible, really being with him. It even meant being hounded by him, obsessing over some passage that resisted translation. And when the poet is Shakespeare—Shakespeare quite specifically—it can be something of paramount importance. In my case, chance brought me into contact with a body of work that had an immediate and profound significance for me, and answered a need.

J.N. Did you know right away what this need was? Can you try to describe it?

Y.B. I'll try, because it will help me to explain the way I see Shakespeare. The need I felt at the time, a need that hasn't changed, was to understand what poetry is, and what act of consciousness allows us to recognize it and to free it from ordinary speech. What are the means by which we can help it to exist, both in our words and in our lives? And why, along with the instinctive practice of poetry, is there this need to understand its nature? It's because this understanding may contribute to an activity that seems to me almost as important as the writing of poetry itself, that is, the thinking we devote to other poets (or painters or any form of artistic creation as it relates to poetry). This kind of thinking allows us to bring together the experiments of many poets and thus to create a kind of poetical brotherhood, which today appears in danger of fragmentation, if not of complete disappearance from the concerns of society. That would be a catastrophic loss.

Now what can answer this need if not works that fully and boldly embrace the question of what poetry is? Works of that kind are fairly rare. But Shakespeare's plays and poems offer an example. We become aware of it when we see Hamlet mindful of something within him that his words can't express, or when we notice how Shakespeare's key plays, from *Romeo and Juliet* to *The*

Winter's Tale and *The Tempest*, construct their fictions—with such discernment and diversity—as critiques of that idealistic transfiguration of the world and of other people, which is the original sin of lyric poetry. Shakespeare speaks about poetry, about its hopes but also about the dangers that threaten it; so I approached his work as a lesson that would be essential to me, provided I could free his thinking from its necessarily indirect expression in the plays and give it form in notions that would remain as close as possible to that great experience which is poetry, resistant by nature to the order of concepts. In a word, it was elucidation that I was attempting, and I didn't accomplish it all at once. I was hardly capable of that, and I certainly don't pretend, as you can imagine, that my effort takes stock of all the immense reality of Shakespeare. I do feel, however, that I now have a better sense of what he was about.

What has struck me most about Shakespeare over the many years that I have been translating him (it's almost half a century now, and I've done eleven plays, together with the poems and around sixty of the sonnets.) is that his thinking about poetry was accompanied by a very particular and specific action: the way he tried to recapture a fuller poetic intuition when it was imperiled both in his life and in his writing by a narrow and even fallacious conception of what poetry has to be. I'm thinking of the poems *Venus and Adonis* and *The Rape of Lucrece,* and especially the sonnets. The sonnets are often magnificent syntheses of rhetoric and poetic sensibility, thanks to the musical power of the words, but the writing is obviously trapped in the kind of representation of the world and existence that is created by the propensity toward the ideal, which loves the beauty of the young man but disastrously undervalues ordinary reality, the reality that bears the mark of finitude. This denial of what is, is revealed in the sonnets through the author's utterly fantastic and truly murderous reading of women, who are reduced to the image of the "dark lady." Clearly, poetry has not yet accomplished its task. It should be the war against conceptual representations, the kind of war that would allow it to experience the immediacy of other beings and to free those beings from the stereotypical interpretations that impoverish them. But here poetry has devoted itself to an intelligible structure that once again removes real beings and replaces them with the values and images this system provides. Underneath the idolatry and the fear, there is a great deal of agitation and anguish in these poems. Their author perceives the trap he has been lured into.

But Shakespeare wrote these sonnets in the 1590s, when sonnets were all the rage and almost everyone in England, from true poets to anonymous rhymesters, was producing them. And I dare say Shakespeare thought about that and concluded that his need for poetry could be filled elsewhere, in the place where he worked almost instinctively—the theater. "I dare say," because I know that at that time, when there was not yet an entirely clear conception of poetry—which hadn't completely freed itself from rhetoric, for example—it was through intuitions that could hardly be put into words that a feeling and a choice of this sort would be made manifest. But I believe this is what happened. The stage offered Shakespeare all the possibilities of the spoken word, characters in whose speech the stereotypical thinking of a society, its sexism for instance, would flourish and abound, but in which more lucid intuitions and even remarks of a subversive nature could also be heard, giving the author a chance to deepen his relation to life, to death, and to aspects of existence that are authentically real. And all along, through the fiction that structures the plays, there are situations, events, and figures that can be presented in such a way as to reflect symbolically or emblematically the playwright's thinking about poetry and poetics. Once again, I can't be as clear as I would like to be, since this isn't the place to develop this line of thought, but let's just say that it's in the current that passes from the lure of timelessness to the experience of finitude that I want to follow Shakespeare. This is the direction I am pursuing in the preface that I am writing for my translation of *As You Like It*. I have written an essay after each one of my translations so as to take my bearings and to determine what other play I should now approach. Shakespeare's meditation on the dignity of women in *Antony and Cleopatra*, on their right to reclaim their own "nobility," to use Cleopatra's word, led me to see the same wish in Desdemona, though in her it was intimidated and scorned. And Desdemona, as victim, prompted me to look more closely at Rosalind, who refuses to be one.

J.N. You have just referred to two of the essays that appear in this book, and this leads me to another question. When you write about an English-language author, when you translate him, don't you encounter different kinds of difficulties with vocabulary from those you were speaking of a moment ago, the ones that had to do with, say, the meanings of words at a different moment in history? I'm thinking of the difficulties that are inherent in the very nature of languages, which all have different ways of raising and resolving great metaphysical questions as well as issues relating to poetics. You make use of a very specific vocabulary when you discuss the plays, and such words as *présence* and *évidence*, which recur frequently, may mean something to you that your translators will have difficulty capturing, especially if they resort to simple English equivalents.

Y.B. You raise questions that ask for several different responses, depending on the relevant activity. When we translate a poet such as Shakespeare, the problem of a "philosophical" vocabulary in his work does in fact come up, but it is not all that serious. A poet is not a philosopher; he only uses philosophical words in a context where there are images, symbols, and other facts to sustain and even clarify the meaning, and the translation of this meaning can only be made in the roundabout way that considers the whole context, which presents problems but of a different sort. And so to look for a more or less exact equivalent of a philosophical term in order to use it in the translation, after having first decided on the meaning of the term in the original text, is useless and even inappropriate. It's better to get to the idea through the phrase as a whole. Take the English word "mind": Here is a word that gives all kinds of difficulty to French translators of English. How should it be translated? What exactly does it mean, and which of the related categories in French can best render this meaning? Should you go with *esprit*, a word that is itself full of difficulties, or rather with *intellect*? What is its relation to our *entendement*, or to *raison*? Isn't it as humble as our *avis*, or *sentiment*, when Rosalind says "all the world was of my father's mind," and doesn't it rise to the level of *âme* when Lucrece exclaims, "Immaculate and spotless is my mind"? But what would be a real headache for me if I were a translator of a philosophical treatise, where the words tend to be restricted to a single, precise meaning, is not at all the case in Shakespeare where the meaning can be approached from every angle of the phrase. I translated Prospero's "the bettering of my mind" by "le perfectionnement de mon esprit." And Hamlet's "in my mind's eye, Horatio" by "avec les yeux de l'âme, Horatio."

But the dissimilarities and incompatibilities between our abstract categories can cause us most concern when we French begin to reflect upon and analyze a poem in English. For we will use our own concepts, and among these we will of course find, or invent, ones that seem appropriate and useful; they will become one with our understanding of the work. But these concepts that we have taken on may not exist in exactly the same way in English, so the problem is knowing how to translate into another language essays that were written with the hope of showing our English-speaking friends that we are merely taking different paths to the same place, a place where we might pursue a common quest for truth. The words are not the same; there is a risk of misunderstanding what has been said, what has been put forward—and, of course, the risk is reciprocal.

I am thinking, for instance, of the concept of *parole*, which is fundamental to the way in which questions about poetry are raised in French. *Parole* is the verbal form that our thinking, our desire, our decisions, our actions take on at moments of existence that are sometimes experienced with great intensity. As such, *parole* is obviously a way of using language, but it is also something more. It seeks to modify the use of language by exposing it to situations that often exceed its capacity to understand. Above all, it's the place in our consciousness where the conceptual order gives up its claim to govern the mind, since the *parole* is concerned with situations and objects that truly exist and are therefore more than what their definitions say about them, and are often even perceived as this overabundance, particularly in situations where feeling is in play. The *parole* is not simply a use of language, if by language we mean the present state of words as they are recorded in a dictionary and reduced to conceptual relations. Even when attached to particular words, *parole* stirs language to its depths. In short, it has more truth than language. And so, how should *parole* be translated? Neither "speech act," nor "utterance," nor "word" provides a convincing solution. Of course there is "Word" with a capital *w*—that is, "the Word"—but its reference to a divine authority that is beyond the reach of ordinary human language shows precisely why attention has not been focused in English thought on the usage, both ordinary and transcendental, that we can make of our *paroles*.

Another word that does not come over easily, though a similar term does exist in English, is the word *évidence* that you asked me about. When a mental operation is at issue, the translation of this word creates no particular problem. A statement, let us say, is *évident* when its truth emerges from its mere articulation, when no one feels the slightest doubt about it. In this case, you have adjectives such as "obvious" or "self-evident" that work perfectly well. But we might speak in French of the *évidence* of the world when, one morning, on leaving home—the mental place that language saturates with its representations and its fantasies—we see the mountain, the trees, the sky as they break free from the mist. What is at issue this time? We need to find a way of signifying that these realities are making themselves known in such a way that nothing about them is kept at a distance by the various interests that might have been pursued by conceptual thinking, so that all their various elements—which are no longer perceived as separate components—are now all in the same foreground, making it possible for us to see a fullness in them, a fullness through which we rediscover the unity, the oneness of the world that had been forgotten. At such moments, things are one with themselves, beyond any formulation we might attempt to produce by conceptual means, even beyond all the evocations that poetry is capable of. In short, *évidence* is silence. To a person who goes out in the morning into the rain just as it is stopping, it teaches that to be *évident* is to be "sufficient." It is what turns things into what I like to call "presences."

These, then, are difficult words. But they do speak of an "experience" that is fundamental to what I identify as the motivating principle of poetry. And so I feel the need to use them in order to understand Shakespeare, since it seems to me that beneath the enormous breadth of his undertaking, which ventures to every level of society and emotional life, it is this very specific dimension of poetry that is trying to emerge in a writer who was, in many ways, the first modern.

J.N. One last question. When you are thinking about Shakespeare, and obviously when you are translating him, your main concern is with poetic speech, but this is less and less a concern of contemporary society. Don't translations such as yours run the risk of speaking only to a happy few, when the plays themselves were and are theatrical works designed to appeal to the largest possible audiences?

Y.B. It's true that poetry has less and less of a place in intellectual society, and in France this is nothing new. But just as it did at other times, poetry touches people who know how to be attentive to what is stirring and searching within them, and there are many people like this, scattered throughout the whole country. If a translation that is concerned with its poetic articulation is also a good, powerful rendering—which is obviously not always the case—it's sure to have its readers and its audience, although with an audience it is essential that those who direct or act in the play be sensitive to this poetic dimension in Shakespeare. The problem is that outside English-speaking countries, there are often only translations that have failed to see that poetic utterance—*la parole*—in all its vehemence is the very soul of the tragedies and the key to their meaning. When Shakespeare is staged in England or the United States, the original text is there, with its rhythms, its resonances, and every actor is thus in a position to discover the poetic resources of the play in whatever way he or she wishes. The play can be presented in all its depth and can lay out its true form, which is the reason why performances of

Shakespeare's works are often so much better in English-speaking countries, especially perhaps, in little theaters—on college campuses, for instance—where actors and directors can give themselves entirely to the text, without having to worry too much about the kind of fashionable interpretation that elsewhere weakens the conception of the production or the direction of the actors. In France we don't have that inexhaustible resource.

And so it's very tempting to see in Shakespeare only the playwright who has his characters say certain things; who delights in putting insinuations and double meanings into words; and whose principal interest is in how the public will receive the actors' retorts, their interjections and rejoinders, their cries and their laughter, all of it punctuated with the appropriate gestures and orchestrated with maximum effect on stage—in short, the Shakespeare who is viewed as the perfect "man of the theater." The concern for theatrical effectiveness certainly exists in Shakespeare; there can be no doubt about that. But where is it implemented? Surely it is in the pentameter, sometimes in the rhymes, and always in the rhythms; and in the great breaks in the words—the "multitudinous seas" the hands of Macbeth will "incarnadine" at the darkest moment of the play—that boldly expose, at the very moment they are spoken, a field of perceptions, worries, values, conflicts, rifts, passions, which constitute for Shakespeare the poetic recovery of existence. They alone allow us to understand the deepest motivations and the most essential aims of the action of the drama. It's in speech, in the depths of an invention that is specifically verbal, that the action—the inner action—is lodged. The truth of this is borne out by Hamlet's soliloquies and other great speeches in Shakespeare in which the sentences are long and seem muddled to those of our contemporaries who do not realize that they must be lived on the level of their birth in the writing, at the point where the writing escapes from ordinary language. When Hamlet, advancing to the front of the stage, says, "To be or not to be," it is to have the spectator or the reader enter into his speech and venture with him onto a stage that obviously, and fortunately, is a mental one—the place where, with little or no setting, Shakespeare sought to place his work.

With Shakespeare, theater and poetry are one. Failing to realize this—and translations abet such failure—can only lead to false problems. Should we give preference to a translation written "to be read" or to one written "for the stage"? The dilemma is a false one that paradoxically risks impoverishing a translation meant to be read rather than performed. For if the importance of poetry in the play is forgotten, we will expect the literary translation

to try to collect all the possible nuances of meaning, which of course is legitimate, but what will this profusion of meaning be? Something that has come
untied, whose various elements, real or imagined, will fly off in every direction. And this will provide a perfect excuse for calling attention to problems
in the text that aren't really there. A perfect excuse, too, for losing sight of the
fundamental mystery of our being-in-the-world, which haunts Hamlet and
shakes old Lear to the core when he suddenly becomes aware of it, but which
can also become pure light at the festive moment when Perdita and Florizel
set the truth of love against the bitter lessons of winter.

TRANSLATED BY JOHN NAUGHTON

Sources

Except for chapters 6 and 7 and the Interview with Yves Bonnefoy, all chapters appeared in *Shakespeare et Yeats* (see bibliog., sec. 2, 1998).

Chapter 1. First published as a preface to Bonnefoy's French translations of *Macbeth* and *Romeo and Juliet* (see bibliog., sec. 4, 1985). Translated by Jean Stewart in *The Act and the Place of Poetry* (see bibliog., sec. 3, 1989). Stewart's English translation was revised by John Naughton for publication in the present volume.

Chapter 2. First published as a preface to Bonnefoy's French translations of these two plays (see bibliog. sec. 4, 1978). An English translation by John Naughton appeared in *New Literary History* 17, no. 3 (Spring 1986): 477–91, and was republished in *The Act and the Place of Poetry* (see bibliog., sec. 3, 1989). Naughton has revised his original English translation for the present volume.

Chapter 3. First published as a preface to Bonnefoy's French translation of *The Winter's Tale* (See bibliog., sec. 4, 1994). Republished in 1996 by Gallimard in the Collection Folio / Théâtre.

Chapter 4. First published as a preface to Bonnefoy's translation of *The Tempest* (see bibliog., sec. 4, 1997).

Chapter 5. First published as a preface to Bonnefoy's translation of *Julius Caesar* (see bibliog., sec. 4, 1995). Republished in 1995 by Gallimard in the Collection Folio / Théâtre.

Chapter 6. First published as a preface to Bonnefoy's translation of *Antony and Cleopatra* (see bibliog., sec. 4, 1999). Revised and republished in *Sous l'horizon du langage* (see bibliog., sec. 2, 2002). The English translation that appears in this volume is based on the 2002 version of the French text.

Chapter 7. First published as a preface to Bonnefoy's translation of *Othello* (see bibliog., sec. 4, 2001). The essay was substantially revised for publication in *Sous l'horizon du langage* (see bibliog., sec. 2, 2002). The English translation that appears in this volume is based on the 2002 version of the French text.

Chapter 8. First published as "Shakespeare et le poète français" in the review *Preuves* 100 (June 1959): 42–48. Revised and republished as part of an afterword to Bonnefoy's French translation of *Hamlet* (see bibliog., sec. 4, 1962). An English translation of the essay was published anonymously the same year in *Encounter* 18, no. 6 (June 1962): 38–47, and a revised version of that translation appeared in *The Act and the Place of Poetry* (see bibliog., sec. 3, 1989). John Naughton has further revised the translation for publication in this volume.

Chapter 9. First published in a somewhat longer version as part of an afterword to Bonnefoy's French translation of *Hamlet* (see bibliog., sec. 4, 1962). An English translation of the essay in its longer form was published anonymously in *Yale French Studies* 33 (December 1964): 120–26. The English translation in this volume is based on the shorter, revised version of the text that appears in *Shakespeare et Yeats* (see bibliog., sec. 2, 1998). It borrows substantially from the earlier translation at those points where the two versions of the French text are the same.

Chapter 10. Lecture given at the annual meeting of the Société des Anglicistes (Shakespeare Year), Toulouse, 1964. First published in *Études anglaises* 17, no. 4 (October–December 1964) in a special number of that review devoted to Shakespeare. Republished as a preface to Bonnefoy's translation of *King Lear* (see bibliog., sec. 4, 1991).

Chapter 11. First published as a preface to *William Shakespeare: Les Poèmes*, Bonnefoy's translations of Shakespeare's *Venus and Adonis*, *The Rape of Lucrece*, and *The Phoenix and the Turtle* (see bibliog., sec. 4, 1993).

Chapter 12. First published as an afterword to Bonnefoy's translations of twenty-four of Shakespeare's sonnets (see bibliog., sec. 4, 1995).

Interview with Yves Bonnefoy. Previously unpublished. The interview was conducted by John Naughton in July 2002 through a series of written questions and answers.

Notes on the Translators

MICHAEL BISHOP is McCulloch Professor of French and Contemporary Studies in the Faculty of Arts and Social Sciences at Dalhousie University in Nova Scotia. He has published extensively in the field of modern and contemporary literature and culture. His books include *Nineteenth-Century French Poetry* (Twayne, 1993); *Contemporary French Women's Poetry*, 2 vols. (Rodopi/Chiasma, 1995); *Women's Poetry in France, 1960–1995: A Bilingual Anthology* (Wake Forest University Press, 1997); *Jacques Prévert: From Film and Theater to Poetry, Art, and Song* (Rodopi/Chiasma, 2002); *Altérités d'André du Bouchet: De Hugo, Shakespeare et Poussin à Celan, Mandelstam et Giacometti* (Rodopi/Chiasma, Collection Monographique, 2003). Michael Bishop is the translator of the work of Salah Stétié, *Cold Water Shielded* (Bloodaxe Books, 1999).

MARY ANN CAWS is Distinguished Professor of English, French, and Comparative Literature at the Graduate School, City University of New York. She has published widely in the field of modern and contemporary literature and culture and has translated a broad range of French writers and poets. Her recent books include *The Surrealist Look: An Erotics of Encounter* (MIT Press, 1997); *Picasso's Weeping Woman: The Life and Art of Dora Maar* (Little Brown/Bulfinch, 2001); *Virginia Woolf: Illustrated Life* (Penguin, Overlook, 2001, 2002); *Marcel Proust: Illustrated Life* (Overlook, 2003). She is the editor of: *Surrealist Painters and Poets: An Anthology* (MIT Press, 2001); *Manifesto: A Century of Isms* (University of Nebraska Press, 2001); *Mallarmé in Prose* (New Directions, 2002); *Vita Sackville-West: Selected Writings* (Palgrave, 2002); *Surrealist Love Poems* (University of Chicago Press, 2002); *The Yale Anthology of Twentieth-Century French Poetry* (Yale University Press, 2004).

MARYANN DE JULIO is professor of French at Kent State University and a member of the American Literary Translators Association. She has translated work by the contemporary French and Italian writers Emmanuel Hocquard and Monica Sarsini, as well as a play by the eighteenth-century French activist Olympe de Gouges. She has published a monograph, *Rhetorical Landscapes: The Poetry and Art Criticism of Jacques Dupin* (Lexington, Kentucky: French Forum Publishers, 1992), as well as articles on Bonnefoy, Du Bouchet, Reverdy, Apollinaire, Artaud, and Joyce Mansour, among others.

MARK HUTCHINSON is the founder-editor of the little magazine *Straight Lines*. He has published widely in reviews such as *Agenda, Grand Street, Modern Poetry in Translation, Poetry Review,* and the *Threepenny Review* and is a regular contributor to the *Times Literary Supplement.* He has published a number of chapbooks and pamphlets, including *A Pretender's Flag* (1986), *April Passage* (1987), and *The Emperor Has No Clothes* (1989). His translations from the French include works by Emmanuel Hocquard (*Of Mists and Clouds,* 1993; *The Gardens of Sallust and Other Writings,* 1995; *The Library at Trieste,* 1995) and René Char (*Hypnos: Notes on the French Resistance* and *René Char: A Thirty-One Gun Salute,* both forthcoming). His translation of Jean Clair's *Everyday Barbarity: Zoran Music at Dachau* is also forthcoming.

JOHN NAUGHTON is professor of Romance languages and literatures and director of the Division of University Studies at Colgate University. In addition to articles on a number of modern French poets, he has published *The Poetics of Yves Bonnefoy* (University of Chicago Press, 1984) and *Louis-René des Forêts* (Rodopi, 1993). He is the editor of *The Act and the Place of Poetry* (University of Chicago Press, 1989) and of *Yves Bonnefoy: New and Selected Poems* (University of Chicago Press / Carcanet Press, 1995). He is the translator of Bonnefoy's *In the Shadow's Light* (University of Chicago Press, 1991).

JAMES PETTERSON is associate professor of French at Wellesley College. He has published articles on a number of French poets from Théophile de Viau to Francis Ponge. He is the author of *Postwar Figures of L'Éphémère: Yves Bonnefoy, Louis-René des Forêts, Jacques Dupin, André du Bouchet* (Bucknell University Press, 2000). He has translated a wide variety of texts in French, including Jacques Dupin's *Miro* (Flammarion/Abrams, 1993). He is currently at work on a book provisionally titled "Poetry Proscribed: The Trials of Poetry in France."

STEPHEN ROMER is Maître de Conférences in the English department at the University of Tours. Recently he has been Distinguished Visiting Professor in the Department of Romance Languages at Colgate University and Visiting Fellow at Sidney Sussex, Cambridge. A frequent reviewer for the *Times Literary Supplement,* he has published three collections of poetry with Oxford University Press: *Idols* (1986), *Plato's Ladder* (1992), and *Tribute* (1998). His anthology, *20th Century French Poems,* was published by Faber in 2002.

ANTHONY RUDOLF has published books of poetry, autobiography, and literary criticism, as well as translations of Russian and French poets, including Yves Bonnefoy. He is coeditor, with John Naughton, of *Yves Bonnefoy: New and Selected Poems* (University of Chicago Press / Carcanet Press, 1995). He has written on art, including an essay on Kitaj for the National Gallery, London. His academic appointments include a visiting lectureship in humanities at London Metropolitan University and a Royal Literary Fund fellowship at the University of Hertfordshire.

The late JEAN STEWART was a prize-winning translator of many French authors. She translated among other works, Louis-René des Forêts' *The Children's Room* (John Calder, 1963) and Yves Bonnefoy's monumental *Alberto Giacometti: A Biography of His Work* (Abbeville Press, 1991).

Selected Bibliography

PRINCIPAL WORKS OF YVES BONNEFOY

1. Poetry

1953. *Du mouvement et de l'immobilité de Douve.* Mercure de France. Translated by Galway Kinnell as *On the Motion and Immobility of Douve.* Ohio University Press, 1968; Bloodaxe Books, 1992. This translation also appears in *Early Poems, 1947–1959* (1990; see below).

1958. *Hier régnant désert.* Mercure de France. Translated by Anthony Rudolf as *Hier régnant désert / Yesterday's Wilderness Kingdom.* MPT Books.2000. Translated by Richard Pevear as *Yesterday's Empty Kingdom,* in *Early Poems, 1947–1959* (1990; see below).

1965. *Pierre écrite.* Mercure de France. Translated by Susanna Lang as *Words in Stone / Pierre écrite.* University of Massachusetts Press, 1976. Translated by Richard Pevear as *Written Stone,* in Yves Bonnefoy, *Poems, 1959–1975* (1985; see below).

1975. *Dans le leurre du seuil.* Mercure de France. Translated by Yves Bonnefoy as *Dans le leurre du seuil / In the Lure of the Threshold,* with etchings by George Nama. Monument Press, 2001. Translated by Richard Pevear as *The Lure of the Threshold,* in *Poems, 1959–1975* (1985; see below). Translated by John Naughton as *In the Lure of the Threshold,* in *Temenos* 6, 1985.

1978. *Poèmes* (1947–1975). Mercure de France. (Includes all the French works listed above.)

1985. *Poems, 1959–1975.* Translated by Richard Pevear. Random House.

1987. *Ce qui fut sans lumière.* Mercure de France. Translated by John Naughton as *In the Shadow's Light.* Bilingual edition. University of Chicago Press, 1991.

1990. *Early Poems, 1947–1959,* translated by Galway Kinnell and Richard Pevear. Ohio University Press, 1990.

1991. *Début et fin de la neige,* followed by *Là où retombe la flèche.* Mercure de France.

2001. *Les planches courbes.* Mercure de France.

2001. *Le Cœur-espace.* Farrago.

2. Prose

1954. *Peintures murales de la France gothique.* Paul Hartmann.

1959. *L'Improbable.* Mercure de France.

1961. *Arthur Rimbaud*. Le Seuil. Translated by Paul Schmidt as *Rimbaud*. Harper and Row, 1973.

1967. *Un Rêve fait à Mantoue*. Mercure de France.

1970. *Rome 1630: l'horizon du premier baroque*. Flammarion.

1972. *L'Arrière-pays*. Skira; Flammarion, 1982.

1974. *L'Ordalie*. Galerie Maeght.

1977. *Le Nuage rouge*. Mercure de France.

1977. *Rue Traversière*. Mercure de France.

1980. *L'Improbable*, followed by *Un Rêve fait à Mantoue*, revised and expanded edition. Mercure de France.

1981. *Dictionnaire des mythologies et des religions des sociétés traditionnelles et du monde antique*, compiled and edited by Yves Bonnefoy. Flammarion. Translated under the direction of Wendy Doniger as *Mythologies*. University of Chicago Press, 1991.

1982. *Leçon inaugurale de la chaire d'Etudes comparées de la fonction poétique*. Collège de France; reprinted as *La Présence et l'image*. Mercure de France, 1983. Translated by John Naughton as "*Image and Presence:* Yves Bonnefoy's Inaugural Address at the Collège de France," New Literary History 15, no. 3 (Spring 1984).

1987. *Récits en rêve*. Mercure de France.

1988. *La Vérité de parole*. Mercure de France.

1989. *Sur un sculpteur et des peintres*. Plon.

1990. *Entretiens sur la poésie*. Mercure de France.

1991. *Alberto Giacometti*. Flammarion. Translated by Jean Stewart as *Alberto Giacometti: A Biography of His Work*. Abbeville Press, 1991.

1992. *Rue Traversière et autres récits en rêve*. Collection Poésie, Gallimard.

1993. *Remarques sur le dessin*. Mercure de France.

1993. *La Vie errante*. Mercure de France.

1994. *Palézieux* (with Florian Rodari). Skira.

1995. *Dessin, couleur et lumière*. Mercure de France.

1995. *La Journée d'Alexandre Hollan*. Le Temps qu'il fait.

1998. *Shakespeare et Yeats*. Mercure de France. Translated in part in the present work.

1999. *Lieux et destins de l'image*. Le Seuil.

2000. *La Communauté des traducteurs*. Presses Universitaires de Strasbourg.

2001. *Breton à l'avant de soi*. Farrago.

2001. *L'Enseignement et l'exemple de Leopardi*. William Blake and Co.

2001. *Poésie et architecture*. William Blake and Co.

2001. *Le Théâtre des enfants*. William Blake and Co.

2002. *Remarques sur le regard*. Calmann Lévy.

2002. *Sous l'horizon du langage*. Mercure de France.

2003. *Goya: les peintures noires*. William Blake and Co.

2003. *La Hantise de Ptyx*. William Blake and Co.

2003. *Le nom du roi d'Asiné*. Virgile. Collection Ulysse fin de siècle.

3. Translations

1957–60. *Henry IV(I); Jules César; Hamlet; Le Conte d'hiver; Vénus et Adonis; Le Viol de Lucrèce.* Club Français du Livre.

1960. *Jules César.* Mercure de France.

1962. *Hamlet,* followed by "Une Idée de la traduction." Mercure de France; new edition, 1988.

1965. *Le Roi Lear.* Mercure de France; new edition, preceded by "Comment traduire Shakespeare?" 1991.

1968. *Roméo et Juliette.* Mercure de France.

1978. *Hamlet / Le Roi Lear,* preceded by "Readiness, Ripeness: Hamlet, Lear." Collection Folio, Gallimard; new edition, Mercure de France, 1988.

1983. *Macbeth.* Mercure de France.

1985. *Roméo et Juliette / Macbeth,* preceded by "L'Inquiétude de Shakespeare." Collection Folio, Gallimard.

1989. *Quarante-cinq poèmes de Yeats,* followed by *Résurrection.* Hermann. Collection Poésie, Gallimard, 1993.

1993. *William Shakespeare: Les Poèmes,* preceded by "Traduire en vers ou en prose." Mercure de France.

1994. *Le Conte d'hiver,* preceded by "Art et Nature: l'arrière-plan du *Conte d'hiver.*" Mercure de France. Collection Folio/Théâtre, Gallimard, 1996.

1995. *Jules César,* preceded by "Brutus, ou le rendez-vous à Philippes." Mercure de France.

1995. *Vingt-quatre sonnets,* followed by "Traduire les sonnets de Shakespeare." Thierry Bouchard and Yves Prié.

1997. *La Tempête,* preceded by "Une Journée dans la vie de Prospéro." Collection Folio / Théâtre.

1999. *Antoine et Cléopatre,* preceded by "La Noblesse de Cléopatre," Collection Folio / Théâtre. Revised for *Sous L'Horizon du Langage.* Mercure de France, 2002.

2000. *Keats et Leopardi.* Mercure de France.

2001. *Othello,* preceded by "La Tête penchée de Desdémone." Collection Folio / Théâtre. Revised for *Sous L'Horizon du Langage.* Mercure de France, 2002.

2003. *Comme il vous plaira,* preceded by "La Décision de Shakespeare." Le Livre de poche.

ENGLISH TRANSLATIONS OF WORKS BY YVES BONNEFOY
(OTHER THAN THOSE LISTED ABOVE)

1968. *Selected Poems,* translated by Anthony Rudolf. Jonathan Cape; Grossman, 1969.

1979. *The Origin of Language and Other Poems,* translated by Susanna Lang, with etchings by George Nama. Monument Press.

1985. *Things Dying Things Newborn: Selected Poems,* translated by Anthony Rudolf. Menard Press.

1987. *Les Raisins de Zeuxis et d'autres fables / The Grapes of Zeuxis and Other Fables*, translated by Richard Stamelman, with etchings by George Nama. Monument Press.

1989. *The Act and the Place of Poetry: Selected Essays*, edited by John Naughton; translated by John Naughton and others. University of Chicago Press. © 1989 by The University of Chicago. All rights reserved.

1989. "Words, Names, Nature, Earth: On the Poetry of Pierre-Albert Jourdan," translated by Richard Stamelman. *Studies in Twentieth-Century Literature* 13 (Winter): 85–97.

1990. *Encore les raisins de Zeuxis / Once More the Grapes of Zeuxis*, translated by Richard Stamelman, with etchings by George Nama. Monument Press.

1991. "The Photosynthesis of Being," translated by Richard Stamelman, in *Edward Hopper*. Tabard Press.

1992. "Henri Cartier-Bresson," translated by Richard Stamelman, in *Henri Cartier-Bresson, Photographer*. Thames and Hudson; Little, Brown and Company.

1993. *Derniers raisins de Zeuxis / The Last Grapes of Zeuxis*, translated by Richard Stamelman, with ethings by George Nama. Monument Press.

1994. *Traité du pianiste*, translated by Anthony Rudolf. The Delos Press.

1995. *The Lure and the Truth of Painting: Selected Essays on Art*, edited by Richard Stamelman; translated by Richard Stamelman and others. University of Chicago Press.

1995. *Yves Bonnefoy: New and Selected Poems*, edited by John Naughton and Anthony Rudolf; translated by Galway Kinnell and others. University of Chicago Press.

1997. *Transmorphosis*, translated by Richard Stamelman, with etchings by George Nama. Monument Press.

2000. *The Primacy of Gaze: Some Remarks about Raymond Mason / La Primauté du regard: Quelques regards sur Raymond Mason*, translated by Anthony Rudolf. Delos Press.

2003. *L'Horizon / The Horizon*, translated by Michael Bishop. Editions VVV Editions.

2003. *In the Lure of Language*, translated by Michael Bishop. Editions VVV Editions.

WORKS ON YVES BONNEFOY PUBLISHED IN ENGLISH

1979. *An Homage to French Poet Yves Bonnefoy*. Special issue, *World Literature Today*, no. 53 (Summer).

1984. Mary Ann Caws, *Yves Bonnefoy*. Twayne Publishing Co.

1984. John T. Naughton, *The Poetics of Yves Bonnefoy*. University of Chicago Press.

1990. *Concordance: Poems by Yves Bonnefoy*, edited by Jean-Jacques Thomas; bilingual ed. Edwin Mellen Press.

1990. Richard Stamelman, *Lost beyond Telling: Representations of Death and Absence in Modern French Poetry*. Cornell University Press.

1992. Special issue, *Modern Poetry in Translation*, n.s., no. 1 (Summer).

2000. James Petterson, *Postwar Figures of 'L'Éphémère': Yves Bonnefoy, Louis-René des Forêts, Jacques Dupin, André du Bouchet*. Bucknell University Press.

Index